WISDOM FOR LIFE

WISDOM

FOR

LIFE

Collections of Proverbs
for Wise Living

JEREMIAH J. E. WIERWILLE

SOTERION PRESS

Soterion Press
An imprint of Spirit & Truth Fellowship International
P.O. Box 1737
Martinsville, IN 46151
stfi.org

Printed in the United States of America

CATALOGING-IN-PUBLICATION DATA
Names: Wierwille, Jeremiah, J. E., 1984—author.
Title: Wisdom For Life: Collections of Proverbs for Wise Living / Jeremiah J. E. Wierwille.
Description: Martinsville: Soterion Press, an imprint Spirit & Truth Fellowship International [2025] | Includes index.
Identifiers: LCCN 2025925713 | ISBN 978-1-970908-00-8 (hardback) | ISBN 979-8-218-83636-8 (paperback) | ISBN 978-1-970908-01-5 (ebook)
Subjects: LCSH: Bible. —Proverbs. | Bible.—Wisdom literature. | Bible.—Reference.
Classification: DDC 223.7/02—dc23/eng/20251222
LC record available at: https://lccn.loc.gov/2025925713

Edited by Renee Dugan
Cover design by Aleksandar Milosavljevic
Interior design by Katelyn Salyers

For those who seek wisdom...

CONTENTS

INTRODUCTION

When I was growing up, my mom and I loved to go to antique flea markets and browse the aisles to see all the various paraphernalia and memorabilia from years gone by, a former age—one which I was wholly unfamiliar with. As I walked through the aisles, I was fascinated by what each vendor had collected and was offering for sale. Some had many items with multiple tables and shelves, while others had a smaller, more consolidated assortment of items that could be displayed on a single table. On one hand, it seemed that each vendor presented an eclectic array of historical merchandise, but on the other, some would specialize in only a single type or category.

There was furniture, such as tables, chairs, or stands, and other home décor items like lamps and fixtures, mirrors, and table settings. There were often dinner and glassware, such as fine plates, cups, real silverware and serving ware, and always some collectible artwork, old books, maps, and miscellaneous memorabilia for sports, photography, music, and so on. Many vendors would have some old jewelry, clothes, and other fashion items, and most would offer tools, kitchenware, or various sorts of jars and bottles. And there were also usually vintage toys and games to be found among the assemblage of stuff.

My favorite type of antiques were always the porcelain figurines, perhaps because my mom had a large collection of dog figurines that she proudly displayed in a China cabinet in the dining room of our house, and which I was enamored by as a child. However, as much as I wanted to, I was never allowed to open it up and touch them...though, I might have done so on several occasions without her knowing. Sorry, Mom!

At the flea markets, I would search the stacks and shelves for little figurines tucked away in nooks and crannies. It became a little bit of a pastime when I was done looking at things but my mom still wanted to peruse the market a while longer. Sometimes I wondered, what if I was able to take all those figurines and line them up on a single, long table? Then I could sort them into groups of similar types, like putting all the animal figurines together, or all the people. This would allow me to see and take note of the differences and similarities among all the figurines in each group.

Well, that is what I have attempted to do in this book, Wisdom For Life. I have perused the "aisles" in the Book of Proverbs countless times and have tried to bring together under common headings all the proverbs which relate to a similar topic—such as finances and work, speech and communication, friendships, marriage, and parenting, as well as how to become a wise and discerning person who excels at making good choices, endures hardship with dignity and composure, and walks with integrity in all aspects of life.

In this book, you will discover the godly principles of wisdom from the Book of Proverbs that, while written thousands of years ago, still speak loudly and ring true today. Whether you are seeking understanding about managing money, choosing friends or a spouse, how to avoid decisions that lead to pain, suffering, and harm, or simply desiring to speak with thoughtfulness and discretion, Proverbs will offer a clear guiding light for your journey to wisdom.

I have not been exhaustive in the selection or categorization of the proverbs, but I have endeavored to be as thorough as possible. First, under each topic, you will find a brief summary of the wisdom that the Book of Proverbs offers. This summary is in no way meant to be comprehensive in its scope, but rather is intended to orient the reader to some of the most salient points of wisdom that Proverbs provides. Furthermore, after each summary you will then find a list of proverbs in canonical order that address the particular topic of the section. Some proverbs speak more directly to the topic, while others might mention the topic more indirectly, or apply in a less obvious way. Thus, each proverb has been included in the particular collection of proverbs precisely because it has something wise to say that relates to the topic.

This volume is primarily designed to be a devotional reader, offering over 75 topics for reading and meditating on the wisdom in the Book of Proverbs. The introductory summaries are fairly consistent in their length, but some topics contain a list of many relevant proverbs, while others only have a few. It all depends since Proverbs focuses on some subjects much more heavily than others, and this will be apparent by the quantity of verses listed under the topic.

Lastly, this book can also be used simply as a topical reference volume on the Book of Proverbs that pastors, students, and general readers of the Bible can consult for a topical arrangement of proverbs. Either way, my prayer is that this book is useful tool and helps you come to know the life-giving wisdom of Proverbs so that you can learn, grow, and become wise.

ANGER/RAGE/HATRED

A nger is a powerful force that, when left unchecked, can be immensely destructive. Those who are quick-tempered often act impulsively, making rash decisions that harm themselves and others. Hatred fuels division, breaking down interpersonal relations, while in contrast love and patience have the power to mend broken relationships and prevent unnecessary disputes. A wise person understands the importance of self-control, choosing to be slow to anger, knowing that a calm and collected demeanor supports peace and resolution.

Hot-tempered individuals frequently fall into cycles of strife and regret, saying and doing things they later wish they hadn't. True strength lies not in overpowering others (whether physically or verbally) but in mastering one's own emotions. Overlooking an offense and responding with patience rather than vitriol is a true mark of wisdom.

Furthermore, associating with those prone to anger is risky, as their temperament can change rapidly and they tend to influence others negatively. Instead, surrounding oneself with patient and peace-loving individuals creates a more harmonious community and life overall.

While bribes or gifts may temporarily pacify anger, true peace comes from living with wisdom and understanding—rather than offering external appeasements, which only can subdue anger for so long before it comes back.

In relationships, especially within a household, an angry and contentious disposition breeds tension and misery for the whole house. Proverbs compares living with an easily angered person to enduring a relentless storm—there never seems to be any peace or relief.

Wisdom teaches that anger should never dictate one's actions. True strength lies in patience, self-restraint, and the pursuit of peace with others. Those who master their emotions will experience stability, contentment, and a life free from the turmoil that uncontrolled anger brings.

A wise person is cautious and turns away from evil,

but a fool is angry and is overconfident.

Proverbs 14:16

A gentle response turns away rage,

but a hurtful word increases anger.

Proverbs 15:1

A hot-tempered person incites strife,

but one who is slow to get angry peacefully settles a dispute.

Proverbs 15:18

A king's rage *is like* messengers of death,

but a wise person will pacify *the anger*.

Proverbs 16:14

A person's foolishness subverts his way,
but his heart rages against Yahweh.

Proverbs 19:3

The king's rage is like the growl of a lion,
but his favor is like the dew upon the grass.

Proverbs 19:12

A person with great anger will bear the penalty;
surely, if you deliver him, then you will have to do it again.

Proverbs 19:19

The terror of a king is like the growl of a lion;
the one who infuriates him does wrong to his *own* life.

Proverbs 20:2

A gift *given* in secret subdues anger,
and a secret bribe *averts* strong wrath.

Proverbs 21:14

It is better to live in a desolate land
than *with* a contentious and angry woman.

Proverbs 21:19

Do not make friends with an angry person,
and do not associate with a person who is hot-tempered,
or you will learn his path
and get yourself *caught in* a snare.

Proverbs 22:24–25

The north wind brings rain,
and a tongue *telling* secrets brings an angry face.

Proverbs 25:23

Like a city broken into, *one* without a wall,
is a person who has no self-control over his emotions.

Proverbs 25:28

A stone is heavy and the sand is weighty,
but vexation by a fool is heavier than both of them.
Rage is cruel and anger is a flood,
but who is able to stand in the presence of jealousy?

Proverbs 27:3–4

Scornful people inflame a city,
but the wise turn away anger.

Proverbs 29:8

A fool lets out all of his emotions,
but a wise person keeps them calm within.

Proverbs 29:11

An angry person stirs up strife,
and a vengeful person *commits* much transgression.

Proverbs 29:22

If you acted foolishly by exalting yourself,
or if you plan *to do so, put* your hand over your mouth!
For the churning of milk brings forth butter,
and the churning of the nose brings forth blood,
so the churning of anger brings forth strife.

Proverbs 30:32–33

BEAUTY

Beauty is often prized as a desirable trait, but it is fleeting and can be deceptive. Outward attractiveness may catch the eye, but it should never be the foundation for admiration or lasting desire. A person can be physically attractive and have a stunning appearance yet completely lacks wisdom and discernment, making their beauty meaningless—like a gold ring in a pig's snout. Instead, true beauty comes from wisdom and resides in a person's inner character, not what they look like on the outside.

Proverbs warns against being captivated by beauty alone, as it can lead to poor choices and misplaced priorities. It can easily become an obsession and a snare, blinding the heart and making the eyes captive to it. Rather than valuing charm or external appeal, the person truly deserving of praise is one who embodies strength, wisdom, and reverence for God. True beauty is found in qualities like dignity, faith, and a heart guided by wisdom—virtues that bring lasting honor and admiration.

When one embraces wisdom, it becomes like a crown—a symbol of honor, dignity, and grace. This kind of beauty is not fleeting, but enduring by bringing value and distinction to a person's life. Words, too, can carry a kind of beauty when spoken at the right time with wisdom and grace. When spoken properly, they are like fine ornaments—beautiful, valuable, and fitting.

Proverbs offers a broad warning about craving appearances in general—whether it's physical beauty, food and drink, or material gain. These things may glitter on the surface and seem important and alluring, but they are ultimately deceptive if pursued apart from wisdom. They can distract one's focus and attention, lead to misplaced trust in one's own perception and understanding, and wear a person out from expending effort in something that ultimately doesn't last.

Proverbs 31 presents a woman whose beauty extends beyond appearance. While she dresses in fine linen and purple, her true adornment is her strength and confidence. She looks to the future without fear, knowing her life is built on wisdom and purpose. Her beauty is not just seen—it is lived.

Rather than chasing superficial assets, Proverbs encourages seeking what is truly valuable: wisdom and understanding from living with the fear of Yahweh. Wisdom is the most beautiful attribute a person could ever possess and exhibit. Truly that person is worthy of praise and to be desired.

She will place on your head a wreath of grace;
she will present to you a beautiful crown."

Proverbs 4:9

Do not desire her beauty in your heart,
and do not allow her to capture you with her eyes.

Proverbs 6:25

Like a gold ring in a pig's snout,
so too is a beautiful woman who turns aside from good judgment.

Proverbs 11:22

Do not crave his tasty foods,

for it is deceptive bread.

Do not wear yourself out by attempting to get rich;

cease from *relying upon* your *own* understanding.

Proverbs 23:3–4

Like apples of gold in settings of silver

is a word spoken at the *proper* moment.

Like an earring of gold or an ornament of *fine* gold

is a wise person reproving a listening ear.

Proverbs 25:11–12

Charm is deceptive and beauty is fleeting,

but a woman who fears Yahweh—she will be praised.

Proverbs 31:30

BLAMELESS/ PURE/UPRIGHT

Being blameless, pure, and upright is established as the way to security, stability, and God's favor. These qualities describe a life marked by moral integrity, sincerity of heart, and faithfulness in conduct. The upright walk a straight path and don't deviate, avoiding deceit, injustice, and corruption. Their lives reflect reverence for God and a commitment to righteousness in both private and public behavior.

The blameless are protected by their integrity. Their steps are guided and preserved, and they are shielded from the destruction that overtakes the wicked. Their prayers are pleasing to God, and their ways are delightful to Him. Uprightness is not perfection, but a consistent alignment with truth, humility, and obedience. The blameless speak honestly, are just in all their dealings, and have a heart that resists evil.

Purity, especially of heart and motive, is highly valued and should be guarded from the corrupting influence of foolishness. The pure speak with grace and act with honor, avoiding both immorality and manipulative behavior. They do not rely on appearances but walk in genuine sincerity, and as they do that, God guards their path and places their feet on solid ground. The upright are also a source of strength and stability for others—their influence brings life, peace, and wisdom to their communities.

In contrast, those who are crooked or double-minded walk a path filled with instability and hidden danger. Their ways may appear smooth and desirable at first, but they only lead to destruction and ruin. Pretending to be upright while hiding wicked motives brings disgrace and incurs God's judgment. The difference between the upright and the corrupt is ultimately exposed by their actions and their end.

To live blamelessly is to walk faithfully under the care and provision of God, with confidence and peace. It is a life of integrity that stands firm when tested and leaves behind a legacy of trust, honor, and blessing.

He has stored up sound advice for the upright—

a shield for those who walk blamelessly—

guarding the paths of justice,

and watching over the way of his loyal ones.

Proverbs 2:7–8

Therefore you are to walk on the road of good people,

and you are to keep to the paths of the righteous.

For the upright will live in the land,

and the blameless will remain in it.

Proverbs 2:20–21

The road of Yahweh is a place of refuge for the blameless person,

but it is destruction for those who act wickedly.

Proverbs 10:29

The righteousness of the blameless person will make

his road straight,

but the wicked person will fall by his wickedness.

The righteousness of the upright will deliver them,

but the unfaithful will be taken captive by their desire.

Proverbs 11:5–6

A twisted heart is an abomination to Yahweh,

but the road of the blameless is his delight.

Proverbs 11:20

The words of the wicked lie in wait for blood,

but the mouth of the upright will deliver them.

The wicked will be overthrown and will be no more,

but the house of the righteous will stand.

Proverbs 12:6–7

The one who walks in his integrity fears Yahweh,

but the one who is devious in his ways shows contempt for him.

Proverbs 14:2

BLESSING/FAVOR

Blessing and favor are the outcomes of a life marked by wisdom, righteousness, kindness/compassion, and reverence for God. The blessings are not merely material rewards, but encompass relational harmony, spiritual peace, honor, and divine favor. Those who walk with integrity, pursue understanding, and act justly attract the favor of both God and others. Their lives are enriched with joy, stability, and meaningful influence.

God's favor rests especially on those who are faithful, generous, and humble. Acts of kindness to the poor, being fair in one's judgments, and seeking honesty in relationships invite God's blessing. A cheerful giver, a peacemaker, and one who seeks the good of others are all honored and exalted. Blessing is also found in wisdom's embrace—those who listen to wisdom, keep her close, and follow her teaching receive life, grace, and peace.

Favor from others is closely tied to good sense, gracious speech, and consistent character. A good name and reputation are more valuable than wealth, and those who seek to do good find favor with others and God. The favor of a ruler or influential person is desirable, but it is ultimately God's favor that grants true and lasting blessing.

Proverbs describes the overflowing blessings of God that come to the person who lives uprightly and trusts in God's guidance. These blessings may include material prosperity, loving relationships, in-

fluence in community, and peace of mind. And even when experiencing discipline or correction, God's blessings are at work for a
person's growth and protection.

God's blessings and favor are not random but are deeply tied to a
person's character and obedience. God blesses and bestows His favor upon those who live righteously before Him. Such blessings are
the fruit of aligning one's life with truth, loving others well, and
living in a way that honors God. Those who do so continually walk
a path of blessing, bringing light to others and enjoying the rewards
of faithful living.

Do not let covenant loyalty and faithfulness leave you;

bind them around your neck;

write them upon the tablet of your heart,

then you will find favor and good judgment

in the eyes of God and people.

Proverbs 3:3–4

Blessed is the person who finds Wisdom,

and the one who obtains discernment,

Proverbs 3:13

She is a tree of life to those taking hold of her,

and blessed are those *who are* holding her fast.

Proverbs 3:18

Yahweh's curse is upon the house of the wicked person,

but he blesses the dwelling of the righteous person.

Proverbs 3:33

Blessed is the one who listens to me,
keeping watch at my doors day after day,
watching at the entrance to my gates,
because the one finding me finds life,
and he will obtain favor from Yahweh.

Proverbs 8:34–35

Blessings are upon the head of a righteous person,
but the mouth of the wicked conceals wrongdoing.

Proverbs 10:6

The blessing from Yahweh is what makes one rich,
and he does not combine pain with *the blessing.*

Proverbs 10:22

By the blessing of the upright a town will be exalted,
but it will be thrown down by the mouth of the wicked.

Proverbs 11:11

The person who blesses *others* will be made prosperous,
and the one who waters, indeed, he himself will be watered.
The people will curse the one who withholds grain,
but a blessing *will be* upon the head of the one who sells grain.
The one who is on the lookout for *what is* good seeks favor,
but the one who is intent on evil, it will come to him.

Proverbs 11:25–27

A good person will obtain favor from Yahweh,
but a person with wicked schemes, he will condemn.

Proverbs 12:2

Good judgment brings favor,
but the road of the unfaithful never changes.

Proverbs 13:15

The one who shows contempt toward his neighbor is sinning,
but blessed are those who show favor to the poor.

Proverbs 14:21

The person who oppresses the poor taunts the one
        who created him,
but the person who shows favor to the needy glorifies him.

Proverbs 14:31

A sacrifice *made by* the wicked is an abomination to Yahweh,
but the prayer of the upright *brings* his favor.

Proverbs 15:8

When Yahweh takes pleasure in a person's ways,
even his enemies will make peace with him.

Proverbs 16:7

The one who comprehends a *wise* saying will find good,
and blessed is the one who trusts in Yahweh.

Proverbs 16:20

He who finds a wife finds a good thing,
and he obtains favor from Yahweh.

Proverbs 18:22

Many will entreat the favor of a generous person,
and everyone is a friend to a person who gives gifts.

Proverbs 19:6

The one who shows favor to a poor person lends to Yahweh,
and he will repay him according to his *good* work.

Proverbs 19:17

A *good* name is to be chosen over great wealth;
favor is better than silver and gold.

Proverbs 22:1

The generous person will be blessed
because he gave some of his bread to the poor.

Proverbs 22:9

These *proverbs* also are for the wise:
To show favoritism in judgment is not good.
The one who says to the wicked person, "You are righteous,"—
peoples will curse him, *and* nations will be indignant with him.
But for those who offer rebuke, it will go well,
and upon them will come a good blessing.

Proverbs 24:23–25

A faithful person *will have* many blessings,
but the one who makes haste to get rich will not go unpunished.

Proverbs 28:20

One who reproves a person will afterward find more favor
than the person who flatters with the tongue.

Proverbs 28:23

BRIBES/GIFTS

Bribes and gifts wield significant power in human interactions and can influence outcomes for both good and evil purposes. A well-timed gift can create opportunities, provide access to influential circles, or help resolve conflicts and disagreements. When given with pure intentions, gifts can serve as a bridge, fostering goodwill and opening doors that might otherwise remain closed. However, the same act of giving, when motivated by corruption, is bribery and can distort justice, compromise integrity, and foster dishonesty.

Bribery is a dangerous force, particularly in legal and moral matters. It skews fairness, undermines trust, and creates inequality and oppression. Those who seek to gain power or wealth through bribes not only harm others but bring trouble upon themselves and their own households. The pursuit of dishonest gain may seem to work in the short term, but it ultimately leads to trouble and punishment. In contrast, those who reject corrupt gifts and instead choose integrity will enjoy stability, security, and a life free from the burdens of deceit and shame.

Proverbs makes the point about the powerful impact that gifts can have, distinguishing between their rightful and wrongful use. While a gift can soothe anger or appease someone's wrath, using wealth as a tool for manipulation is deceptive and dangerous. The wicked accept bribes to twist the truth and pervert justice, allowing corruption to flourish. By contrast, the righteous recognize the destructive consequences of bribery and refuse to be swayed by dishonest gain.

There is also a warning against false generosity—those who make empty promises about their giving but fail to follow through. True generosity is not about flashy displays or self-serving motives, but about sincerity and wisdom in giving and being true to one's word when they pledge a gift.

The teaching of Proverbs is for a person to gain discernment in how gifts are to be used. There is a fine line between generosity that fosters growth and creates opportunity, and bribery that breeds evil and corruption. The wise person understands the difference and chooses integrity over greed, righteousness over dishonesty. By doing so, they not only secure their own well-being, but contribute to a just and fair society.

The one who pursues unjust gain troubles his household,
but the one who hates gifts *that influence* will live.

Proverbs 15:27

A bribe is a 'magic stone' in the eyes of its owner;
every direction he turns, he prospers.

Proverbs 17:8

A wicked person takes a secret bribe
to twist the paths of justice.

Proverbs 17:23

A person's gift creates opportunity for him
and leads him before great people.

Proverbs 18:16

Many will entreat the favor of a generous person,
and everyone is a friend to a person who gives gifts.

Proverbs 19:6

A gift *given* in secret subdues anger,
and a secret bribe *averts* strong wrath.

Proverbs 21:14

Like clouds and wind but no rain
is a person who boasts of a gift never given.

Proverbs 25:14

BUSINESS

S uccess in business and finance must be built on honesty, dili-gence, and fairness. Proverbs warns that dishonest gain—such as deceitful practices, bribery, and unjust interest—may bring temporary profit but ultimately lead to ruin. True prosperity comes from practicing righteousness and integrity, which bring lasting success, a good reputation, and God's favor.

Hard work is the foundation of financial success and stability. This is because diligence leads to a steady increase in profit, while la-ziness or chasing unrealistic dreams results in poverty. A skilled and hardworking person will be recognized and given opportu-nities, while those who are trying to cut corners and take short-cuts will struggle.

Wealth, however, must be pursued with wisdom and balance. Those who relentlessly pursue riches may find that they quickly slip away, while those who seek moderation in wealth—avoiding both extreme wealth and poverty—will find a life of contentment. Also, wise financial management, generosity toward the poor, and ethical business practices are what create lasting security and true prosperity.

The righteous understand that wealth is not just for personal gain but should be used to care for others, especially the poor. Those who are generous and fair earn honor, while those who exploit others or hoard resources will face consequences. Money is not bad in itself, but trusting in wealth alone is dangerous, and ultimately, disappointing. Rather, those who trust in God and apply wisdom in business will experience true and lasting success and fulfillment.

Ethical business practices require wisdom, self-control, and discipline. The prudent consider their actions carefully, while the reckless expose their own incompetence. Success in business and leadership comes to those who make wise, measured decisions, while those who act impulsively or dishonestly bring about their own downfall. This is because rushing into financial decisions without careful thought often leads to disaster. Arrogance and impulsiveness are a gateway to poor judgments and missed opportunities, but honesty and humility foster trust and long-term prosperity because those who plan wisely and work diligently will build something that lasts.

My son, if you have put up security for your neighbor,

if you have entered into an agreement with a stranger,

then you have been ensnared by the words of your mouth,

you have been captured by the words of your mouth.

Do this now, my son, and be set free,

for you have put yourself into the hand of your neighbor.

Go! Humble yourself and pressure your neighbor.

Do not give *any* sleep to your eyes,

or slumber to your eyelids.

Be rescued like a gazelle from a hunter,

and like a bird from the hand of a fowler.

Proverbs 6:1–5

Treasures *gained* by wickedness profit nothing,
but righteousness will deliver from death.

Proverbs 10:2

Deceitful balances are an abomination to Yahweh,
but a fair weight is his delight.

Proverbs 11:1

The one who puts up security *for* a stranger will suffer badly,
but the one who hates making *such* deals is secure.

Proverbs 11:15

The wicked person makes a deceptive wage,
but the one who sows righteousness *receives* a true reward;

Proverbs 11:18

There is one who generously scatters *wealth*, and it is
    continually added *to him,*
and one who is withholding *what is* right, *which* surely *will*
    end in poverty.
The person who blesses *others* will be made prosperous,
and the one who waters, indeed, he himself will be watered.
The people will curse the one who withholds grain,
but a blessing *will be* upon the head of the one who sells grain.

Proverbs 11:24–26

Wealth *obtained* by fraud will dwindle away,
but the one who gathers little by little increases *his wealth.*

Proverbs 13:11

In all hard work there is profit,
but *mere* words from the lips surely *lead* to poverty.

Proverbs 14:23

The one who pursues unjust gain troubles his household,
but the one who hates gifts *that influence* will live.

Proverbs 15:27

Better is a little with righteousness,
than great income without justice.

Proverbs 16:8

A just balance and scales are according to Yahweh;
all the weights in the bag are established by him.

Proverbs 16:11

Righteous lips are the delight of kings,
and the one who speaks with integrity will be loved.

Proverbs 16:13

A laborer's appetite labors for him,
for his mouth urges him on.

Proverbs 16:26

A person lacking sense shakes hands on an agreement,
making a solemn pledge in the presence of his neighbor.

Proverbs 17:18

Unequal weights and unequal measures;
both of them are an abomination to Yahweh.

Proverbs 20:10

"Bad! Bad!" says the buyer,
but when he goes his way, he boasts.

Proverbs 20:14

Take his garment since he has *agreed to* give security for a stranger;
hold it as security *when he has pledged* for a foreigner.

Proverbs 20:16

Unequal weights are an abomination to Yahweh,
and deceitful scales are not good.

Proverbs 20:23

The plans of a diligent person surely *will lead* to abundance,
but everyone who acts hastily surely *will come to* poverty.

Proverbs 21:5

The rich person rules over the poor,
and the borrower is a slave to the lender.

Proverbs 22:7

Do not be among those who shake hands *in a pledge*,
among those who put up security for loans.
If you have nothing with which to pay,
why should he take your bed out from under you?

Proverbs 22:26–27

Like an archer who wounds everyone,
so is the one who hires a fool or hires those who are
      just passing by.

Proverbs 26:10

Take his garment since he has *agreed to* give security for a stranger;
hold it as security *when he has pledged* for a foreign woman.

Proverbs 27:13

The one who guards a fig tree will eat of its fruit,
and the one who watches over his master will be honored.

Proverbs 27:18

The person who increases his wealth by interest and
      by profiteering
collects it for the one who shows favor to the poor.

Proverbs 28:8

A ruler who lacks understanding *commits* many extortions,
but the one who hates unjust gain will prolong *his* days.

Proverbs 28:16

CALAMITY/DISASTER

A ccording to Proverbs, calamity and disaster do not simply fall upon people arbitrarily. Rather, they are often the natural and inevitable result of a person ignoring wisdom, rejecting discipline, and persisting in behavior that leads to injury and misfortune. Calamity is experienced as a consequence when a person ignores repeated warnings or when the voice of godly counsel and advice is disregarded or silenced. When people reject correction and harden their hearts, they invite disaster to visit them. It can strike suddenly and leave no room for recovery—like a whirlwind or violent storm sweeping away everything in its path.

Calamity and disaster can occur in various forms. Many are external and material, such as loss of money, property, possessions, employment, membership/privileges, and so on. But others are immaterial, such as status/reputation, relationships, and still others are internal, such as mental and emotional malignity, regret, and shame.

In Proverbs, a sharp contrast exists between the experience of the righteous and that of the wicked. While the righteous are preserved, protected, and established even when the storms of life come, the wicked are exposed, swept away, and decimated with their foundation crumbling beneath them. Those who act with integrity and keep a guarded heart avoid many of the traps that ensnare the foolish. In contrast, those who speak recklessly, incite quarrels and strife, and scheme wickedness, find themselves the architects of their own downfall.

The seeds people sow—whether of wisdom or of wickedness—determine what they will reap. Those who pursue evil will find that evil relentlessly pursues them in return. Disaster becomes what a person harvests from injustice, arrogance, and perversion. Even mocking the suffering and misfortune of others provokes divine judgment, showing how deeply injustice assaults the moral order of life established by God.

Continuing to seek wisdom, maintain humility, and receive correction are safeguards against calamity and disaster. While some applaud audacious and risk-taking attitudes, being cautious is deemed wise and a blessing—it keeps one alert to potential dangers and aligned with the road that leads to life and peace. Those who mock, deceive, or remain unteachable set themselves on a course for personal ruin, while the one who listens and is responsive to wisdom can avoid great loss.

True security and safety are found not in a life free of any trouble or hardship, but in walking with integrity and discernment. Those who cultivate such a life are resilient, even when challenges arise, whereas those who walk on the road of foolishness and refuse to submit to the authority of Yahweh and choose wisdom, walk a path that ends in sudden, and often irreversible, distress and tragedy.

But since you refused me when I called,

I stretched out my hand but no one paid attention,

and you neglected all my counsel,

and you did not want my reproof—

I also will laugh at your distress;

I will mock when what you dread comes,

when your terror comes like a violent storm,
and your calamity like a whirlwind,
and trouble and distress come upon you all.

Proverbs 1:24–27

Keep your road far from her,
and do not go near to the door of her house,
otherwise you might give your honor to others,
and your years to a cruel person;
otherwise strangers might eat their fill from your strength,
and your hard-earned goods *end up* in the house of a foreigner,
and in the end you groan
when your flesh—even your body—are used up.
Then you will say, "O how I have hated discipline,
and my heart has spurned reproof.
I did not listen to the voice of my teachers,
nor did I incline my ear to those instructing me.
I was soon in all sorts of trouble
in the midst of the assembly and congregation."

Proverbs 5:8–14

With perversions in his heart he devises evil,
at every moment he sows strife.
Therefore, his calamity will come suddenly,
in an instant he will be broken and there will be no remedy.

Proverbs 6:14–15

The wise store up knowledge,
but the mouth of the fool *brings* destruction near.

Proverbs 10:14

When the storm passes through, then the wicked
      person is no more,
but the righteous person *has* a foundation that endures.

Proverbs 10:25

The road of Yahweh is a place of refuge for the blameless person,
but it is destruction for those who act wickedly.

Proverbs 10:29

The one who is on the lookout for *what* is good seeks favor,
but the one who is intent on evil, it will come to him.

Proverbs 11:27

By the transgression of *his* lips an evil person *will fall into* a snare,
but the righteous person will escape from trouble.

Proverbs 12:13

No disaster will come upon the righteous person,
but the wicked are filled *with* misfortune.

Proverbs 12:21

The one who guards his mouth watches over his life;
destruction will come to the one who opens his lips wide.

Proverbs 13:3

A wicked messenger will fall into evil,
but a faithful messenger *brings* healing.

Proverbs 13:17

Evil pursues sinners,
but goodness will reward the righteous.

Proverbs 13:21

The house of the righteous person *has* great treasure,
but trouble is stirred up by the revenue of the wicked person.

Proverbs 15:6

The one who mocks the poor taunts the one who created him;
the one who is joyful at a calamity will not go unpunished.

Proverbs 17:5

The one who sows injustice will reap wickedness,
and the rod of his anger will fail.

Proverbs 22:8

My son, fear Yahweh and the king;
do not get involved with those who think otherwise,
for disaster will suddenly arise from them,
and who knows the ruin *that can come* from the two of them?

Proverbs 24:21–22

Do not forsake your friend or your father's friend,
and do not enter into your brother's house on the day
     of your distress;
better is a neighbor nearby than a brother far away.

Proverbs 27:10

Blessed is the person who trembles *before God* continually,
but the one who hardens his heart will fall into evil.

Proverbs 28:14

A person who stiffens his neck *after multiple* rebukes
will suddenly be broken and there will be no remedy.

Proverbs 29:1

CONDUCT/BEHAVIOR

A person's conduct and behavior shape their reputation, relationships, and future outcomes. Walking in wisdom, integrity, and righteousness leads to security and favor, while foolishness and wickedness bring problems and consequences. Wisdom teaches that self-control is superior to strength, and having good judgment reflects deep understanding.

Associating with wise people fosters personal growth in one's life, while companionship with fools leads to adopting bad habits and dishonorable behavior. Furthermore, a person's conduct and behavior extends beyond mere actions to include their words as well.

Pride often affects one's behavior and precipitates struggles and issues in life, whereas humility and careful self-examination in one's manner of conduct help avoid disaster. A wise person listens to advice and accepts correction, while fools stubbornly follow their own way. Seeking justice and fairness in dealings is highly valued, and revenge should not be pursued; instead, trusting in divine justice is the better path.

A person's true character is evident in their daily actions, even from youth. Guarding one's words, avoiding gossip, and being thoughtful before speaking prevent unnecessary trouble. Conduct that aligns with wisdom and righteousness brings stability, peace, and honor, while reckless behavior results in regret and destruction.

My son, if sinners entice you,

do not consent.

If they say, "Come with us, let's lie in wait to *shed* blood,

let's ambush an innocent person for no *good* reason.

We will swallow them alive, just as Sheol does,

and whole, just as those who go down into the pit.

We will find all sorts of valuable things;

we will fill our houses with plunder.

Throw your lot in with us;

we will all share the loot."

My son, do not walk on *that* road with them;

keep your feet from their pathway,

for their feet run to *do* evil,

and they make haste to shed blood.

For in vain the net is spread

in the sight of a bird,

but these lie in wait for their own blood;

they set an ambush for their *own* souls!

This is the way of everyone who pursues unjust gain;

it takes away the life of its owners.

Proverbs 1:10–19

Therefore you are to walk on the road of good people,

and you are to keep to the paths of the righteous.

For the upright will live in the land,

and the blameless will remain in it.

But the wicked will be cut off from the land,

and the unfaithful will be uprooted from it.

Proverbs 2:20–22

My son, do not forget my instruction,

and let your heart guard my commandments,

for they will add to you length of days,

years of life, and peace.

Do not let covenant loyalty and faithfulness leave you;

bind them around your neck;

write them upon the tablet of your heart,

then you will find favor and good judgment

in the eyes of God and people.

Trust in Yahweh with all your heart,

and do not lean upon your own understanding;

in all your ways be mindful of Him,

and He will make your paths straight.

Do not be wise in your own eyes;

fear Yahweh and turn away from evil.

Proverbs 3:1–7

Do not withhold a good thing from those to whom it is due,

when it is *in* the power of your hands to do *it*.

Do not tell your neighbors, "Go, and come back,

and tomorrow I will give *it*," when it is with you.

Do not devise evil against your neighbor;

he lives near you and trusts *you*.

Do not quarrel with someone for no reason

if he has not committed evil against you.

Do not envy a violent person,

and do not choose any of his ways.

Proverbs 3:27–31

More than anything else you protect, guard your heart,

because from it *flow* the issues of life.

Put away from you a crooked mouth,

and put deceitful lips far away from you.

Focus your eyes in front of you,

and let your eyelids *look* straight ahead of you.

Carefully weigh the path of your feet,

and let all your roads be established.

Do not turn to the right or to the left;

keep your foot away from evil.

Proverbs 4:23–27

The one who walks blamelessly walks securely,

but the one who perverts his ways will be made known.

Proverbs 10:9

The one who heeds *sound* teaching is *on* the path to life,

but the one who ignores reproof goes astray.

Proverbs 10:17

The integrity of the upright will lead them,

but the perversity of the unfaithful will destroy them.

Proverbs 11:3

The one who shows contempt for his neighbor lacks sense,

but a person with understanding remains silent.

A gossip walks around revealing secrets,

but the person who is of a faithful spirit conceals a matter.

Without wise guidance people will fall,

but with a multitude of advisors there is deliverance.

Proverbs 11:12–14

The road of a fool is right in his own eyes,

but a wise person listens to counsel.

The anger of a fool is known at once,

but a prudent person conceals dishonor.

The one who speaks *what is* faithful declares an honest testimony,

but a false witness *utters* deceit.

There is one who speaks recklessly, like the stabbings of a sword,

but the tongue of the wise is healing.

Proverbs 12:15–18

The one who walks with the wise will become wise,

but the one who associates with fools will suffer harm.

Proverbs 13:20

A wise person is cautious and turns away from evil,

but a fool is angry and is overconfident.

An easily angered person acts foolishly,

and a schemer will be hated.

Proverbs 14:16–17

The beginning of strife is *like* letting water out,

so abandon the dispute before it breaks out.

Proverbs 17:14

A fool does not delight in understanding,

but only in expressing his own mind.

Proverbs 18:2

A person's good judgment makes him slow to anger,
and it is his honor to overlook an offense.

Proverbs 19:11

The one who keeps the commandment watches over his life,
but the one who has contempt for his road will die.

Proverbs 19:16

Even a young boy is known by his actions,
whether *or not* his conduct is pure and upright.

Proverbs 20:11

The one who watches over his mouth and his tongue
guards his life from trouble.

Proverbs 21:23

CONFLICT/STRIFE

C onflict can arise for many different reasons—pride, anger, jealousy, gossip, wrongdoing, and so on. Those who stir up discord do so often on account of arrogance, deception, and slander, thriving on the hurt and division it causes. This kind of strife utterly destroys peace and unity, and God absolutely detests it.

First, pride is a major source of conflict. When people insist on their own way and refuse wise counsel, tensions can escalate and erupt into an all-out war. While arrogance fuels division and further conflict, humility engenders healing and harmony. Anger, too, is a key contributor that often accompanies pride. A hot-tempered person provokes quarrels and contention, but those who exercise patience and self-control bring peace.

Words have the power to either inflame or resolve conflict. Fools speak recklessly, inciting fights, while the wise seek to be calm and restore order. Gossip and slander are especially destructive, spreading misinformation and breaking down trust between people. Removing a contentious person or refusing to engage in gossip can put an end to much strife, just as taking away fuel extinguishes a fire.

Proverbs instructs that the best way to handle conflict is to avoid unnecessary disputes in the first place. Arguments only invite greater turmoil, and the wise know when to walk away rather than further engage. Most often, responding to a conflict only incites further conflict.

Strife is often generated by those who love division and chaos, meddling in matters that don't concern them and only invite trouble. They enjoy stirring the pot and seeing what happens. Their tendency to cause conflict often reveals a deep issue of unresolved conflict within themselves.

True peace comes through humility, wisdom, and trust in God. Those who avoid quarrels, speak with grace, and act in love will experience harmony and strong relationships, while those who feed on discord and strife will find themselves isolated and consumed by conflict.

There are six things that Yahweh hates,

indeed, seven things are abominations to his soul:

prideful eyes, a lying tongue,

and hands shedding innocent blood;

a heart that devises wicked thoughts,

feet that are swift to run to *do* evil,

a false witness who breathes out lies,

and one who sows strife among brothers.

Proverbs 6:16–19

Hatred stirs up strife,

but love covers over all transgressions.

Proverbs 10:12

The one hiding *his* hatred *has* deceitful lips,
and the one spreading slander, he is a fool.

Proverbs 10:18

Arrogance only causes strife,
but wisdom is with those who accept advice.

Proverbs 13:10

Fools mock at a guilt offering,
but among the upright is favor.

Proverbs 14:9

A gentle response turns away rage,
but a hurtful word increases anger.

Proverbs 15:1

Better is a meal of vegetables when love is present,
than a fattened ox and hatred with it.
A hot-tempered person incites strife,
but one who is slow to get angry peacefully settles a dispute.

Proverbs 15:17–18

When Yahweh takes pleasure in a person's ways,
even his enemies will make peace with him.

Proverbs 16:7

A perverse person sows strife,
and a gossip separates close friends.

Proverbs 16:28

Better is a dry *piece of* bread and peace with it,
than a household full of feasting with strife.

Proverbs 17:1

The one who covers over a transgression seeks love,
but the one who repeats the issue separates close friends.

Proverbs 17:9

The beginning of strife is *like* letting water out,
so abandon the dispute before it breaks out.

Proverbs 17:14

The one who loves transgression loves strife,
the one who exalts his doorway seeks disaster.

Proverbs 17:19

When a wicked person enters, contempt also enters,
and with dishonor *comes* scorn.

Proverbs 18:3

The lips of a fool bring strife,
and his mouth calls for beatings.

Proverbs 18:6

Casting lots *causes* quarrels to cease
and decides between mighty *opponents*.
An offended brother is *harder to win* than a strong city,
and contentions are like the barred *gate* of a castle.

Proverbs 18:18–19

It is an honor for a person to cease from strife,
but every fool will quarrel.

Proverbs 20:3

A gift *given* in secret subdues anger,
and a secret bribe *averts* strong wrath.

Proverbs 21:14

Drive out the mocker and strife will go out,

and quarrelling and insults will cease.

Proverbs 22:10

Who has woe? Who has sorrow?

Who has contentions? Who has a complaint?

Who has wounds without cause? Who has bleary eyes?

It is those who linger over wine;

those who come in to taste mixed wine.

Proverbs 23:29–30

Like one who removes clothing on a cold day,

or vinegar upon a wound,

is one who sings a song to a heavy heart.

Proverbs 25:20

The north wind brings rain,

and a tongue *telling* secrets brings an angry face.

Proverbs 25:23

Like a person who seizes a dog by its ears

is one who while passing by gets angry over a dispute that

is not his own.

Like a maniac shooting flaming arrows,

arrows, and death,

so is a person who deceives his neighbor,

then says, "Was I not simply joking?"

Proverbs 26:17–19

When the wood is gone, a fire will go out,

and when there is no gossip, contentions will grow quiet.

Like charcoal for hot coals and wood for fire,

so is a contentious person for kindling strife.

Proverbs 26:20–21

A greedy soul stirs up strife,

but the person who trusts in Yahweh will be made prosperous.

Proverbs 28:25

Scornful people inflame a city,

but the wise turn away anger.

If a wise person disputes with a foolish person,

he rages or laughs, but there is no calm.

Proverbs 29:8–9

An angry person stirs up strife,

and a vengeful person *commits* much transgression.

Proverbs 29:22

If you acted foolishly by exalting yourself,

or if you plan *to do so, put* your hand over your mouth!

For the churning of milk brings forth butter,

and the churning of the nose brings forth blood,

so the churning of anger brings forth strife.

Proverbs 30:32–33

DECEIT/FRAUD

Deceit and dishonesty may promise gain, but they ultimately lead to one's own ruin, while on the other hand, standing with integrity brings security and lasting blessings. A person who walks in truth has nothing to hide, but those who rely on deception have to lurk in the shadows but will eventually be exposed. God despises dishonesty, especially in business, where unfair tactics and fraudulent dealings exploit and harm others. One deceives themselves in thinking that wealth gained through trickery will be rewarding and long-lasting. It won't. It will be gone before one can notice. But honest work leads to steady prosperity and the accumulation of true wealth.

Lies not only trap the one who tells them, but they also hurt those who trust in them. Though deception may offer temporary advantages, it leads to disgrace and punishment in the end. The righteous reject falsehood, knowing that truth builds strong relationships and preserves life. On the other hand, those who embrace dishonesty find themselves ensnared by their own schemes and will face the shame and destruction of their own making.

Justice is the foundation of a well-ordered society, so those who twist justice through bribery and deceit contribute to social disorder and chaos, oppressing the weak for their own benefit. True wisdom teaches that honesty is the surest path, as God delights in fairness and integrity. While deceivers may think they are clever, their own tricks will eventually backfire, and they won't be the ones laughing in the end.

What seems sweet at first—gaining riches or getting ahead by fraud—soon turns bitter, leading to regret and hardship. Wealth gained through deception is short-lived, but honest labor brings lasting reward. Proverbs clearly says that deceit and dishonesty will be uncovered and punished, while integrity provides stability and peace. Dishonest business practices, such as false weights and misleading negotiations, are detestable to God and result in ruin.

Ultimately, one must be careful and discerning since appearances can be misleading. Whether it's the charm of a person, the illusion of wealth, or an enticing offer, not everything is as it seems.

The one who walks blamelessly walks securely,

but the one who perverts his ways will be made known.

Proverbs 10:9

Deceitful balances are an abomination to Yahweh,

but a fair weight is his delight.

Proverbs 11:1

The integrity of the upright will lead them,

but the perversity of the unfaithful will destroy them.

Proverbs 11:3

The wicked person makes a deceptive wage,

but the one who sows righteousness *receives* a true reward;

Proverbs 11:18

The thoughts of the righteous are just,
but the guidance of the wicked is deceitful.

Proverbs 12:5

The one who speaks *what is* faithful declares an honest testimony,
but a false witness *utters* deceit.

Proverbs 12:17

Deceit *is* in the heart of those who devise evil,
but those who counsel peace *have* joy.

Proverbs 12:20

There is one who pretends to be rich, but *has* nothing;
another pretends to be poor *but has* great wealth.

Proverbs 13:7

Wealth *obtained* by fraud will dwindle away,
but the one who gathers little by little increases *his wealth.*

Proverbs 13:11

A faithful witness will not lie,
but a deceptive witness breathes out lies.

Proverbs 14:5

The wisdom of a prudent person is to understand his road,
but the foolishness of fools is deceit.

Proverbs 14:8

The one who winks his eyes devises perversions;
the one who purses his lips brings evil to pass.

Proverbs 16:30

A twisted heart will not find good,
and the one who has a double tongue will fall into evil.

Proverbs 17:20

A rich person's wealth is his strong city,
indeed, *it is* like a high wall in his imagination.

Proverbs 18:11

The first person to present his case in a dispute *seems* right
until a neighbor comes and questions him.

Proverbs 18:17

A false witness will not go unpunished,
and the one who tells lies will not escape.

Proverbs 19:5

A false witness will not go unpunished,
and the one who tells lies will perish.

Proverbs 19:9

"Bad! Bad!" says the buyer,
but when he goes his way, he boasts.

Proverbs 20:14

Bread *gained* by deceit is sweet to a person,
but afterwards his mouth will be filled with gravel.

Proverbs 20:17

Unequal weights are an abomination to Yahweh,
and deceitful scales are not good.

Proverbs 20:23

Acquiring treasures by a lying tongue
is a fleeting vapor *of* those who seek death.

Proverbs 21:6

When you sit to eat with a ruler,
carefully discern who is before you,
and put a knife in your throat

if you *have* a greedy appetite.
Do not crave his tasty foods,
for it is deceptive bread.

Proverbs 23:1–3

Like clouds and wind but no rain
is a person who boasts of a gift never given.

Proverbs 25:14

Like a maniac shooting flaming arrows,
arrows, and death,
so is a person who deceives his neighbor,
then says, "Was I not simply joking?"

Proverbs 26:18–19

A person who hates disguises himself with his lips,
but he harbors deceit in his inner being;
when his speech is gracious, do not believe him,
for in his heart are seven abominations.
Though his hatred is covered by deception,
his evil will be exposed in *the midst of* the congregation.

Proverbs 26:24–26

Charm is deceptive and beauty is fleeting,
but a woman who fears Yahweh—she will be praised.

Proverbs 31:30

DILIGENCE/WORK ETHIC

D iligence brings prosperity, success, and stability, while laziness leads to poverty, frustration, and shame. Proverbs repeatedly emphasizes that hard work results in satisfaction and provision. Just as the ant instinctively prepares for the future, wise individuals take initiative, working diligently without needing constant oversight. In contrast, those who avoid responsibility and prioritize comfort over effort will eventually face hardship and suffering.

A diligent person seizes opportunities and works at the appropriate time. Their reliability and determination pave the way for success and prosperity. On the other hand, the lazy person procrastinates, makes excuses, and allows fear to hinder their progress. Because they fail to act when effort is required, they miss out on benefiting from the opportunity, and eventually they suffer the consequences of their foolishness and inaction.

Laziness is not only self-destructive but also frustrating to others. Just as vinegar irritates the teeth and smoke stings the eyes, an unreliable person is a burden to those who depend on them. They evade responsibility, waste opportunities, and choose ease over discipline. Even when given chances to succeed, a lazy person squanders them by neglecting the simplest tasks that could advance them in life and provide additional opportunity.

This neglect leads to ruin—financially, materially, and even morally. Proverbs illustrates this vividly with the image of a lazy person's field overgrown with thorns and broken walls, symbolizing how idleness allows disorder and decay to take over one's life. Those who ignore this warning will face increasing hardship. However, those who embrace diligence, discipline, and wisdom will find success, financial security, and the ability to help others.

Hard work is not just about achieving financial gain, though. It reveals one's character. A diligent person is resourceful, dependable, and respected by others, while a lazy person is wasteful, unreliable, and always in need of something. The wise understand that success comes through consistent effort, and they embrace the necessary labor to obtain it rather than take the "easy" route in life and avoid it.

Beyond financial consequences, laziness damages personal relationships as well. A lazy person jeopardizes others' trust in them and inevitably lets those around them down, because they fail to follow through on promises made or fulfill basic duties to support and demonstrate commitment.

In the end, diligence is a sign of wisdom, while laziness indicates foolishness. The wise work hard, make the most of opportunities, and refuse to be ruled by excuses. Meanwhile, laziness leads to missed chances, unfulfilled desires, and eventual hardship and devastation. The choice between diligence and idleness ultimately determines whether one's life is marked by abundance or scarcity.

The poor person works with an idle palm,

but a diligent hand makes *one* rich.

The one who gathers in the summer is an insightful son;

the one who is fast asleep at the harvest is a shameful son.

Proverbs 10:4–5

The one who works his land will be satisfied with food,
but the one who pursues worthless things lacks sense.
The wicked person desires the spoils of evil people,
but the root of the righteous produces *its own fruit*.

Proverbs 12:11–12

From the fruit of his mouth a person is satisfied with good,
and the accomplishments of a person's hands will return to him.

Proverbs 12:14

The hand of the diligent will rule,
but the slack *hand* will become a forced laborer.

Proverbs 12:24

A lazy person will not catch his prey,
but the diligent *will obtain* precious wealth.

Proverbs 12:27

The appetite of the lazy person craves yet *gets* nothing,
but the desire of the diligent person will be fully satisfied.

Proverbs 13:4

Wealth *obtained* by fraud will dwindle away,
but the one who gathers little by little increases *his wealth*.

Proverbs 13:11

In all hard work there is profit,
but *mere* words from the lips surely *lead* to poverty.

Proverbs 14:23

A laborer's appetite labors for him,
for his mouth urges him on.

Proverbs 16:26

The plans of a diligent person surely *will lead* to abundance,
but everyone who acts hastily surely *will come to* poverty.

Proverbs 21:5

Do you see a man skilled in his occupation?
He will stand in the presence of kings;
he will not stand in the presence of obscure people.

Proverbs 22:29

Prepare your outdoor work,
and carefully prepare it for yourself in the field;
afterwards, then, build your house.

Proverbs 24:27

The one who guards a fig tree will eat of its fruit,
and the one who watches over his master will be honored.

Proverbs 27:18

The one who works his land will be satisfied with food,
but the one who pursues worthless things will be
        "satisfied" with poverty.

Proverbs 28:19

DISCERNMENT/ DISCRETION

Discernment and discretion are vital for living a life rooted in wisdom. They serve as safeguards, steering individuals away from deception and harmful choices. True discernment is cultivated through attentive listening, a thirst for understanding, and valuing wisdom like a priceless treasure. Those who develop this quality recognize truth and apply it wisely in their lives, thereby avoiding reckless decisions and the tempting allure of foolishness.

Discretion, in turn, is a basis for making sound judgments. It enables one to approach challenges with healthy caution and awareness rather than impulsive reactions. A person with discernment and discretion is mindful in their interactions, slow to speak, and aware that silence can often be more powerful than responding quickly with hasty words. Such individuals do not belittle others through their composed demeanor but are being careful and intentional in the situation.

Ultimately, true discernment comes from God. He is the one who provides reliable insight and understanding in life. Thus, those who seek discernment find not only guidance and protection, but also the ability to act with wisdom. A person with discretion carefully chooses their words, influencing others through thoughtfulness rather than reckless speech. Wisdom is not just intellectual knowledge—it is practical, shaping character and decision-making.

It leads to security, constructive relationships, and a reputation built on integrity. A life led by discernment brings favor, peace, and prosperity, shielding one from the pitfalls of foolishness.

Proverbs emphasize the significance of wisdom, discernment, and discretion in making sound decisions and leading a righteous life. Wisdom is more than knowledge; it is the ability to apply insight skillfully. Those who pursue wisdom find stability and protection, ensuring they walk in integrity and avoid deception.

A discerning person listens closely, seeks knowledge, and uncovers deeper truths, drawing wisdom like water from a deep well. Where wisdom thrives, society and individuals prosper. In contrast, a lack of wisdom leads to disorder, as seen when a land suffers under many unstable rulers.

Discretion protects against deception and immorality, allowing one to judge fairly and recognize hidden motives. A fool delights in reckless behavior, but the wise find joy in understanding. Even silence can signal wisdom, as a quiet fool may be mistaken for one who is wise.

Those who seek Yahweh and His wisdom gain insight into justice and truth, while the wicked remain blind. Discernment reveals false appearances, whether in the self-assured wealthy or in situations that demand careful judgment. A life guided by wisdom and discretion leads to peace, stability, and divine blessing.

The proverbs of Solomon, the son of David, king of Israel:

To know wisdom and teaching,

to understand words *that give* understanding,

to receive wise teaching

in righteousness, justice, and integrity;

to give prudence to the naive,

knowledge and discretion to the youth.

A wise person will listen and increase in learning,

and a discerning person will get wise guidance,

to understand a proverb and an obscure expression,

words of the wise and their riddles.

Proverbs 1:1–6

For wisdom will come into your heart,

and knowledge will be pleasant to your soul;

discretion will watch over you,

and discernment will guard you,

Proverbs 2:10–11

Blessed is the person who finds Wisdom,

and the one who obtains discernment,

Proverbs 3:13

My son, do not let these depart from *before* your eyes:

guard sound advice and discretion,

Proverbs 3:21

My son, pay attention to my wisdom;

incline your ear to my discernment,

in order that you keep discretion,

and your lips guard knowledge.

Proverbs 5:1–2

"I, Wisdom, dwell with prudence,

and I find knowledge and discretion.

Proverbs 8:12

Wisdom is found upon the lips of the discerning,

but a rod *will strike* the back of the one lacking sense.

Proverbs 10:13

Acting indecently is pleasure to a fool,
so also is wisdom for a person with discernment.

Proverbs 10:23

Wisdom rests in the heart of the one who has understanding,
and *even* among fools she makes herself known.

Proverbs 14:33

A person with a wise heart will be called "one who understands,"
and the sweetness of *his* lips will increase persuasiveness.

Proverbs 16:21

Even a fool who remains silent is thought to be wise;
when he shuts his lips, he is *considered* to be discerning.

Proverbs 17:28

The heart of one who understands acquires knowledge,
and the ear of the wise seeks knowledge.

Proverbs 18:15

Strike a mocker and a naive person will act prudently,
and if you reprove the one who has understanding, he will
       discern knowledge.

Proverbs 19:25

The counsel in a person's heart is *like* deep water,
but a person with discernment will draw it out.

Proverbs 20:5

On account of the transgression of the land, many are its rulers,
but by a person with understanding *and* knowledge order
       will be prolonged.

Proverbs 28:2

Evil people do not understand justice,

but those who are seeking Yahweh will come to understand it all.

Proverbs 28:5

A rich person is wise in his own eyes,

but the poor person with understanding sees right through him.

Proverbs 28:11

DISCIPLINE

Discipline is essential for a life of wisdom and success. Those who reject discipline walk a path of dishonor, poverty, ruin, and even death. But discipline is not meant to harm or be destructive. Rather, it is a safeguard, a gentle, guiding hand that steers a person onto the right path. Those who embrace discipline grow in wisdom, avoid life's pitfalls, and ultimately experience honor and blessing.

To ignore discipline is to invite ignorance and suffering into one's life. True knowledge and understanding comes to those who are willing to be corrected, and they flourish because of it. This is especially true for children, whose natural inclination toward foolishness must be curbed and refashioned through discipline. Without correction, a child will naturally grow up with harmful and destructive habits. But when properly guided and trained, they can acquire wisdom. Parents play a crucial role in this, ensuring that early discipline instills character and sound judgment in children as they grow.

The foundation of wisdom is built on discipline, and rejecting it leads only to one's injury and regret. Far from being oppressive, discipline is a beneficial tool for growth that produces self-control and righteousness. It requires humility and a willingness to listen, but those who accept the correction of discipline and are humble to change and adapt reap lasting rewards—wisdom, success, and divine favor.

Parental discipline, in particular, is an act of love. A father or mother who truly cares for their child will provide correction, knowing that allowing foolishness to dominate their child leads to dishonor, hardship, and pain. In contrast, proper instruction, even when it might seem overbearing and harsh, shapes a child's character and sets them on the right path in life. A well-trained child will carry wisdom into adulthood, making good choices that honor both God and their family.

But discipline is not just for children—it is a lifelong process. Those who reject reproof will suffer loss, whether in reputation, material wealth, or even their life. Correction, though sometimes painful, purifies and strengthens a person, purging foolishness and immaturity from their heart. The wise welcome a rebuke, knowing it deepens one's knowledge and understanding and builds strong character. On the other hand, fools resist and detest all rebuke and correction, thus dooming themselves to repeat their foolishness and suffering the consequences over and over again.

The fear of Yahweh is the beginning of knowledge,

but fools show contempt for wisdom and *sound* teaching.

Proverbs 1:7

My son, do not reject the discipline of Yahweh,

and do not abhor his reproof.

For the one whom Yahweh loves, he reproves,

like a father to his cherished son.

Proverbs 3:11–12

and in the end you groan
when your flesh—even your body—are used up.
Then you will say, "O how I have hated discipline,
and my heart has spurned reproof.
I did not listen to the voice of my teachers,
nor did I incline my ear to those instructing me.
I was soon in all sorts of trouble
in the midst of the assembly and congregation."

Proverbs 5:11–14

The one acting wickedly—his *own* iniquities will capture him,
and he will be seized by the cords of his *own* sin.
He will die because of lack of discipline,
and in the abundance of his foolishness he goes astray.

Proverbs 5:22–23

For the commandment is a lamp and the instruction is a light,
and reproofs *that offer* correction are a road *leading to* life,
to keep you from the evil woman,
from the flattering tongue of the foreign woman.

Proverbs 6:23–24

Wisdom is found upon the lips of the discerning,
but a rod *will strike* the back of the one lacking sense.

Proverbs 10:13

A wise son *listens to his* father's discipline,
but a mocker does not listen to rebuke.

Proverbs 13:1

The one who ignores discipline *will get* poverty and dishonor,
but the one who heeds reproof will be honored.

Proverbs 13:18

The one who withholds his rod hates his son,
but the one who loves him desires discipline for him.

Proverbs 13:24

A fool spurns discipline from his father,
but the one who heeds reproof acts prudently.

Proverbs 15:5

Harsh discipline is for the one who abandons the path;
the one who hates reproof will die.

Proverbs 15:10

The one who ignores discipline despises his *own* soul,
but the one who listens to reproof acquires *good* sense.

Proverbs 15:32

A rebuke goes deeper into a person who has understanding
than a hundred blows on a fool.

Proverbs 17:10

Correct your son, for there is hope,
and do not be intent on causing his death.

Proverbs 19:18

Listen to counsel and accept discipline
in order that you may be wise in your latter *days*.

Proverbs 19:20

Blows that wound cleanse away evil,
and beatings *cleanse* the innermost being.

Proverbs 20:30

Train a child in the way he should go;
even when he grows old he will not turn aside from it.

Proverbs 22:6

Foolishness is bound up in the heart of a child;
a rod of discipline will remove it far from him.

Proverbs 22:15

Apply your heart to *sound* teaching,
and *apply* your ears to words of knowledge.
Do not withhold discipline from a child;
if you strike him with the rod, he will not die.
If you strike him with the rod,
you will deliver his soul from Sheol.

Proverbs 23:12–14

A rod and reproof give wisdom,
but a child who is left *to himself* puts his mother to shame.

Proverbs 29:15

Correct your son, and he will give you rest,
and he will give delight to your soul.

Proverbs 29:17

A servant cannot be corrected *simply* with words,
for he understands, but he does not respond.

Proverbs 29:19

DIVINE PROVIDENCE

Trusting in God—and not oneself or others—is wise and brings stability, guidance, and security. While human efforts are limited, God directs the course of life. Those who commit their ways to Him will find their paths straight and sure, while those who rely solely on their own understanding will struggle and fall.

The schemes of the wicked will fail, but God's purposes will always prevail. Nothing is hidden from God's sight—He sees both the righteous and the wicked, ensuring justice in His perfect timing. Proverbs presents God's providence extending over rulers and nations alike, for even the hearts of kings are said to be in His hands. While people may seek favor and justice from those in power, true justice and favor come only from God.

In times of adversity or in situations where the unrighteous and wicked seem to prosper, patience and trust in God are essential. Instead of seeking revenge or depending on human strength to fix things, wisdom calls for waiting on God's deliverance and for Him to act. No human wisdom, power, or strategy can stand against Him.

Everything belongs to God, and He governs all things with perfect wisdom. Trusting in Him brings peace and confidence, knowing that His plans cannot be shaken and His purpose never fails. When life feels uncertain, trusting in God provides an unshakable foundation that guides those who trust in Him toward a secure future based on His power, and not our own.

Trust in Yahweh with all your heart,
and do not lean upon your own understanding;
in all your ways be mindful of Him,
and He will make your paths straight.

Proverbs 3:5–6

Do not be afraid of sudden terror,
and of the devastation of the wicked when it comes,
for Yahweh will be your confidence,
and he will keep your foot from being caught.

Proverbs 3:25–26

For a person's ways are before the eyes of Yahweh,
and he weighs all his paths.

Proverbs 5:21

The blessing from Yahweh is what makes one rich,
and he does not combine pain with *the blessing.*

Proverbs 10:22

Sheol and Abaddon are in the sight of Yahweh,
how much more are human hearts!

Proverbs 15:11

The plans of the heart *belong* to the person,
but the answer of the tongue *comes* from Yahweh.
All a person's ways are pure in his own eyes,

but Yahweh examines the motives.
Commit your works to Yahweh,
and your plans will be established.
Yahweh made everything with an answer to it,
and even the wicked person on a day of evil.

Proverbs 16:1–4

A person's heart devises his way,
but Yahweh prepares his steps.

Proverbs 16:9

The lot is cast into the lap,
but each of its judgments is from Yahweh.

Proverbs 16:33

Many plans are in a person's heart,
but Yahweh's counsel will stand.

Proverbs 19:21

Do not say, "I will repay evil!"
Wait for Yahweh and he will deliver you.

Proverbs 20:22

A person's steps are *directed* by Yahweh;
how then can a person understand his road?

Proverbs 20:24

The breath of a person is the lamp of Yahweh,
searching out his innermost being.

Proverbs 20:27

The heart of a king is *like* water canals in Yahweh's hand;
he turns it wherever he delights.

Proverbs 21:1

There is no wisdom and no discernment
and no counsel that can stand against Yahweh.
A horse is prepared for a day of battle,
but the deliverance belongs to Yahweh.

Proverbs 21:30–31

The eyes of Yahweh guard knowledge,
but he overturns the words of the one acting unfaithfully.

Proverbs 22:12

The poor person and the one who oppresses *others* have
        this in common:
Yahweh gives light to the eyes of them both.

Proverbs 29:13

The fear of people will bring a snare,
but the one who trusts in Yahweh will be protected.
Many seek the attention of the one who rules,
but a person *receives* justice from Yahweh.

Proverbs 29:25–26

Who has ascended into heaven and come down?
Who has gathered the wind into the palms of both hands?
Who has bound up the waters into *his* garment?
Who has set up all the ends of the earth?
What is his name, and what is the name of his son?
Surely you know!

Proverbs 30:4

DRINKING/
DRUNKENNESS

E xcessive drinking leads to self-destruction in many aspects of life. Alcohol dulls judgment, making people act recklessly, speak carelessly, and make poor choices that end very badly. The result of such foolishness with alcohol is that it brings deep sorrow, conflict, regret, vulnerability to exploitation, and often leads to financial ruin as personal resources are squandered.

Though alcohol may appear enticing and fun, the effects of its misuse (such as over-consumption) are deadly. Like a serpent's bite, it will suddenly bring disaster upon a person when they least expect it. The drunkard loses self-awareness, putting themselves in danger, much like a sailor who is tossed by waves at sea and doesn't know what direction they are heading. Despite seeing firsthand the damage and consequences that excess drinking brings, many people remain trapped in a cycle of abusing it, seeking escape from their distress...only to exacerbate the problem and deepen their troubles.

Sobriety, by contrast, is linked to wisdom and self-control. Those in leadership are especially warned against drinking, as sound judgment is essential for justice and proper oversight. Alcohol impairs decision-making, leading to poor leadership decisions and injustice. So, while alcohol may offer temporary relief to those who are downcast and sorrowful, relying on it to numb pain is foolish. Using it as a remedy is nothing but a deep, dark pit filled with more pain.

Excessive drinking is deceptive—it promises pleasure but results in mockery, reckless behavior, and all forms of foolishness. And a love of alcohol and indulgence leads to wastefulness, financial loss, and erosion of one's character. Furthermore, drunkenness brings blurred vision, incoherent speech, and distorted judgment. Those who are caught in its grip wake up from their stupor only to seek more, illustrating alcohol's addictive nature.

True wisdom calls for moderation and self-control in all things. Avoiding excessive alcohol consumption preserves one's clarity of mind and personal integrity. Choosing to live disciplined rather than giving in to indulgence leads to a life that is directed by wisdom rather than desire and addiction.

Wine is a mocker, beer is a loudmouth,

and everyone who goes astray by them is not wise.

Proverbs 20:1

The one who loves pleasure *will become* a poor person;

the one who loves wine and oil will not become rich.

Proverbs 21:17

You, my son, must listen and be wise,

and direct your heart on the *upright* road.

Do not be among those who drink too much wine,

or with gluttonous meat-eaters.

For the drunkard and the glutton will become impoverished,

and drowsiness wears rags.

Proverbs 23:19–21

Who has woe? Who has sorrow?

Who has contentions? Who has a complaint?

Who has wounds without cause? Who has bleary eyes?

It is those who linger over wine;

those who come in to taste mixed wine.

Do not look at the wine when it sparkles with red,

when it gleams in the cup,

when it goes down smoothly.

In the end it bites like a serpent,

and it poisons like a viper.

Your eyes will see strange things,

and your heart will speak perverse things.

And you will become like one who lies down in the

middle of the sea,

or like one who lies down on the top of a ship's mast.

"They struck me, *but* I did not feel pain.

They hit me, *but* I did not know *it.*

When will I awaken? I will seek another *drink.*"

Proverbs 23:29–35

It is not for kings, O Lemuel,

not for kings to drink wine,

nor for those who rule *to drink* beer.

Otherwise, they will drink and forget what has been decreed,

and alter the legal claim of all the afflicted people.

Give beer to the person who is disheartened,

and wine to the bitter soul.

Let him drink and forget his poverty,

and no longer remember his troubles.

Proverbs 31:4–7

EMOTIONS

E motions play a significant role in nearly every aspect of life, influencing decision-making, relationships, and overall well-being. Wisdom calls for one to rule over their emotions rather than being ruled by emotions. Uncontrolled emotions lead to impulsive reactions and foolish behavior that result in personal suffering or harm to others.

Anger can be a particularly destructive emotion when left unchecked. A hot-tempered person stirs up conflict and makes foolish decisions, while those who remain calm and slow to anger display understanding, patience, and strength. So powerful are emotions that the ability to control one's emotions is compared to having greater power than even someone who conquers a city. Having self-control is truly a great victory in life.

Other emotions like anxiety and sorrow can weigh down the heart, but kind and encouraging words bring gladness. And a joyful heart is like medicine, bringing life and health to a person, while envy, bitterness, and a crushed spirit drain vitality and lead to suffering.

While fools don't regulate their emotions and openly display them without any restraint, the wise exercise discretion and keep their feelings properly in check. Without emotional control, a person is like a defenseless city with broken walls—vulnerable and easily overtaken. Thus, emotions can be thought of as a gate or door, and negligence or carelessness in handling them is like opening yourself up to be conquered and destroyed.

The hope of the righteous is joy,
but the expectation of the wicked will perish.

Proverbs 10:28

The anger of a fool is known at once,
but a prudent person conceals dishonor.

Proverbs 12:16

Anxiety in a person's heart weighs it down,
but a good word makes it glad.

Proverbs 12:25

Even in laughter the heart *might* be in pain,
and the end of joy *may be* grief.

Proverbs 14:13

A wise person is cautious and turns away from evil,
but a fool is angry and is overconfident.
An easily angered person acts foolishly,
and a schemer will be hated.

Proverbs 14:16–17

The one who is slow to get angry *possesses* great understanding,
but the one who is easily angered displays foolishness.
A peaceful heart is the life of the flesh,
but envy is decay to the bones.

Proverbs 14:29–30

A hot-tempered person incites strife,
but one who is slow to get angry peacefully settles a dispute.

Proverbs 15:18

Bright eyes make the heart glad,
and good news fattens the bones.

Proverbs 15:30

The one who is slow to get angry is better than a mighty person,
and one who rules his spirit is *better* than one who captures a city.

Proverbs 16:32

A cheerful heart is a good cure,
but a broken spirit dries up the bones.

Proverbs 17:22

The one who holds back his words has *attained* knowledge,
and the one who has a cool spirit is a person of understanding.

Proverbs 17:27

A person's good judgment makes him slow to anger,
and it is his honor to overlook an offense.

Proverbs 19:11

Like a city broken into, *one* without a wall,
is a person who has no self-control over his emotions.

Proverbs 25:28

A fool lets out all of his emotions,
but a wise person keeps them calm within.

Proverbs 29:11

FAITHFULNESS

Faithfulness is a defining characteristic of a person with integrity. It earns favor from both God and others because it reflects reliability, trustworthiness, and commitment. A faithful person keeps their promises, avoids gossip, and protects relationships by preserving trust. Their presence has a positive impact on those around them and brings stability to their communities, serving as a godly example to those around them.

Closely tied to righteousness, faithfulness shields individuals from harm, while unfaithfulness leads to destruction and self-entrapment. Those who remain faithful in their relationships and dealings bring blessings to others, rescue people from entering dangerous arrangements, and contribute to the greater good.

A true test of faithfulness is consistency—doing what is right even when no one is watching. Many claim to have loyalty and allegiance, but few truly live it out. Actions, not just words, reveal a person's character and whether or not they are steadfast and trustworthy.

Faithfulness is especially vital in leadership. A person who governs with faithfulness and integrity ensures stability, gains respect, and secures a lasting legacy. This principle extends beyond rulers and leaders—it applies to anyone entrusted with responsibility. Those who act with faithfulness are protected and honored, while those who betray trust bring only pain and disappointment, both upon themselves and all those involved.

In regard to words, a faithful person is a trustworthy person who keeps secrets, speaks the truth, and upholds justice. Their counterpart is a liar or gossip who goes around causing mischief and destruction. Trusting an unfaithful person in a time of need is like leaning on a broken crutch—it only leads to falling down and getting hurt.

Faithfulness is more than just words; it is a way of life. It fosters trust, leads to prosperity, and strengthens relationships with both God and others. Those who walk in faithfulness will find stability, respect, and abundant blessings in life.

He has stored up sound advice for the upright—

a shield for those who walk blamelessly—

guarding the paths of justice,

and watching over the way of his loyal ones.

Proverbs 2:7–8

Do not let covenant loyalty and faithfulness leave you;

bind them around your neck;

write them upon the tablet of your heart,

then you will find favor and good judgment

in the eyes of God and people.

Proverbs 3:3–4

Honor Yahweh from your wealth,

and from the firstfruits of all your revenue,

and your storehouses will be completely filled,
and your wine vats will overflow with new wine.

Proverbs 3:9–10

A gossip walks around revealing secrets,
but the person who is of a faithful spirit conceals a matter.

Proverbs 11:13

Lying lips are an abomination to Yahweh,
but those who do *what is* faithful *obtain* his favor.

Proverbs 12:22

A wicked messenger will fall into evil,
but a faithful messenger *brings* healing.

Proverbs 13:17

A faithful witness will not lie,
but a deceptive witness breathes out lies.

Proverbs 14:5

Do not those who plan evil go astray?
But loyalty and faithfulness *are with* those who plan good.

Proverbs 14:22

A faithful witness rescues lives,
but the one who breathes out lies is treacherous.

Proverbs 14:25

Iniquity is atoned for by covenant loyalty and faithfulness,
and by the fear of Yahweh one turns away from evil.

Proverbs 16:6

Many people claim to be loyal,
but a faithful man, who can find?

Proverbs 20:6

Covenant loyalty and faithfulness guard the king,
yes, he upholds his throne by covenant loyalty.

Proverbs 20:28

to make known to you true words of faithfulness,
and to return words of faithfulness to those who sent you?

Proverbs 22:21

Like the cold of snow at the time of harvest
is a faithful messenger to those who send him,
for he refreshes the soul of his masters.

Proverbs 25:13

Like a bad tooth or a foot that slips
is confidence in a person who acts unfaithfully in a
        time of distress.

Proverbs 25:19

A faithful person *will have* many blessings,
but the one who makes haste to get rich will not go unpunished.

Proverbs 28:20

FAMILY RELATIONSHIPS

F amily relationships thrive on exercising wisdom and love. Parents play a crucial role in guiding their children toward righteous living through instruction and correction. A child who listens to wisdom brings joy to their parents, while a rebellious one causes grief and shame. Though discipline may be difficult and unpleasant in the moment, it is essential for a child's growth and long-term well-being.

Proverbs highlights the importance of children honoring both their father and mother. Those who respect and follow their parents' guidance walk the path of wisdom, while those who mock or despise them face serious consequences and do so at their own peril. A strong family is built on wisdom and righteousness, ensuring blessings for generations to come.

Marriage is also a cornerstone of family life. A wise and virtuous spouse is a gift, bringing stability and honor to the household. In contrast, a contentious spouse breeds constant conflict and unrest. It is the diligent and faithful person who is praiseworthy for supporting their family and earning the love and admiration of their spouse and children.

Respect for parents is also intrinsic to a healthy family. When children submit to parental authority and honor them, it leads to peace, stability, and blessings. Children who betray or mistreat their parents bring shame and hurt upon themselves.

There are six things that Yahweh hates,
indeed, seven things are abominations to his soul:
prideful eyes, a lying tongue,
and hands shedding innocent blood;
a heart that devises wicked thoughts,
feet that are swift to run to *do* evil,
a false witness who breathes out lies,
and one who sows strife among brothers.

Proverbs 6:16–19

The proverbs of Solomon:
A wise son makes *his* father glad,
but a foolish son *brings* grief *to* his mother.

Proverbs 10:1

A wise son makes a father glad,
but a foolish person shows contempt for his mother.

Proverbs 15:20

An insightful servant will rule over a shameful son,
and he will share the inheritance among brothers.

Proverbs 17:2

The crown of old men is *their* children's children,
and the glory of children is their fathers.

Proverbs 17:6

A friend loves at all times,
and a brother is born for *times of* distress.

Proverbs 17:17

He who fathers a fool *does so* to his own grief,
and the father of a godless person will have no joy.

Proverbs 17:21

A foolish son *brings* destruction to his father,
and the contentions of a wife are *like* a constant drip.

Proverbs 19:13

Correct your son, for there is hope,
and do not be intent on causing his death.

Proverbs 19:18

He who assaults *his* father and drives *his* mother away
is a shameful and disgraceful son.

Proverbs 19:26

A righteous person who walks in his integrity—
blessed are his children after him.

Proverbs 20:7

The one who curses his father or his mother,
his lamp will go out in a time of darkness.

Proverbs 20:20

Train a child in the way he should go;
even when he grows old he will not turn aside from it.

Proverbs 22:6

Do not withhold discipline from a child;
if you strike him with the rod, he will not die.

If you strike him with the rod,
you will deliver his soul from Sheol.

Proverbs 23:13–14

Listen to your father who begot you,
and do not show contempt for your mother when she is old.
Get truth and do not sell it;
get wisdom and teaching and understanding.
The father of a righteous person will rejoice exceedingly,
and the man who fathers a wise *son* will delight in him;
may your father and your mother be glad,
and may she who gave birth to you rejoice.

Proverbs 23:22–25

Like a bird that wanders from her nest,
so is a person who wanders from his place.

Proverbs 27:8

He who keeps the Law is a discerning son,
but he who associates with those who lack restraint brings shame
        upon his father.

Proverbs 28:7

The person who robs his father or his mother and says, "It is not a
        transgression,"
he is a friend of a person *who causes* destruction.

Proverbs 28:24

A person who loves wisdom makes his father glad,
but the man who gets involved with prostitutes
        destroys his wealth.

Proverbs 29:3

A rod and reproof give wisdom,
but a child who is left *to himself* puts his mother to shame.

Proverbs 29:15

Correct your son, and he will give you rest,
and he will give delight to your soul.

Proverbs 29:17

There is a generation that curses its father
and that does not bless its mother.

Proverbs 30:11

An eye that mocks at his father
and despises obedience to his mother—
ravens of the valley will peck it out,
and the offspring of a vulture will eat it.

Proverbs 30:17

FEAR OF YAHWEH/ TRUSTING IN YAHWEH

B oth the fear of Yahweh and trusting in Yahweh are foundational themes in Proverbs, presented as the beginning of wisdom and the key to a life of blessing, stability, and true understanding. To fear the Lord is to live with reverence, awe, and humble submission to God's rule, recognizing His power and authority and living according to law. This involves turning away from evil and wickedness, seeking what is right, and aligning one's life with God's will, knowing that God's commandments, as the Creator and Designer of life, are for the benefit and well-being of all creation.

This reverent fear of Yahweh is not crippling terror but a guiding awareness of God's presence and standards for how to best live. Submitting to God's rule leads to wisdom, protection, prosperity in all facets of life, and a deep sense of purpose. Those who fear Yahweh receive insight, are confident, and have a place of refuge in times of trouble. Having reverence for God and his law is a fountain of life, keeping one from the snares of death and offering safety, stability, and peace, even in the face of danger.

Trusting in Yahweh means not leaning on one's own understanding or abilities but acknowledging their need for God in every decision, desire, challenge, joy, sorrow, and experience. It is an act of total surrender, resting upon God's wisdom, strength, and timing. Those who trust in God are kept safe from fear of people, selfish ambition, greed, and unforeseen circumstances. Their paths are made straight, and they enjoy God's favor, peace, and the success and contentment that only he can bestow.

Both the fear of and trust in Yahweh shape one's character, cultivating humility, obedience, and a deep reliance upon and respect for God in all things. The opposite of this mindset is arrogance and pride, a rebellious heart, self-reliance and over-confidence, and a disregard for God's provision and protection, all of which lead to disappointment and suffering. But the rewards of fearing and trusting in Yahweh include long life, honor, spiritual insight and understanding, and enduring hope that will never fail.

These qualities form the core of wise living, and they draw a person close to God's heart, anchor the soul in truth, and provide a foundation to excel in every other godly virtue and conduct. There is nothing to lose and everything to gain, because the one who fears and trusts in Yahweh walks a path that is secure and richly blessed.

The fear of Yahweh is the beginning of knowledge,

but fools show contempt for wisdom and *sound* teaching.

Proverbs 1:7

Because they hated knowledge,

and they did not choose the fear of Yahweh;

they were not interested in my counsel,

and they spurned all my reproof,

so they will eat from the fruit of their *own* way,

and from their *own* schemes they will have *their* fill.

Proverbs 1:29–31

My son, if you receive my words,

and store up my commandments with you,

making your ear attentive to Wisdom,

directing your heart to discernment,

for if you call out to understanding,

if you raise your voice to discernment,

if you seek her like silver,

and search for her like hidden treasure,

then you will understand the fear of Yahweh,

and you will find the knowledge of God.

Proverbs 2:1–5

Trust in Yahweh with all your heart,

and do not lean upon your own understanding;

in all your ways be mindful of Him,

and He will make your paths straight.

Proverbs 3:5–6

Do not be wise in your own eyes;

fear Yahweh and turn away from evil.

Proverbs 3:7

The fear of Yahweh is to hate evil—

pride and arrogance and the path of evil

and a perverse mouth, I hate.

Proverbs 8:13

The fear of Yahweh is the starting point of wisdom,

and the knowledge of the Holy One is *the starting point*

of understanding.

Proverbs 9:10

The fear of Yahweh adds to *one's* days,
but the years of the wicked will be cut short.

Proverbs 10:27

The one who despises a word *of instruction* will come to ruin,
but the one who fears the commandment will be rewarded.

Proverbs 13:13

The one who walks in his integrity fears Yahweh,
but the one who is devious in his ways shows contempt for him.

Proverbs 14:2

In the fear of Yahweh there is strong confidence,
and he will be a shelter for his children.
The fear of Yahweh is a fountain of life,
that one may turn aside from the snares of death.

Proverbs 14:26–27

Better is a little with the fear of Yahweh
than great treasure and turmoil with it.

Proverbs 15:16

The fear of Yahweh is what wisdom teaches,
and humility goes before glory.

Proverbs 15:33

Iniquity is atoned for by covenant loyalty and faithfulness,
and by the fear of Yahweh one turns away from evil.

Proverbs 16:6

The fear of Yahweh *leads* to life,
and the one *who has it* will sleep satisfied through the night *and*
    not be visited by evil.

Proverbs 19:23

The reward of humility—the fear of Yahweh—
is wealth, glory, and life.

Proverbs 22:4

So that your trust may be in Yahweh,
I have made *them* known to you today—yes, you.

Proverbs 22:19

Do not let your heart be envious of the sinners;
rather, fear Yahweh all day *long*,
for certainly there is a future,
and your hope will not be cut off.

Proverbs 23:17–18

My son, fear Yahweh and the king;
do not get involved with those who think otherwise,
for disaster will suddenly arise from them,
and who knows the ruin *that can come* from the two of them?

Proverbs 24:21–22

A greedy soul stirs up strife,
but the person who trusts in Yahweh will be made prosperous.

Proverbs 28:25

The fear of people will bring a snare,
but the one who trusts in Yahweh will be protected.

Proverbs 29:25

Charm is deceptive and beauty is fleeting,
but a woman who fears Yahweh—she will be praised.

Proverbs 31:30

FIDELITY

F idelity relates to faithfulness in a relationship and forms the foundation upon which every relationship is built. It is especially meaningful in marriage where it guards the life-long covenant relationship between husband and wife. Remaining true to one's spouse is depicted as a source of blessing and satisfaction, while infidelity leads to destruction, disgrace, and horrible regret. Those who engage in unfaithfulness are warned that their actions lead to ruin and death, like stepping into a trap from which there is no escape.

However, fidelity in general is not just limited to marriage; it extends to all aspects of life, including speech, commitments, and business dealings. A trustworthy person maintains fidelity by guarding secrets reveal to them in confidence, speaking truthfully, and not deceiving others.

Wisdom teaches that true satisfaction comes from remaining devoted to one's commitments. Seeking fulfillment through being unfaithful is a dangerous self-deception that leads only to emptiness and harm. Life is always worse on the other side than if infidelity was never committed to begin with.

Proverbs emphasizes that being faithful—whether in marriage, friendships, or responsibilities—brings favor from both God and people. In contrast, disloyalty, deceit, and treachery undermine trust and ultimately result in personal harm, financial loss, and dishonor.

A faithful person is a source of healing and security to those around them, while an unfaithful one brings harm and sorrow. The wise person understands that true happiness is found in steadfast love and integrity, not by indulging in fleeting temptations or betrayal.

For wisdom will come into your heart,
 and knowledge will be pleasant to your soul;
discretion will watch over you, *and* discernment will guard you,
 ...to deliver you from the forbidden woman,
from the foreign woman *who is* flattering *with* her words,
who leaves the mate of her youth,
and has forgotten the covenant she made before her God,
for her house sinks down to death,
and her paths *lead* to the dead.
All who go to her do not return;
they will not reach the paths of life.

Proverbs 2:10–11, 16–19

Drink water from your own cistern,
and fresh water from the midst of your own well.
Should your springs overflow outside,
streams of water in the public plazas?
Let them be for you alone,
and not for strangers with you.
Let your fountain be continually blessed,
and rejoice because of the wife of your youth.

She is a loving doe and a graceful mountain goat;

let her breasts satisfy you at every *opportune* time—

going astray in her love.

So why go astray, my son, with a forbidden woman,

and *why* do you embrace the bosom of a foreign woman?

Proverbs 5:15–20

For the commandment is a lamp and the instruction is a light,

and reproofs *that offer* correction are a road *leading to* life,

to keep you from the evil woman,

from the flattering tongue of the foreign woman.

Do not desire her beauty in your heart,

and do not allow her to capture you with her eyes.

For on account of a prostitute *a man is reduced to* a piece of bread,

and an adulteress hunts for a precious life.

Can a man snatch up fire against his chest

and his clothes not be burnt?

Or can a man walk upon hot coals

and his feet not get burned?

So is the one who goes into his neighbor's wife;

all who touch her will not go unpunished.

Proverbs 6:23–29

The man committing adultery with a woman lacks sense;

he who does this is destroying his *own* soul.

He will find affliction and dishonor,

and his disgrace will not be blotted out.

For jealousy enrages a husband,

and he will not spare *him* in the day of *his* vengeance.

He will not be persuaded by any ransom,

nor will he be satisfied when you make many bribes.

Proverbs 6:32–35

Do not allow your heart to turn aside to her ways;

do not wander off onto her paths,

for she has brought down many victims,

and numerous are all her slain.

Her house *has many* paths to Sheol,

descending to the chambers of death.

Proverbs 7:25–27

The righteousness of the upright will deliver them,

but the unfaithful will be taken captive by their desire.

Proverbs 11:6

A gossip walks around revealing secrets,

but the person who is of a faithful spirit conceals a matter.

Proverbs 11:13

A person's delight is his loyalty,

and it is better to be poor than one who tells lies.

Proverbs 19:22

Many people claim to be loyal,

but a faithful man, who can find?

Proverbs 20:6

Covenant loyalty and faithfulness guard the king,

yes, he upholds his throne by covenant loyalty.

Proverbs 20:28

The mouth of the forbidden women is a deep pit;

the person with whom Yahweh is angry will fall in there.

Proverbs 22:14

My son, give your heart to me,

and let your eyes observe my ways,

for a prostitute is a deep pit,

and a foreign woman is a narrow well.

Indeed, she lies in wait like a robber,

and she increases *the number of* unfaithful people.

Proverbs 23:26–28

FOOL/FOOLISHNESS

A fool is more than just a person who has a habit of being careless. They are impulsive, arrogant, resistant to correction, quick to anger, reckless with their words and actions, find enjoyment in their foolishness, and show contempt for knowledge and discipline.

At the heart of foolishness lies a rejection of the fear of Yahweh—the foundational step toward knowledge. Fools scorn correction, refuse to learn from rebuke, and persist in behaviors that lead to harm, both for themselves and those around them.

A fool is described as brash and opinionated, often speaking without understanding and acting impulsively. Their speech is reckless, their anger rises quickly, and their choices are driven by pride and self-interest. Even when presented with wisdom, a fool remains unteachable, returning to their foolishness like a dog to its vomit. This inability to grow or accept counsel isolates them morally, spiritually, and socially, leading them down paths of destruction.

Fools often bring grief and shame to their families and friends by stirring up strife in their relationships and communities. People who are around them suffer because their words provoke conflict, and their presence is a burden to others. Engaging with a fool can result in frustration and further aggression by the fool. Thus, it is prudent to avoid becoming entangled in their arguments and dramas. Furthermore, a fool is marked by their inability to remain silent on account of their deep desire to air their own opinions without any true knowledge or understanding, and their tendency to meddle in business that is not their own.

The contrast between the wise and the foolish is stark: while the wise store knowledge, seek counsel, and govern their spirits, fools exalt shame, mock justice, and lack self-control.

The path of the fool is a descent into shame and death, and their end is marked by ruin, despite their self-confidence to the contrary. Proverbs even highlights that the hope for a fool is minimal because their pride blocks their ability to walk on the road of understanding. And so, their end is only one of misery and destruction.

The fear of Yahweh is the beginning of knowledge,

but fools show contempt for wisdom and *sound* teaching.

Proverbs 1:7

Then they will call upon me, but I will not answer;

they will diligently seek me, but will not find me.

Because they hated knowledge,

and they did not choose the fear of Yahweh;

they were not interested in my counsel,

and they spurned all my reproof,

so they will eat from the fruit of their *own* way,

and from their *own* schemes they will have *their* fill.

For the turning away of the naive will kill them,

and the *false* security of fools will destroy them.

But the one who listens to me will live in safety,

and will be at ease from the dread of evil."

Proverbs 1:28–33

The wise will inherit glory,

but fools exalt shame.

Proverbs 3:35

The one who rebukes a mocker brings shame upon himself,

and the one who reproves a wicked person *brings*

injury upon himself.

Proverbs 9:7

Lady Folly is boisterous,

she lacks understanding and does not know anything.

And she sits at the entrance of her house,

on a throne at the heights of the city,

calling out to those passing by *on* the road,

to the ones making their paths straight,

"Whoever is naive, let him turn in here."

And she says to the one lacking sense,

"Stolen waters are sweet,

and food *eaten in* secret is pleasant."

But he does not know that the dead are there;

the ones who have accepted her *invitation* are in the

depths of Sheol.

Proverbs 9:13–18

A wise son makes *his* father glad,

but a foolish son *brings* grief *to* his mother.

Proverbs 10:1

The wise heart accepts commandments,
but the one who is foolish with his lips will come to ruin.

Proverbs 10:8

The one winking *his* eye causes pain,
and the one who is foolish with his lips will come to ruin.

Proverbs 10:10

The lips of a righteous person will shepherd many people,
but fools will die for a lack of sense.

Proverbs 10:21

Acting indecently is pleasure to a fool,
so also is wisdom for a person with discernment.

Proverbs 10:23

The one who troubles his household will inherit wind,
and the fool will be a servant to one who is wise of heart.

Proverbs 11:29

The road of a fool is right in his own eyes,
but a wise person listens to counsel.
The anger of a fool is known at once,
but a prudent person conceals dishonor.

Proverbs 12:15–16

Every prudent person acts with knowledge,
but a fool displays foolishness.

Proverbs 13:16

A desire fulfilled is sweet to the soul,
but it is an abomination to fools to turn away from evil.

The one who walks with the wise will become wise,

but the one who associates with fools will suffer harm.

Proverbs 13:19–20

Lady Wisdom builds her house,

but *Lady* Folly tears it down with her hands.

The one who walks in his integrity fears Yahweh,

but the one who is devious in his ways shows contempt for him.

In the mouth of a fool is a prideful rod,

but the lips of the wise will watch over them.

Proverbs 14:1–3

Walk away from the presence of a foolish person,

for *there* you will not know lips *that speak* knowledge.

The wisdom of a prudent person is to understand his road,

but the foolishness of fools is deceit.

Fools mock at a guilt offering,

but among the upright is favor.

Proverbs 14:7–9

A wise person is cautious and turns away from evil,

but a fool is angry and is overconfident.

Proverbs 14:16

The naive inherit foolishness,

but the prudent are crowned with knowledge.

Proverbs 14:18

The crown of the wise is *their* wealth,

but the foolishness of fools is *still* foolishness.

Proverbs 14:24

The one who is slow to get angry *possesses* great understanding,
but the one who is easily angered displays foolishness.

Proverbs 14:29

The tongue of the wise produces good knowledge,
but the mouth of fools pours out foolishness.

Proverbs 15:2

A fool spurns discipline from his father,
but the one who heeds reproof acts prudently.

Proverbs 15:5

The heart of the one who has understanding seeks knowledge,
but the mouth of fools feeds on foolishness.

Proverbs 15:14

A wise son makes a father glad,
but a foolish person shows contempt for his mother.
Foolishness is a joy to the one who lacks *good* sense,
but a person with understanding walks with integrity.

Proverbs 15:20–21

Good judgment is a fountain of life *for* its owner,
but the teaching of fools is foolishness.

Proverbs 16:22

There is a road *that seems* upright to a person,
but its end is the road *leading to* death.

Proverbs 16:25

Eloquent speech is not fitting for a godless person,
how much less *fitting* are deceptive lips for a nobleman?

Proverbs 17:7

Better for a person to encounter a bear deprived of her cubs
than *to encounter* a fool in his foolishness.

Proverbs 17:12

Why is there payment in the hand of a fool to buy wisdom
when *he has* no sense?

Proverbs 17:16

He who fathers a fool *does so* to his own grief,
and the father of a godless person will have no joy.

Proverbs 17:21

Wisdom is with the one who understands,
but the eyes of a fool are on the ends of the earth.
A foolish son is grief to his father
and bitterness to the woman who bore him.

Proverbs 17:24–25

Even a fool who remains silent is thought to be wise;
when he shuts his lips, he is *considered* to be discerning.

Proverbs 17:28

A fool does not delight in understanding,
but only in expressing his own mind.

Proverbs 18:2

The lips of a fool bring strife,
and his mouth calls for beatings.
The mouth of a fool *will bring* destruction to him,
and his lips are a snare to his soul.

Proverbs 18:6–7

The person who gives an answer before he listens—
foolishness and disgrace belong to him.

Proverbs 18:13

A person's foolishness subverts his way,
but his heart rages against Yahweh.

Proverbs 19:3

A foolish son *brings* destruction to his father,
and the contentions of a wife are *like* a constant drip.

Proverbs 19:13

Judgments have been prepared for mockers,
and beatings *have been prepared* for the backs of fools.

Proverbs 19:29

It is an honor for a person to cease from strife,
but every fool will quarrel.

Proverbs 20:3

Desirable treasure and oil are in the dwelling place of
        the wise person,
but the foolish person consumes it.

Proverbs 21:20

Foolishness is bound up in the heart of a child;
a rod of discipline will remove it far from him.

Proverbs 22:15

Do not speak into the ears of a fool,
for he will have contempt for the prudence of your words.

Proverbs 23:9

Wisdom is too high for a fool;
he does not open his mouth at the *city* gate.

He who devises to do evil,

they will call him, "Schemer."

A foolish plan is sin,

and a mocker is an abomination to humankind.

Proverbs 24:7–9

Like snow in the summer and rain during the harvest,

so too honor is not fitting for a fool.

Proverbs 26:1

A whip is for the horse, a bridle is for the donkey,

and a rod is for the backs of fools.

Do not answer a fool according to his foolishness,

or you, too, will become just like him.

Answer a fool according to his foolishness,

so that he does not become wise in his own eyes.

One who cuts off *his own* feet, *and* one who drinks violence,

is a person who sends a message by the hand of a fool.

Like the legs of a lame person that dangle *uselessly*,

so is a proverb in the mouth of fools.

Like one who entangles a stone in a sling,

so is a person who gives honor to a fool.

Like a thorn that goes into the hand of a drunkard,

so is a proverb in the mouth of fools.

Like an archer who wounds everyone,

so is the one who hires a fool or hires those who are

       just passing by.

Like a dog that returns to its vomit,

so a fool repeats his foolishness.

Do you see a person who is wise in his own eyes?
There is more hope for a fool than for him.

Proverbs 26:3–12

A stone is heavy and the sand is weighty,
but vexation by a fool is heavier than both of them.

Proverbs 27:3

Like a bird that wanders from her nest,
so is a person who wanders from his place.

Proverbs 27:8

Although you grind the fool with a pestle
among the grain in the mortar,
his foolishness will not depart from him.

Proverbs 27:22

The person who trusts in his own heart—he is a fool;
but the one who walks in wisdom—he will be delivered.

Proverbs 28:26

A person who loves wisdom makes his father glad,
but the man who gets involved with prostitutes
        destroys his wealth.

Proverbs 29:3

If a wise person disputes with a foolish person,
he rages or laughs, but there is no calm.

Proverbs 29:9

A fool lets out all of his emotions,
but a wise person keeps them calm within.

Proverbs 29:11

Do you see a person who is hasty with his words?

There is more hope for a fool than for him.

Proverbs 29:20

The words of Agur, son of Yakeh—an inspired utterance.

The declaration of *this* man to Ithiel,

to Ithiel and Ucal.

Surely I am more stupid than anyone,

and I do not have the understanding of a man.

And I did not learn wisdom,

nor do I know the knowledge of the Holy One.

Who has ascended into heaven and come down?

Who has gathered the wind into the palms of both hands?

Who has bound up the waters into *his* garment?

Who has set up all the ends of the earth?

What is his name, and what is the name of his son?

Surely you know!

Proverbs 30:1–4

FRIENDSHIP/FRIENDS

Wisdom is necessary for cultivating healthy, godly relationships with family, friends, and neighbors. It recognizes both the blessings and the potential pitfalls in human interactions, teaching that relationships must be grounded in truth, loyalty, humility, and being gracious with each other.

True friendship is steadfast and sacrificial. It is marked by loyalty in times of adversity and the courage to speak hard truths when needed. A real friend is not simply someone who offers comfort or tries to cheer others up in times of sadness, but someone whose words are trustworthy and whose advice brings truth, healing, and positive direction in life. These kinds of friends are rare treasures, and their counsel is likened to sweet incense that is soothing and meaningful.

At the same time, Proverbs warns against those who are careless in their relationships, such as gossipers, flatterers, and deceivers. Gossip is especially dangerous and can sever even close friendships, while patronizing or deceptive speech, along with mockery and sarcasm, can betray trust and cause deep relational wounds that quickly destroy relationships. Engaging with others in rash or manipulative ways—such as through hasty accusations, careless humor, or telling secrets that were told in confidence—also damages and destroys relationships, resulting in one's shame and social isolation.

A wise person uses discretion and protects proper boundaries in relationships. Overfamiliarity in a relationship can wear out even good friendships, and rushing into judgment about others will only lead to strife. Instead, the wise person handles conflicts discreetly and respectfully where spoken words are carefully measured and thought through before being uttered.

Furthermore, external factors like wealth can also greatly affect relationships, often forging superficial connections with others who then vanish in times of need. By contrast, a faithful friend remains through adversity and proves potentially more valuable than even family in times of crisis.

Thus, a blueprint for wise living in relationships is to cherish loyal friends, walk with integrity, guard how you use your words, respect others' boundaries, and treat others with fairness and kindness. Such wisdom not only builds strong, lasting relationships, but reflects the heart of God in everyday life for healthy families, friends, and communities.

My son, if sinners entice you,

do not consent.

If they say, "Come with us, let's lie in wait to *shed* blood,

let's ambush an innocent person for no *good* reason.

We will swallow them alive, just as Sheol does,

and whole, just as those who go down into the pit.

We will find all sorts of valuable things;

we will fill our houses with plunder.

Throw your lot in with us;

we will all share the loot."

My son, do not walk on *that* road with them;

keep your feet from their pathway,

for their feet run to *do* evil,

and they make haste to shed blood.

Proverbs 1:10–16

Do not envy a violent person,

and do not choose any of his ways.

For devious people are an abomination to Yahweh,

but his counsel is with the upright.

Proverbs 3:31–32

My son, if you have put up security for your neighbor,

if you have entered into an agreement with a stranger,

then you have been ensnared by the words of your mouth,

you have been captured by the words of your mouth.

Do this now, my son, and be set free,

for you have put yourself into the hand of your neighbor.

Go! Humble yourself and pressure your neighbor.

Do not give *any* sleep to your eyes,

or slumber to your eyelids.

Be rescued like a gazelle from a hunter,

and like a bird from the hand of a fowler.

Proverbs 6:1–5

The godless person ruins his neighbor with *his* mouth,

but the righteous will be delivered by knowledge.

Proverbs 11:9

The one who shows contempt for his neighbor lacks sense,

but a person with understanding remains silent.

Proverbs 11:12

A poor person is hated even by his neighbor,
but there are many who love the rich.

Proverbs 14:20

A perverse person sows strife,
and a gossip separates close friends.
A violent person entices his neighbor,
and he leads him on a road that is not good.

Proverbs 16:28–29

The one who covers over a transgression seeks love,
but the one who repeats the issue separates close friends.

Proverbs 17:9

A friend loves at all times,
and a brother is born for *times of* distress.
A person lacking sense shakes hands on an agreement,
making a solemn pledge in the presence of his neighbor.

Proverbs 17:17–18

The one who isolates himself seeks his *own* desire;
he quarrels with every piece of sound advice.

Proverbs 18:1

The first person to present his case in a dispute *seems* right
until a neighbor comes and questions him.

Proverbs 18:17

A person has many friends to socialize with,
but there is one who loves *him* who sticks closer than a brother.

Proverbs 18:24

Wealth will add many friends,
but a poor person will be separated from his friend.

Proverbs 19:4

Many will entreat the favor of a generous person,
and everyone is a friend to a person who gives gifts.
All the brothers of a poor person hate him;
indeed, how much more do his friends distance
themselves from him.
He pursues *them with* words, *but* they do not *respond.*

Proverbs 19:6–7

Many people claim to be loyal,
but a faithful man, who can find?

Proverbs 20:6

The soul of the wicked person desires evil;
his neighbor finds no favor in his eyes.

Proverbs 21:10

The person who loves a pure heart,
whose lips are gracious—a king is his friend.

Proverbs 22:11

Do not make friends with an angry person,
and do not associate with a person who is hot-tempered,
or you will learn his path
and get yourself *caught in* a snare.

Proverbs 22:24–25

Do not move an ancient boundary marker,
and do not enter into the fields of orphans,

for the one who redeems them is strong;
he will defend their case against you.

Proverbs 23:10–11

The wounds of a friend are faithful,
but an enemy multiplies kisses.

Proverbs 27:6

Oil and incense make the heart glad,
and the sweetness of a friend is better than one's own counsel.
Do not forsake your friend or your father's friend,
and do not enter into your brother's house on the day
        of your distress;
better is a neighbor nearby than a brother far away.

Proverbs 27:9–10

The one who blesses his friend with a loud voice in
        the early morning,
it will be regarded as a curse to him.

Proverbs 27:14

Iron sharpens iron,
and a person sharpens his friend.

Proverbs 27:17

He who keeps the Law is a discerning son,
but he who associates with those who lack restraint brings shame
        upon his father.

Proverbs 28:7

GENEROSITY

Generosity is portrayed throughout Proverbs as a vital expression of righteousness and a source of personal blessing. It is not merely a moral obligation, but a powerful life principle that aligns with God's justice and brings a lasting reward.

A generous person is ready to give when it is within their power. Delaying aid or withholding what is due is a denial of responsibility and reflects a lack of compassion. In contrast, the one who shares freely, especially with those in need, does not suffer loss but is enriched. This principle is repeatedly affirmed: those who give generously see increase, those who bless others are themselves blessed, and those who share with others are shown like-favor in return.

The heart of generosity lies in empathy for others and a deep reverence for God. Helping the poor is not just charity—it is lending to Yahweh Himself. Such acts will not go unnoticed or unrewarded. On the other hand, being selfish and ignoring the cry of the poor leads to Yahweh's silence when the selfish person is in need. Oppressing the poor or favoring the rich for personal gain is also condemned and will result in poverty.

Generosity also encompasses unexpected mercy, such as feeding one's enemy. These surprising acts of kindness disarm hostility and invite God's reward. Furthermore, Proverbs link a generous life to one that is focused on social justice and showing dignity to others.

Treating others with fairness, not exploiting them for profit, and choosing to bless rather than hoard are all signs of a righteous life.

A generous heart is one that trust in God's provision. The generous person gives without fear of lack, while the selfish—driven by craving and greed—find themselves deprived, wanting, and cursed. Living generously fosters community, engenders Yahweh's favor, and creates a reciprocal effect of blessing that benefits both the giver and receiver.

Do not withhold a good thing from those to whom it is due,

when it is *in* the power of your hands to do *it*.

Do not tell your neighbors, "Go, and come back,

and tomorrow I will give *it*," when it is with you.

Proverbs 3:27–28

There is one who generously scatters *wealth*, and it is

 continually added *to him*,

and one who is withholding *what is* right, *which* surely *will*

 end in poverty.

The person who blesses *others* will be made prosperous,

and the one who waters, indeed, he himself will be watered.

The people will curse the one who withholds grain,

but a blessing *will be* upon the head of the one who sells grain.

Proverbs 11:24–26

The one who shows contempt toward his neighbor is sinning,

but blessed are those who show favor to the poor.

Proverbs 14:21

The person who oppresses the poor taunts the one
      who created him,
but the person who shows favor to the needy glorifies him.

Proverbs 14:31

Many will entreat the favor of a generous person,
and everyone is a friend to a person who gives gifts.

Proverbs 19:6

The one who shows favor to a poor person lends to Yahweh,
and he will repay him according to his *good* work.

Proverbs 19:17

The one who closes his ear to the cry of the poor,
he will also cry out and not be answered.

Proverbs 21:13

All day *long* he craves *what he* desires,
but the righteous person gives and does not withhold
      his generosity.

Proverbs 21:26

The generous person will be blessed
because he gave some of his bread to the poor.

Proverbs 22:9

The one who oppresses the poor for his own gain,
and the one who gives to the rich—both will come to poverty.

Proverbs 22:16

If the one who hates you is hungry, give him food to eat,
and if he is thirsty, give him water to drink,

for you will heap burning coals upon his head,
and Yahweh will reward you.

Proverbs 25:21–22

The person who increases his wealth by interest and
          by profiteering
collects it for the one who shows favor to the poor.

Proverbs 28:8

The person who gives to the poor will not *be in* need,
but the one who shuts his eyes *to them will receive* many curses.

Proverbs 28:27

GLUTTONY/EXCESS

E xcessive indulgence—whether in food, drink, or pleasure—
often leads to negative and harmful consequences. Over-
eating and gluttony are not just physical habits; they often
reveal deeper struggles and unhealed wounds of the heart. When
a person fails to control their appetite, sickness, regret, and even
financial hardship can follow. The striking image of putting a knife
to one's throat serves as a serious warning against unchecked crav-
ings, emphasizing the dangers of impulsive indulgence.

Gluttony is deceptive. It promises satisfaction but often delivers
discomfort, waste, and shame. Even good things, like food, become
harmful when consumed without restraint. This principle extends
beyond eating—any pleasure, when pursued without moderation,
leads to emptiness rather than fulfillment. Ironically, the more one
chases pleasure without limits, the more it eludes them.

Moreover, gluttony is closely tied to laziness and poverty. Those
who overeat and overdrink are warned that such habits lead to
sluggishness and an unproductive life. A lack of self-control results
in financial and social decline as indulgence replaces responsibility.
This underscores the importance of discipline and moderation in
maintaining health and well-being in one's life.

Wisdom calls for balance. Enjoying food and drink is not forbidden,
but it must be tempered with restraint and self-awareness. A wise

person knows when to stop before pleasure turns harmful. True satisfaction comes not from excess, but from exercising discipline while enjoying what God has created.

When you sit to eat with a ruler,

carefully discern who is before you,

and put a knife in your throat

if you *have* a greedy appetite.

Do not crave his tasty foods,

for it is deceptive bread.

Proverbs 23:1–3

You, my son, must listen and be wise,

and direct your heart on the *upright* road.

Do not be among those who drink too much wine,

or with gluttonous meat-eaters.

For the drunkard and the glutton will become impoverished,

and drowsiness wears rags.

Proverbs 23:19–21

Did you find some honey? Eat just enough for you,

so that you do not have too much of it and then vomit it up.

Proverbs 25:16

It is not good to eat much honey,

nor *for people* to seek glory *on top of* glory.

Proverbs 25:27

A satisfied soul tramples on a honeycomb,

but *to* a hungry soul every bitter thing is sweet.

Proverbs 27:7

He who keeps the Law is a discerning son,

but he who associates with those who lack restraint brings shame

upon his father.

Proverbs 28:7

GOSSIP/RUMORS/
SLANDER/MOCKERY

Proverbs speaks in very stark terms about the destructiveness of gossip, slander, and mockery, painting these behaviors as deeply corrosive to relationships and communities. Gossip is likened to delicacies—tempting and easily consumed—but its impact is far from harmless. It reaches deep into a person, stirring conflict, mistrust, and emotional damage. Repeatedly, gossip is shown to cause separation between close friends, damage to reputations, and strife to ignite where there would otherwise be peace.

Those who indulge in spreading secrets or speaking maliciously are characterized as fools, evildoers, and those having perverse mouths. Their words act like fire—burning bridges, kindling disputes, and creating lasting wounds. Even more dangerous is the deceit that often cloaks gossip and slander. Lips that hide hatred behind pleasant words are considered particularly treacherous. This kind of duplicity—speaking against others while pretending to be at peace with them—is not only harmful but also morally corrupt and highly offensive in the eyes of Yahweh.

Mockery also shares in this destructive power. Mockers are shown to be instigators of strife and disrespect. Their presence fosters quarrels, tension, and even widespread disorder. Proverbs encourages the wise to cast out the mocker in order to restore peace and civility, suggesting that a mocker's influence is fundamentally disruptive and aimed at stirring up quarrels. Moreover, mocking others is portrayed as a sin that breeds contempt and disgust from those who value wisdom.

Proverbs urges people to guard their words and their ears. Refusing to listen to or repeat gossip is a mark of moral strength and fortitude. Turning away from slander and choosing to walk with understanding not only spares others from harm but protects one's own integrity and peace of mind. This wisdom is a powerful call to speak with integrity, protect people's character and our relationships, and uphold truthfulness in all that we say and do.

There are six things that Yahweh hates,

indeed, seven things are abominations to his soul:

...a false witness who breathes out lies,

and one who sows strife among brothers.

Proverbs 6:16, 19

The one who rebukes a mocker brings shame upon himself,

and the one who reproves a wicked person *brings*

injury upon himself.

Proverbs 9:7

The one hiding *his* hatred *has* deceitful lips,

and the one spreading slander, he is a fool.

Proverbs 10:18

The godless person ruins his neighbor with *his* mouth,

but the righteous will be delivered by knowledge.

Proverbs 11:9

The one who shows contempt for his neighbor lacks sense,

but a person with understanding remains silent.

A gossip walks around revealing secrets,
but the person who is of a faithful spirit conceals a matter.

Proverbs 11:12–13

A person of Belial digs up evil,
and *the words* upon his lips are like a burning fire.
A perverse person sows strife,
and a gossip separates close friends.

Proverbs 16:27–28

An evildoer pays attention to wicked lips;
a liar listens to a destructive tongue.

Proverbs 17:4

The one who covers over a transgression seeks love,
but the one who repeats the issue separates close friends.

Proverbs 17:9

When a wicked person enters, contempt also enters,
and with dishonor *comes* scorn.

Proverbs 18:3

The words of a gossip are like delicacies,
and they go down into one's innermost being.

Proverbs 18:8

A gossip walks around revealing secrets,
so do not get involved with a person who speaks
        loosely with his lips.

Proverbs 20:19

Drive out the mocker and strife will go out,
and quarrelling and insults will cease.

Proverbs 22:10

A foolish plan is sin,
and a mocker is an abomination to humankind.

Proverbs 24:9

What your eyes have seen,
do not go out to argue your dispute too hastily;
otherwise, what will you do in the end
when your neighbor humiliates you?
Argue your dispute with your neighbor,
but do not reveal another person's secret,
or the one who hears *it* might put you to shame,
and your bad reputation will not go away.

Proverbs 25:7c-10

The north wind brings rain,
and a tongue *telling* secrets brings an angry face.

Proverbs 25:23

When the wood is gone, a fire will go out,
and when there is no gossip, contentions will grow quiet.
Like charcoal for hot coals and wood for fire,
so is a contentious person for kindling strife.
The words of a gossip are like delicacies,
and they go down into one's innermost being.

Proverbs 26:20–22

Scornful people inflame a city,
but the wise turn away anger.

Proverbs 29:8

Do not slander a servant to his master,
or he will curse you and you will be found guilty.

Proverbs 30:10

GREED

G reed distorts the heart and leads people to pursue wealth in ways that are shortsighted, destructive, and ultimately self-defeating. Greed is portrayed as a harmful and deceptive force, leading individuals into paths that ultimately result in suffering and conflict. It fosters a mindset of self-prioritization, where the desire to accumulate for oneself surpasses the desire to act generously and compassionately toward others. The person who clings tightly to their wealth, refusing to share, is not only socially scorned but also headed on a path for eventual poverty (financially, relationally, and spiritually). In contrast, those who are generous (i.e., open-handed) find themselves enriched and continually blessed.

The hunger to get rich quickly or dishonestly is shown to be a path that ends in nothing but disappointment. Whether acting through fraud, unjust gain, or simply wanting to acquire inherited wealth too hastily, the end result is the same—financial decline and disfavor with others. Greed breeds rash and poor decision making, and those who grasp at amassing wealth often overlook the benefit and stability of the slow and steady path of faithful, diligent stewardship, which actually brings lasting increase and blessing in one's life.

In contrast, generosity and faithfulness are shown to bring increase. A person who shares freely, even when they might feel uncertain, finds themselves growing in prosperity and goodwill. Steady, honest accumulation of wealth—gathered little by little over time—is to be valued over rapid or dishonest gain, which quickly vanishes. Wealth achieved through unjust means is portrayed as fleeting, destined to disappear as soon as one thinks they have it or when they least expect to lose it.

Moreover, greed is inherently isolating. It disrupts relationships and stirs up conflict, as the greedy person prioritizes their personal gain over peace. It also blinds people to the transient nature of wealth. Riches, if idolized or pursued at the cost of integrity and wisdom, will vanish just when one thinks they are secure. Even the stingy person, who may think they are saving themselves from being in a state of need or want, are unknowingly bringing the very poverty upon themselves that they so fear.

At its heart, greed reveals a lack of trust in God and in his provision for people who live righteously and wisely. But the alternative is clear: trust, generosity, and patience lead to enrichment in both material and spiritual life, while greed leads down a road of eventual ruin.

There is one who generously scatters *wealth*, and it is
     continually added *to him,*
and one who is withholding *what is* right, *which* surely *will*
     end in poverty.

Proverbs 11:24

The people will curse the one who withholds grain,
but a blessing *will be* upon the head of the one who sells grain.

Proverbs 11:26

The one who trusts in his wealth, he will fall,
but the righteous will bud like a leaf.

Proverbs 11:28

Wealth *obtained* by fraud will dwindle away,
but the one who gathers little by little increases *his wealth*.

Proverbs 13:11

An inheritance *gained* quickly at the beginning
will not be blessed in the end.

Proverbs 20:21

Do not wear yourself out by attempting to get rich;
cease from *relying upon* your *own* understanding.
If your eyes fly to it, then it is gone,
for it surely makes wings for itself like an eagle,
and it flies *into* the sky.

Proverbs 23:4–5

The person who increases his wealth by interest and
        by profiteering
collects it for the one who shows favor to the poor.

Proverbs 28:8

A faithful person *will have* many blessings,
but the one who makes haste to get rich will not go unpunished.

Proverbs 28:20

A stingy person makes haste toward wealth,
but he does not know that poverty will come to him.

Proverbs 28:22

A greedy soul stirs up strife,
but the person who trusts in Yahweh will be made prosperous.

Proverbs 28:25

HEART

The heart is portrayed as the center of one's thoughts, emotions, and moral character, shaping a person's entire life and who they are. It is where wisdom must be rooted, since discernment and understanding are cultivated by directing the heart toward teaching and instruction. And to this end, Proverbs makes clear that guarding one's heart is of utmost importance, as it is the wellspring from which a person's life flows. The condition of the heart influences every aspect of life: one's words, behavior, decisions, and relationships. Whether a heart is doing well or ill has a dramatic effect, as a wise and joyful heart brings life, health, and clarity, while a foolish and sorrowful heart leads to misdirection, ruin, and inner decay.

Trusting in God with one's whole heart rather than relying on one's own understanding is a hallmark of the wise. The heart that humbly receives instruction and cherishes wisdom is a heart that produces good judgment and gains favor with both God and people. In contrast, the heart filled with pride, deceit, or foolishness is destructive and misleads others. Negative emotional states like anxiety, bitterness, or jealousy burden the heart, affecting a person's physical, mental, and spiritual health, while a cheerful and glad heart has a restorative effect, resulting in the strengthening of one's mind and soul.

The hidden nature of the heart means it must be continually examined and purified, for even outward actions cannot always reveal inner motives. A person's heart must be actively trained and corrected, especially in one's youth, in order to avoid paths of destruction and to cultivate a life of purpose, peace, and joy. In all things, the heart's orientation will determine the trajectory and destination of one's life. Furthermore, Proverbs emphasizes God's role in testing and guiding a person's heart, as all human plans and choices are ultimately evaluated by Him.

The state of one's heart also affects all personal relationships, since loyalty, love, and honesty all stem from it. One cannot have a sick heart and healthy relationships. The state of one's heart will inevitably affect relationships, either strengthening and building them up, or weakening and destroying them. To shape the heart rightly, one must seek wisdom, treasure understanding, and turn away from the influences of temptation and foolishness.

Careful attention must be given to what is in one's heart because it is the seat of all desires and motivation, carrying the true source of all actions and decisions. Thus, when the heart is stirred by selfish ambition or envy, it becomes a source of corruption that damages relationships and brings about one's downfall and injury. But when the heart is shaped by humility, kindness, and living with the fear of Yahweh, it becomes a source of light and guidance, preserving one's integrity even in the midst of adversity or suffering.

Just as water reflects a face like a mirror, a person's heart reflects their true self. A wise person therefore pays careful attention to their heart, aligning it with what is good, true, and just, so their life may flourish with wisdom and discernment that bring joy, peace, and long life.

My son, if you receive my words,
and store up my commandments with you,
making your ear attentive to Wisdom,
directing your heart to discernment,

Proverbs 2:1–2

For wisdom will come into your heart,
and knowledge will be pleasant to your soul;

Proverbs 2:10

My son, do not forget my instruction,
and let your heart guard my commandments,

Proverbs 3:1

Do not let covenant loyalty and faithfulness leave you;
bind them around your neck;
write them upon the tablet of your heart,

Proverbs 3:3

Trust in Yahweh with all your heart,
and do not lean upon your own understanding;

Proverbs 3:5

When I was a son with my father,
a tender and only son in the sight of my mother,
he taught me and said to me, "Let your heart hold on to my words,
keep my commandments and live.

Proverbs 4:3–4

My son, pay attention to my words,
incline your ear to my sayings.
Do not let them depart from *before* your eyes;
keep them in the midst of your heart.

Proverbs 4:20–21

More than anything else you protect, guard your heart,
because from it *flow* the issues of life.

Proverbs 4:23

With perversions in his heart he devises evil,
at every moment he sows strife.

Proverbs 6:14

My son, keep your father's commandments,
and do not ignore the instruction of your mother.
Bind them upon your heart always,
tie them around your neck.

Proverbs 6:20–21

Do not desire her beauty in your heart,
and do not allow her to capture you with her eyes.

Proverbs 6:25

Keep my commandments and live,
and my instruction as the pupil of your eye.
Bind them upon your fingers;
write them upon the tablet of your heart.

Proverbs 7:2–3

Do not allow your heart to turn aside to her ways;
do not wander off onto her paths,

Proverbs 7:25

The wise heart accepts commandments,
but the one who is foolish with his lips will come to ruin.

Proverbs 10:8

The tongue of a righteous person is choice silver;
the heart of the wicked is *worth* little.

Proverbs 10:20

A twisted heart is an abomination to Yahweh,
but the road of the blameless is his delight.

Proverbs 11:20

A person will be praised for his insightful mouth,
but the one who has a twisted heart will be *viewed with* contempt.

Proverbs 12:8

Deceit *is* in the heart of those who devise evil,
but those who counsel peace *have* joy.

Proverbs 12:20

A prudent person conceals knowledge,
but the heart of fools proclaims foolishness.

Proverbs 12:23

Anxiety in a person's heart weighs it down,
but a good word makes it glad.

Proverbs 12:25

Hope delayed makes the heart sick,
but a desire that arrives is a tree of life.

Proverbs 13:12

The heart knows its own bitterness,
and a stranger does not take part in *its* joy.

Proverbs 14:10

Even in laughter the heart *might* be in pain,
and the end of joy *may be* grief.

The one who is disloyal in *his* heart will be satisfied
      from his *own* ways,
but a good person *will be satisfied* from his deeds.

Proverbs 14:13–14

A peaceful heart is the life of the flesh,
but envy is decay to the bones.

Proverbs 14:30

Wisdom rests in the heart of the one who has understanding,
and *even* among fools she makes herself known.

Proverbs 14:33

The lips of the wise spread knowledge,
but it is not so *with* the heart of fools.

Proverbs 15:7

Sheol and Abaddon are in the sight of Yahweh,
how much more are human hearts!

Proverbs 15:11

A joyful heart makes a face cheerful,
but a sorrowful heart *produces* a broken spirit.
The heart of the one who has understanding seeks knowledge,
but the mouth of fools feeds on foolishness.
All the days of the afflicted person are bad,
but a merry heart *has* a lasting banquet.

Proverbs 15:13–15

The heart of a righteous person considers how to answer,
but the mouth of the wicked pours out evil things.

Proverbs 15:28

Bright eyes make the heart glad,
and good news fattens the bones.

Proverbs 15:30

The plans of the heart *belong* to the person,
but the answer of the tongue *comes* from Yahweh.

Proverbs 16:1

Every arrogant heart is an abomination to Yahweh;
be assured, he will not go unpunished.

Proverbs 16:5

A person's heart devises his way,
but Yahweh prepares his steps.

Proverbs 16:9

A person with a wise heart will be called "one who understands,"
and the sweetness of *his* lips will increase persuasiveness.

Proverbs 16:21

The heart of a wise person gives insight to his mouth,
and it increases the persuasiveness of his lips.

Proverbs 16:23

A crucible is for silver and a furnace is for gold,
but Yahweh tests hearts.

Proverbs 17:3

A twisted heart will not find good,
and the one who has a double tongue will fall into evil.

Proverbs 17:20

A cheerful heart is a good cure,
but a broken spirit dries up the bones.

Proverbs 17:22

Before disaster the heart of a person is puffed up,
but humility goes before glory.

Proverbs 18:12

The heart of one who understands acquires knowledge,
and the ear of the wise seeks knowledge.

Proverbs 18:15

A person's foolishness subverts his way,
but his heart rages against Yahweh.

Proverbs 19:3

Many plans are in a person's heart,
but Yahweh's counsel will stand.

Proverbs 19:21

The counsel in a person's heart is *like* deep water,
but a person with discernment will draw it out.

Proverbs 20:5

Who can declare, "I have made my heart pure,
I am cleansed from my sin"?

Proverbs 20:9

The heart of a king is *like* water canals in Yahweh's hand;
he turns it wherever he delights.
Every person's road is right in his own eyes,
but Yahweh examines the hearts.

Proverbs 21:1–2

Haughty eyes and an arrogant heart—
the lamp of the wicked—is sin.

Proverbs 21:4

The person who loves a pure heart,
whose lips are gracious—a king is his friend.

Proverbs 22:11

Foolishness is bound up in the heart of a child;
a rod of discipline will remove it far from him.

Proverbs 22:15

Incline your ear and listen to the words of the wise,
and apply your heart to my knowledge,

Proverbs 22:17

Do not eat the bread of a stingy person,
and do not crave his tasty foods.
For as he calculates in his soul, so he is.
"Eat and drink," he says to you,
but his heart is not with you.
The piece *of bread* you ate, you will vomit,
and you have wasted your pleasant words.

Proverbs 23:6–8

Apply your heart to *sound* teaching,
and *apply* your ears to words of knowledge.

Proverbs 23:12

My son, if your heart is wise,
my own heart will indeed rejoice.
My inward parts will rejoice
when your lips speak with great integrity.
Do not let your heart be envious of the sinners;
rather, fear Yahweh all day *long*,

Proverbs 23:15–17

You, my son, must listen and be wise,
and direct your heart on the *upright* road.

Proverbs 23:19

My son, give your heart to me,
and let your eyes observe my ways,

Proverbs 23:26

Your eyes will see strange things,
and your heart will speak perverse things.

Proverbs 23:33

Do not rejoice when your enemy falls,
and let not your heart celebrate when he stumbles,

Proverbs 24:17

When I noticed, I paid attention;
I observed, *and* I learned *this* lesson:

Proverbs 24:32

As the heavens are high and the earth is deep,
so the hearts of kings are unsearchable.

Proverbs 25:3

Like one who removes clothing on a cold day,
or vinegar upon a wound,
is one who sings a song to a heavy heart.

Proverbs 25:20

Like a clay vessel covered with silver dross
are smooth lips and a wicked heart.

Proverbs 26:23

Oil and incense make the heart glad,
and the sweetness of a friend is better than one's own counsel.

Proverbs 27:9

Become wise, my son, and make my heart glad,
so that I may give an answer to the one who reproaches me.

Proverbs 27:11

As the surface of the water reflects a face,
so the heart of a person reflects a person.

Proverbs 27:19

Blessed is the person who trembles *before God* continually,
but the one who hardens his heart will fall into evil.

Proverbs 28:14

The person who trusts in his own heart—he is a fool;
but the one who walks in wisdom—he will be delivered.

Proverbs 28:26

An excellent wife, who can find?
For her value is far more than gems.
The heart of her husband trusts in her,
and he will have no lack of gain.

Proverbs 31:10–11

HEALTH/WELL-BEING

A person's health and well-being are deeply connected to spiritual discipline, emotional balance, wise living, and self-restraint. Rather than presenting health as a purely physical issue, Proverbs frames it as something that results from the quality of one's inner life, personal choices, and attitude toward God. Living with humility and turning away from evil results in healing and growth. When the heart embraces instruction and stores up knowledge, it becomes a wellspring of life, offering insight and emotional resilience even in hard times. Joy strengthens one's spirit, while jealousy, sorrow, and a crushed spirit figuratively "rot the bones," deteriorating well-being. Moreover, hope and desires that are fulfilled bring life and restoration, while despair makes the heart sick and drains one's energy.

The heart plays a vital role in one's health—not just emotionally, but physically—where joy and hope bring strength, while anxiety and brokenness deplete it. A peaceful, content heart leads to physical flourishing, and pleasant words, a cheerful disposition, and encouragement from others are likened to medicine and nourishment for the body and soul.

Proverbs also strongly emphasizes the importance of moderation and self-control in habits, such as eating and drinking. Overindulgence in food, drink, or any appetite leads to ruin, poverty, and ill health. Those who lack self-restraint are compared to a defenseless city—vulnerable and easily broken into and conquered. The abuse of alcohol is especially condemned and is described vividly as being deceptive in its initial appeal but highly destructive in the end, causing confusion, pain, and simply a craving for more to cope with the effects. Healthy living, then, includes avoiding gluttony and intoxication, and advocates for moderation in all things.

In addition, Proverbs says that practicing generosity, speaking positive and uplifting words, and trusting in God produce health in a person that physical nourishment alone can't provide. It is the person who fears Yahweh who enjoys a satisfied, secure life, untouched by needless harm and trouble. Even having healthy relationships positively affects one's well-being—such as a faithful spouse or trusted friends.

Ultimately, well-being is holistic: it is drawn from all dimensions of life—physical, emotional, mental, spiritual, and social—all intertwined and rooted in wise, humble, generous, and disciplined living.

Do not be wise in your own eyes;

fear Yahweh and turn away from evil.

It will be healing for your flesh,

and a refreshing drink to your bones.

Proverbs 3:7–8

My son, pay attention to my words,

incline your ear to my sayings.

Do not let them depart from *before* your eyes;

keep them in the midst of your heart.

For they are life to the ones who discover them,
and health to a person's whole body.

Proverbs 4:20–22

The fear of Yahweh adds to *one's* days,
but the years of the wicked will be cut short.

Proverbs 10:27

An excellent wife is the crown of her husband,
but she who acts shamefully is like decay in his bones.

Proverbs 12:4

There is one who speaks recklessly, like the stabbings of a sword,
but the tongue of the wise is healing.

Proverbs 12:18

Anxiety in a person's heart weighs it down,
but a good word makes it glad.

Proverbs 12:25

Hope delayed makes the heart sick,
but a desire that arrives is a tree of life.

Proverbs 13:12

The instruction of a wise person is a fountain of life,
that one may turn aside from the snares of death.

Proverbs 13:14

A wicked messenger will fall into evil,
but a faithful messenger *brings* healing.

Proverbs 13:17

A peaceful heart is the life of the flesh,
but envy is decay to the bones.

Proverbs 14:30

A joyful heart makes a face cheerful,
but a sorrowful heart *produces* a broken spirit.

Proverbs 15:13

All the days of the afflicted person are bad,
but a merry heart *has* a lasting banquet.

Proverbs 15:15

Bright eyes make the heart glad,
and good news fattens the bones.

Proverbs 15:30

Pleasant words are a honeycomb,
sweet to the soul and healing to the bones.

Proverbs 16:24

A cheerful heart is a good cure,
but a broken spirit dries up the bones.

Proverbs 17:22

A person's spirit can endure his sickness,
but a broken spirit, who can bear that?

Proverbs 18:14

The fear of Yahweh *leads* to life,
and the one *who has it* will sleep satisfied through the night *and*
     not be visited by evil.

Proverbs 19:23

Wine is a mocker, beer is a loudmouth,
and everyone who goes astray by them is not wise.

Proverbs 20:1

Do not be among those who drink too much wine,
or with gluttonous meat-eaters.

For the drunkard and the glutton will become impoverished,
and drowsiness wears rags.

Proverbs 23:20–21

Who has woe? Who has sorrow?
Who has contentions? Who has a complaint?
Who has wounds without cause? Who has bleary eyes?
It is those who linger over wine;
those who come in to taste mixed wine.
Do not look at the wine when it sparkles with red,
when it gleams in the cup,
when it goes down smoothly.
In the end it bites like a serpent,
and it poisons like a viper.
Your eyes will see strange things,
and your heart will speak perverse things.
And you will become like one who lies down in the
       middle of the sea,
or like one who lies down on the top of a ship's mast.
"They struck me, *but* I did not feel pain.
They hit me, *but* I did not know *it.*
When will I awaken? I will seek another *drink.*"

Proverbs 23:29–35

Did you find some honey? Eat just enough for you,
so that you do not have too much of it and then vomit it up.

Proverbs 25:16

It is not good to eat much honey,
nor *for people* to seek glory *on top of* glory.

Like a city broken into, *one* without a wall,

is a person who has no self-control over his emotions.

Proverbs 25:27–28

The person who gives to the poor will not *be in* need,

but the one who shuts his eyes *to them will receive* many curses.

Proverbs 28:27

HONESTY

Honesty is revealed as a pillar of wisdom, integrity, and security in life. Speaking truthfully, even when it might (or does) cost something or is uncomfortable, is portrayed not just as being morally good, but as a trait that wins people's trust, respect, and favor.

Honest words are like a kiss, which affirms their value in fostering connection and closeness with others. Those who speak truthfully not only benefit others but are themselves protected and honored, and those who are faithful in their testimony, who refuse to distort the truth or manipulate facts, are ones who create a stable and desirable community.

Dishonesty, by contrast, is shown to have destructive consequences. It leads to broken households, societal corruption, and the erosion of justice. The greedy who accept bribes or alter long-standing moral or legal agreements for their own gain are exposed as people who destabilize social relationships by sacrificing their integrity. Even small compromises are condemned as wicked and dishonest, especially when they prey on the vulnerable. Such actions don't go unnoticed—there is a strong warning that God himself defends the innocent and helpless, and he will bring justice to those who act unjustly against them.

Hiding one's wrongdoing may seem safe in the moment and something that will prevent consequences, but it blocks the path to growth, and it ultimately will decrease favor. True honesty isn't just about speaking the truth and dealing rightly with others—it also involves being truthful with oneself, owning up to faults and striving to live better. The upright—those who value and protect truth—show compassion and care for others who do the same, even at potential risk to themselves. In this way, honesty becomes not only a personal virtue but a source of strength, peace, and blessing in every part of one's life.

Put away from you a crooked mouth,
and put deceitful lips far away from you.

Proverbs 4:24

The one who speaks *what is* faithful declares an honest testimony,
but a false witness *utters* deceit.

Proverbs 12:17

A faithful witness will not lie,
but a deceptive witness breathes out lies.

Proverbs 14:5

The one who pursues unjust gain troubles his household,
but the one who hates gifts *that influence* will live.

Proverbs 15:27

Righteous lips are the delight of kings,
and the one who speaks with integrity will be loved.

Proverbs 16:13

It is not good to issue a fine to a righteous person,
nor to beat nobles for *their* uprightness.

Proverbs 17:26

Do not move the ancient boundary marker
that your fathers made.

Proverbs 22:28

Do not move an ancient boundary marker,
and do not enter into the fields of orphans,
for the one who redeems them is strong;
he will defend their case against you.

Proverbs 23:10–11

He kisses the lips—he who replies with a straight answer.

Proverbs 24:26

The person who hides his transgressions will not prosper,
but the person who confesses and forsakes *them* will
be shown mercy.

Proverbs 28:13

People who cause bloodshed hate a blameless person,
but the upright show concern for his life.

Proverbs 29:10

HONOR/GLORY

onor is the fruit of a life grounded in humility, wisdom, faithfulness, and integrity. It is not something that can be grasped through force or pretension; rather, it is a gift that comes naturally to those who live with righteousness. Those who embrace wisdom and exalt her are themselves lifted up and honored in return. Such honor is not some fleeting admiration, but a lasting recognition by others that is rooted in the display of virtue, godly character, and wise living.

The pathway to honor is often perceived as the "low road"—one that is marked by humility, discipline, service, and compassion. Those who fear Yahweh, listen to correction, and pursue what is right are promised honor. It is likened to a reward found in the company of virtues like riches and long life offered by Wisdom herself to those who embrace her. This kind of honor is not a momentary applause or accolade, but a lasting dignity which is rooted in how a person lives, speaks, and treats others.

Conversely, those who live pridefully, oppress the vulnerable, ignore correction, or display foolishness are foreign to true honor. Trying to assign honor to a fool is as unnatural as snow in the summer—it is completely out of place and mistaken. Those who are filled with pride may seem to rise on occasion, but it is only temporary; their arrogance eventually leads to their downfall. This is not so for the humble; though they may start low, they will rise to lasting places of great esteem.

True honor, then, is not merely about being "seen," but rather being properly recognized for a life of wisdom, humility, grace, and faithfulness. It is not a badge that a person claims for themselves, but a quality that is bestowed on them from those who see the fruit in their life that is borne from consistently choosing what is good, right, and godly.

In her right hand is length of days,
in her left hand are riches and glory.

Proverbs 3:16

The wise will inherit glory,
but fools exalt shame.

Proverbs 3:35

Exalt her and she will lift you up;
she will honor you because you embrace her.

Proverbs 4:8

Riches and glory are with me,
enduring prosperity and righteousness.

Proverbs 8:18

A gracious woman will attain glory,
but ruthless men will attain riches.

Proverbs 11:16

The one who ignores discipline *will get* poverty and dishonor,
but the one who heeds reproof will be honored.

Proverbs 13:18

The person who oppresses the poor taunts the one
    who created him,
but the person who shows favor to the needy glorifies him.

Proverbs 14:31

The fear of Yahweh is what wisdom teaches,
and humility goes before glory.

Proverbs 15:33

Before disaster the heart of a person is puffed up,
but humility goes before glory.

Proverbs 18:12

It is an honor for a person to cease from strife,
but every fool will quarrel.

Proverbs 20:3

The one who pursues righteousness and loyalty
will find life, righteousness, and glory.

Proverbs 21:21

The reward of humility—the fear of Yahweh—
is wealth, glory, and life.

Proverbs 22:4

Like snow in the summer and rain during the harvest,
so too honor is not fitting for a fool.

Proverbs 26:1

The one who guards a fig tree will eat of its fruit,
and the one who watches over his master will be honored.

Proverbs 27:18

A person's pride will bring him low,
but a humble spirit will obtain glory.

Proverbs 29:23

HOPE

ope is a sustaining force—something that anchors a person's spirit, lifts their outlook, and shapes how they endure challenges and setbacks. For the righteous, hope is a source of joy, a confident expectation that good will come in time. Even when desires are delayed, they are not lost; rather, they hold the potential to blossom into fulfillment, like a "tree of life" that nourishes the soul.

Yet, this hope is not naive optimism. It is grounded in the fear of Yahweh, seeking wisdom, and living with moral uprightness. It warns against envying the ways of sinners or putting confidence in fleeting wealth, for such hopes will perish along with their corrupt foundations. The wicked may have dreams and hope for things, but their expectations ultimately end in judgment and disappointment.

Correction and discipline—especially in parenting—are seen as acts of hope. To correct a child is to believe in their ability to have a positive future and to act in a way that seeks to prevent their ruin. In contrast, failing to correct, or worse, giving up on training a child, is tantamount to surrendering all hope.

True hope is not just wishful thinking; it is an outlook toward the future built on wisdom, humility, and reverence for Yahweh. It sustains those who live rightly, leading them through times of waiting and assuring them that their efforts are not in vain.

The hope of the righteous is joy,
but the expectation of the wicked will perish.

Proverbs 10:28

When a wicked person dies, his hope perishes,
and *his* hope of wealth perishes.

Proverbs 11:7

The desire of the righteous *ends* only *in* good,
but the hope of the wicked *ends in* wrath.

Proverbs 11:23

Hope delayed makes the heart sick,
but a desire that arrives is a tree of life.

Proverbs 13:12

Correct your son, for there is hope,
and do not be intent on causing his death.

Proverbs 19:18

Do not let your heart be envious of the sinners;
rather, fear Yahweh all day *long*,
for certainly there is a future,
and your hope will not be cut off.

Proverbs 23:17–18

My son, eat some honey, for it is good,
 and honey from the comb is sweet in your mouth;
likewise, know that wisdom is *sweet* to your soul.

If you find it, then there will be a future,
and your hope will not be cut off.

Proverbs 24:13–14

Do you see a person who is wise in his own eyes?
There is more hope for a fool than for him.

Proverbs 26:12

Do you see a person who is hasty with his words?
There is more hope for a fool than for him.

Proverbs 29:20

HUMILITY

Humility is depicted as a central trait of wisdom and a key to living a life that is both honorable and blessed. It begins with a sober view of oneself—rejecting self-conceit and instead revering God and turning away from evil. This leads to spiritual growth and maturity that fosters a life filled with peace and wholeness.

The humble are teachable and open to correction, knowing how to avoid the strife and destruction that come from arrogance. Humility often involves modesty, which is not about self-deprecation, but self-awareness and a correct perspective that makes someone stronger and more confident. Humility cultivates peace, deserves honor, and ultimately leads to success, prosperity, and fullness of life.

In contrast, pride sets a person on a path to disgrace and downfall. Those who exalt themselves or seek recognition for themselves will face humiliation and shame, while those who wait patiently and serve faithfully with a humble heart will be elevated in due time. Even success becomes a test—how one handles the praise of others reveals their true character and whether they are humble or just pretending on the outside. Those who can quietly serve and let others praise them demonstrate real humility and inner strength.

Genuine humility also extends to how one treats others, especially enemies or those in lower positions. Wisdom cautions against gloating over a rival's misfortune and downfall or seeking to overstep one's proper place. True honor comes not from exalting oneself, but from being recognized and esteemed by others. Letting others offer praise about you instead of boasting about yourself guards against the danger of an improper, inflated view of oneself. Even success and praise can be temptations to bask in one's own glory, but they reveal whether one will remain grounded in humility or allow their ego to take root and grow.

At its core, humility guards against self-sabotage. It sets a person on a stable path, is rewarded with Yahweh's favor, and paves the way for a long-lasting and good reputation with others. Pride may build quickly but collapses just as fast, while humility requires a consistent attitude and heart position that creates a deep, steady life orientation and strength that withstands the tests of time and the temptations from others' applause and admiration.

Do not be wise in your own eyes;
fear Yahweh and turn away from evil.
It will be healing for your flesh,
and a refreshing drink to your bones.

Proverbs 3:7–8

He mocks at the mockers,
but he gives grace to the humble.

Proverbs 3:34

Arrogance comes, then dishonor comes,
but wisdom is with the modest.

Proverbs 11:2

Better is one who is dishonored and *has* a servant for himself,
than one who glorifies himself and lacks bread.

Proverbs 12:9

Arrogance only causes strife,
but wisdom is with those who accept advice.

Proverbs 13:10

The fear of Yahweh is what wisdom teaches,
and humility goes before glory.

Proverbs 15:33

Better to be humble in spirit with the poor
than to share the plunder with the proud.

Proverbs 16:19

Before disaster the heart of a person is puffed up,
but humility goes before glory.

Proverbs 18:12

The reward of humility—the fear of Yahweh—
is wealth, glory, and life.

Proverbs 22:4

Do not rejoice when your enemy falls,
and let not your heart celebrate when he stumbles,
otherwise Yahweh will see *it*, and it is evil in his eyes,
and he might turn away his anger from him.

Proverbs 24:17–18

Do not honor yourself in the presence of the king,
and do not stand among great people;
for it is better that it be said to you, "Come up here,"
than to be placed lower in the presence of a noble.

Proverbs 25:6–7

Let another praise you and not your *own* mouth—
a stranger—and not your *own* lips.

Proverbs 27:2

A crucible is for silver and a furnace is for gold,
and a person is *tested* by the praise he receives.

Proverbs 27:21

A person's pride will bring him low,
but a humble spirit will obtain glory.

Proverbs 29:23

IMPULSIVENESS

While there are times when decisive action must be taken, impulsiveness is a negative trait that leads to embarrassment, sin, and missed opportunities. A person who acts or speaks in haste, without listening or reflecting first on what would be the best course of action, exposes themselves to receiving shame and experiencing undesired error and loss. It is the quick tempers and rash reactions that mark a lack of understanding, while measured responses reflect deep insight and self-mastery. A fool spills out all their emotions uncensored and without regard for the effect they will have, and their quick temper tends to incite or escalate conflict, damaging relationships and undermining peace. On the contrary, a wise person exercises emotional restraint and control and does not vent all their feelings or opinions as they arise. Instead, they remain composed and thoughtful, guarding both their words and their actions.

Rushing into decisions, especially without knowledge or careful planning, can lead to regret and even spiritual peril. Making vows or declarations without due consideration becomes a trap that one later may struggle to escape from. Whether in speech, personal commitments, or in the midst of conflict, impulsiveness opens the door to humiliation and ruin. In contrast, diligence, patience, and strategic planning create a path toward safety, stability, and success. A fool's emotions spill out unfiltered, and their quick temper instigates and exacerbates strife, harming their reputation and their relationships with others.

Sometimes a quick decision in the moment can save the day, but especially in disagreements or conflict, a hasty response can quickly backfire. It's better to delay action and assess a situation thoroughly rather than to charge forward and end up doing something careless that brings disgrace. Slowing down and seeking full understanding before responding not only protects one from foolishness but fosters wiser and more beneficial outcomes for all.

Restraint, forethought, and emotional control are the antidotes to impulsiveness. A wise person is the master of their emotions. They listen before speaking and plan diligently before acting. In doing so, they cultivate peace, maintain dignity, and navigate life with clarity and success, steering clear of the pitfalls that hasty words and hot tempers bring. The wise learn to govern themselves before attempting to advise or govern others, thereby making them trustworthy and honorable in the eyes of those around them.

The anger of a fool is known at once,
but a prudent person conceals dishonor.

Proverbs 12:16

There is one who speaks recklessly, like the stabbings of a sword,
but the tongue of the wise is healing.

Proverbs 12:18

An easily angered person acts foolishly,
and a schemer will be hated.

Proverbs 14:17

The one who is slow to get angry *possesses* great understanding,
but the one who is easily angered displays foolishness.

Proverbs 14:29

The tongue of the wise produces good knowledge,
but the mouth of fools pours out foolishness.

Proverbs 15:2

A hot-tempered person incites strife,
but one who is slow to get angry peacefully settles a dispute.

Proverbs 15:18

The heart of a righteous person considers how to answer,
but the mouth of the wicked pours out evil things.

Proverbs 15:28

Even a fool who remains silent is thought to be wise;
when he shuts his lips, he is *considered* to be discerning.

Proverbs 17:28

The person who gives an answer before he listens—
foolishness and disgrace belong to him.

Proverbs 18:13

It is not good *to have* a desire without knowledge,
and one who makes haste with his feet commits sin.

Proverbs 19:2

Do not say, "I will repay evil!"
Wait for Yahweh and he will deliver you.

Proverbs 20:22

It is a snare for a person to carelessly declare, "It is holy!"
and *then* to inquire *about it* after making his vows.

Proverbs 20:25

The plans of a diligent person surely *will lead* to abundance,
but everyone who acts hastily surely *will come to* poverty.

Proverbs 21:5

It is better to live in a desolate land
than *with* a contentious and angry woman.

Proverbs 21:19

A fool lets out all of his emotions,
but a wise person keeps them calm within.

Proverbs 29:11

INSTRUCTION/REPROOF

I nstruction and reproof are essential pathways to gaining wisdom. They are not merely the correction of wrong knowledge or behavior but are meant to train a person in righteous and faithful living before Yahweh. Those who embrace discipline show a love for knowledge and a heart inclined toward learning. They are not afraid to be wrong and learn better next time. The wise are teachable, humble, and open to being guided—whether through parental instruction, spiritual teaching, or wise counsel from friends or others. In contrast, those who reject reproof are portrayed as foolish, self-destructive, and resistant to wisdom. They choose to lead themselves and others down the road of destruction.

In Proverbs, receiving correction is likened to a light that illuminates the path of life, steering a person away from danger and guiding them toward a life that is pleasing and honorable to Yahweh. A wise person values this feedback, understanding that growth comes through being challenged and corrected—something everyone needs. Even painful rebukes are seen as acts of love—signs of care from a parent or from God—and meant to increase understanding and produce maturity and strength. Ignoring these moments of instruction brings undesirable consequences, such as dishonor, poverty, death. Neglecting or diminishing the value of correction ends up leading to missed opportunities for personal transformation and blessing.

On the other hand, a person with a teachable spirit is marked by their ability to listen deeply and authentically and then make appropriate changes in their life as necessary. This willingness to hear and respond to guidance from others preserves one's life—both physically and spiritually—and enriches relationships through promoting peace, growth, and understanding.

Moreover, instruction and reproof are framed as gifts: life-giving, protective, and necessary for anyone who desires to walk in wisdom. They mold a person's character, shape their perspective and outlook on life, and pave the way for a living with integrity and prudence, having a lasting impact on those around them.

Listen, my son, to your father's teaching,

and do not ignore the instruction of your mother,

because they are a wreath of grace for your head,

and a necklace for your neck.

Proverbs 1:8–9

My son, do not reject the discipline of Yahweh,

and do not abhor his reproof.

For the one whom Yahweh loves, he reproves,

like a father to his cherished son.

Proverbs 3:11–12

and in the end you groan

when your flesh—even your body—are used up.

Then you will say, "O how I have hated discipline,

and my heart has spurned reproof.

I did not listen to the voice of my teachers,

nor did I incline my ear to those instructing me.
I was soon in all sorts of trouble
in the midst of the assembly and congregation."

Proverbs 5:11–14

The one acting wickedly—his *own* iniquities will capture him,
and he will be seized by the cords of his *own* sin.
He will die because of lack of discipline,
and in the abundance of his foolishness he goes astray.

Proverbs 5:22–23

For the commandment is a lamp and the instruction is a light,
and reproofs *that offer* correction are a road *leading to* life,
to keep you from the evil woman,
from the flattering tongue of the foreign woman.

Proverbs 6:23–24

Keep my commandments and live,
and my instruction as the pupil of your eye.

Proverbs 7:2

Take my teaching, and not silver,
and knowledge rather than choice gold.

Proverbs 8:10

Listen to *my* teaching and become wise,
and do not neglect it.

Proverbs 8:33

The one who rebukes a mocker brings shame upon himself,
and the one who reproves a wicked person *brings*
injury upon himself.
Do not reprove a mocker or he will hate you;
reprove a wise man and he will love you.

Give *instruction* to a wise person and he will become even wiser;
teach a righteous person and he will increase in learning.

Proverbs 9:7–9

The wise heart accepts commandments,
but the one who is foolish with his lips will come to ruin.

Proverbs 10:8

The one who heeds *sound* teaching is *on* the path to life,
but the one who ignores reproof goes astray.

Proverbs 10:17

Without wise guidance people will fall,
but with a multitude of advisors there is deliverance.

Proverbs 11:14

The one who loves discipline loves knowledge,
but the one who hates reproof is stupid.

Proverbs 12:1

The road of a fool is right in his own eyes,
but a wise person listens to counsel.

Proverbs 12:15

A wise son *listens to his* father's discipline,
but a mocker does not listen to rebuke.

Proverbs 13:1

Arrogance only causes strife,
but wisdom is with those who accept advice.

Proverbs 13:10

The one who despises a word *of instruction* will come to ruin,
but the one who fears the commandment will be rewarded.

The instruction of a wise person is a fountain of life,
that one may turn aside from the snares of death.

Proverbs 13:13–14

The one who ignores discipline *will get* poverty and dishonor,
but the one who heeds reproof will be honored.

Proverbs 13:18

A fool spurns discipline from his father,
but the one who heeds reproof acts prudently.

Proverbs 15:5

Harsh discipline is for the one who abandons the path;
the one who hates reproof will die.

Proverbs 15:10

A mocker will not love *anyone* who reproves him;
he will not go to the wise.

Proverbs 15:12

By a lack of counsel, plans are shattered,
but with a multitude of advisors *a plan* will stand.

Proverbs 15:22

An ear that listens to life-giving reproof
will dwell among the wise.
The one who ignores discipline despises his *own* soul,
but the one who listens to reproof acquires *good* sense.

Proverbs 15:31–32

A rebuke goes deeper into a person who has understanding
than a hundred blows on a fool.

Proverbs 17:10

The one who isolates himself seeks his *own* desire;
he quarrels with every piece of sound advice.
A fool does not delight in understanding,
but only in expressing his own mind.

Proverbs 18:1–2

The heart of one who understands acquires knowledge,
and the ear of the wise seeks knowledge.

Proverbs 18:15

The one who keeps the commandment watches over his life,
but the one who has contempt for his road will die.

Proverbs 19:16

Listen to counsel and accept discipline
in order that you may be wise in your latter *days*.

Proverbs 19:20

Strike a mocker and a naive person will act prudently,
and if you reprove the one who has understanding, he will
        discern knowledge.

Proverbs 19:25

My son, cease listening to teaching
and you will go astray from words of knowledge.

Proverbs 19:27

The counsel in a person's heart is *like* deep water,
but a person with discernment will draw it out.

Proverbs 20:5

Plans are established by counsel,
so make war by wise guidance.

Proverbs 20:18

When a mocker gets punished, the naive person becomes wise,
and when a wise person is instructed, he accepts knowledge.

Proverbs 21:11

Do not speak into the ears of a fool,
for he will have contempt for the prudence of your words.

Proverbs 23:9

Apply your heart to *sound* teaching,
and *apply* your ears to words of knowledge.

Proverbs 23:12

Get truth and do not sell it;
get wisdom and teaching and understanding.

Proverbs 23:23

A wise man is strong,
and a person with knowledge grows in strength.
For with *wise* guidance you should wage your war,
and with a multitude of advisors there is deliverance.

Proverbs 24:5–6

Like apples of gold in settings of silver
is a word spoken at the *proper* moment.
Like an earring of gold or an ornament of *fine* gold
is a wise person reproving a listening ear.

Proverbs 25:11–12

Iron sharpens iron,
and a person sharpens his friend.

Proverbs 27:17

One who reproves a person will afterward find more favor
than the person who flatters with the tongue.

Proverbs 28:23

A person who stiffens his neck *after multiple* rebukes
will suddenly be broken and there will be no remedy.

Proverbs 29:1

A servant cannot be corrected *simply* with words,
for he understands, but he does not respond.

Proverbs 29:19

INTEGRITY

I ntegrity is a steady, unwavering commitment to uprightness in character, speech, and action. It is the quality of being consistently truthful, just, and morally sound—regardless of who is watching or what is at stake. A person of integrity walks a straight path, avoiding deceit, manipulation, and corruption. Their lives are marked by trustworthiness and reliability, which serve as a shield of protection against evil and a source of honor and favor from Yahweh.

It is certain that a life of integrity is not one free from hardship, but it does offer security, prosperity, and long-term reward. Integrity brings clarity to decision-making and builds a reputation for remaining strong and reliable under pressure. A person of integrity contrasts with the unstable and dangerous path of those who act with duplicity or dishonesty, whose foolish choices lead to ruin, shame, and broken relationships.

Living with integrity requires courage, especially when surrounded by the temptations of the world, such as the allure of money, sex, and fame. Yet, integrity guards the way of those who practice it, making paths straight and ensuring the outcomes of decisions are stable and enduring. Integrity requires living with wisdom, as those who are wise recognize that short-term success gained through exploitation, selfish ambition, or deceit will eventually collapse, while righteousness and sound decisions are what establish a good reputation and a lasting legacy.

People of integrity are also peacemakers and truth-tellers. They are careful with their words, honest in their dealings, and show respect for justice. This moral uprightness extends not only to public behavior but to all personal dealings and relationships, forming a life that is consistent in both the private as well as the public sphere. Lastly, integrity is not just about doing the right thing only at one moment—it's about being the quality of person for whom right action is a natural expression of who they are at every moment.

Then you will understand righteousness and justice
and integrity—every good path.

Proverbs 2:9

The one who walks blamelessly walks securely,
but the one who perverts his ways will be made known.

Proverbs 10:9

The integrity of the upright will lead them,
but the perversity of the unfaithful will destroy them.

Proverbs 11:3

A gossip walks around revealing secrets,
but the person who is of a faithful spirit conceals a matter.

Proverbs 11:13

Righteousness guards the one whose way is blameless,
but wickedness overthrows a sinner.

Proverbs 13:6

A wicked messenger will fall into evil,
but a faithful messenger *brings* healing.

Proverbs 13:17

The one who walks in his integrity fears Yahweh,
but the one who is devious in his ways shows contempt for him.

Proverbs 14:2

The one who is disloyal in *his* heart will be satisfied
        from his *own* ways,
but a good person *will be satisfied* from his deeds.

Proverbs 14:14

Foolishness is a joy to the one who lacks *good* sense,
but a person with understanding walks with integrity.

Proverbs 15:21

Righteous lips are the delight of kings,
and the one who speaks with integrity will be loved.

Proverbs 16:13

Better is a poor person who walks in his integrity
than one who has twisted lips and is a fool.

Proverbs 19:1

A righteous person who walks in his integrity—
blessed are his children after him.

Proverbs 20:7

Better is a poor person who walks in his integrity
than a person who is crooked in his ways, even though he is rich.

Proverbs 28:6

The one who walks blamelessly will be delivered,
but the one who is crooked in his ways will fall suddenly.

Proverbs 28:18

JOY/HAPPINESS

J oy and happiness, according to Proverbs, are not derived from fleeting pleasures, entertainment, or material abundance, but are found in a life directed by wisdom, righteousness, and submission to Yahweh's authority. True joy flows from the heart and is deeply connected to inner peace, moral integrity, and harmonious relationships. A joyful heart is like a continual feast—it sustains a person through life's challenges and uplifts their spirit even in difficult times and in the face of adversity. It brings health to the body, a brightness and warmth to the face, and vitality to the soul.

Joy and happiness are found in wise living: listening to instruction, pursuing understanding, speaking truthfully, and acting justly. Hey are the result of living with integrity, practicing kindness, and walking the path of righteousness. Those who are slow to anger, generous, and diligent in their work experience the blessing of joyful contentment. Wisdom brings delight to those who embrace her, and having peaceful relationships multiplies one's joy.

By contrast, fools who reject wisdom, stir up strife, or who give in to envy, deceit, or laziness are repeatedly shown to bring sorrow upon themselves and others. Their happiness is often superficial and short-lived and can hide underlying bitterness or instability and insecurity.

One of the most important foundations of lasting happiness is heathy relationships—loving families, faithful friendships, and communing with Yahweh, the Creator. A home that is filled with love, and which has perhaps only the most modest means, produces a far more satisfying and joy-filled life than a family of wealth that engenders shallow relationships, conflict, and isolation.

In essence, joy is not something pursued directly in itself, but rather something that emerges as a byproduct of living with wisdom, humility, and righteousness. It springs from the heart of the one who fears Yahweh, cherishes understanding, and seeks a life of peace, gratitude, and virtue.

Blessed is the person who finds Wisdom,

and the one who obtains discernment,

for the gain from her is better than the gain from silver,

and her revenue *is better* than gold.

She is more precious than gems,

and nothing you desire can compare with her.

Proverbs 3:13–15

She is a tree of life to those taking hold of her,

and blessed are those *who are* holding her fast.

Proverbs 3:18

So now, O sons, listen to me;

blessed are those who keep my ways.

Proverbs 8:32

Blessed is the one who listens to me,
keeping watch at my doors day after day,
watching at the entrance to my gates,

Proverbs 8:34

A wise son makes *his* father glad,
but a foolish son *brings* grief *to* his mother.

Proverbs 10:1

The hope of the righteous is joy,
but the expectation of the wicked will perish.

Proverbs 10:28

Deceit *is* in the heart of those who devise evil,
but those who counsel peace *have* joy.

Proverbs 12:20

Anxiety in a person's heart weighs it down,
but a good word makes it glad.

Proverbs 12:25

Even in laughter the heart *might* be in pain,
and the end of joy *may be* grief.

Proverbs 14:13

The one who shows contempt toward his neighbor is sinning,
but blessed are those who show favor to the poor.

Proverbs 14:21

A joyful heart makes a face cheerful,
but a sorrowful heart *produces* a broken spirit.

Proverbs 15:13

All the days of the afflicted person are bad,
but a merry heart *has* a lasting banquet.

Proverbs 15:15

Bright eyes make the heart glad,
and good news fattens the bones.

Proverbs 15:30

The one who comprehends a *wise* saying will find good,
and blessed is the one who trusts in Yahweh.

Proverbs 16:20

A cheerful heart is a good cure,
but a broken spirit dries up the bones.

Proverbs 17:22

A person's spirit can endure his sickness,
but a broken spirit, who can bear that?

Proverbs 18:14

A righteous person who walks in his integrity—
blessed are his children after him.

Proverbs 20:7

The father of a righteous person will rejoice exceedingly,
and the man who fathers a wise *son* will delight in him;
may your father and your mother be glad,
and may she who gave birth to you rejoice.

Proverbs 23:24–25

Become wise, my son, and make my heart glad,
so that I may give an answer to the one who reproaches me.

Proverbs 27:11

Blessed is the person who trembles *before God* continually,
but the one who hardens his heart will fall into evil.

Proverbs 28:14

When there is no vision, people are unrestrained,
but blessed is the one who keeps the Law.

Proverbs 29:18

JUSTICE

A s a cornerstone of wise and godly living, justice is to govern not only social order but personal conduct. It is more than simply executing fairness in domestic disputes or criminal punishment; it is exhibited in the character of someone who acts with honesty, defends what is right, and treats others with equity and compassion. Those who pursue justice actively seek to uphold truth, protect the weak and innocent, and resist the corrupting influence of others. Their decisions are guided by understanding, discernment, and a deep sense of moral responsibility.

A person who walks in justice contributes to the stability of their community and earns the trust and respect of others. They don't twist the truth for personal gain, show favoritism, or ignore the cries of the oppressed. Instead, they are careful with their words and fair in their judgments, understanding that every choice is to uphold the rule of Yahweh and the ethic of his kingdom. Moreover, those who desire justice are concerned about those who cannot stand up for themselves and seek to intervene and defend the weak and vulnerable.

In contrast, those who pervert justice—by accepting bribes, spreading lies, or oppressing others—set themselves on a path of destruction. Their actions sow discord, breed resentment, and invite God's judgment upon them. Injustice not only harms its victims but also brings affliction and trouble upon the perpetrator, corroding their soul and leading to spiritual ruin.

True justice is inseparable from righteousness and mercy. It must not be viewed as cold or harsh, but tempered with compassion and truth. When rooted in the fear of Yahweh and a love for wisdom, justice becomes a powerful force for good—restoring what is broken, protecting those who can't protect themselves, and establishing a stable life and society that reflects the goodness and graciousness of the Creator.

He has stored up sound advice for the upright—
a shield for those who walk blamelessly—
guarding the paths of justice,
and watching over the way of his loyal ones.

Proverbs 2:7–8

Do not withhold a good thing from those to whom it is due,
when it is *in* the power of your hands to do *it.*
Do not tell your neighbors, "Go, and come back,
and tomorrow I will give *it,*" when it is with you.
Do not devise evil against your neighbor;
he lives near you and trusts *you.*
Do not quarrel with someone for no reason
if he has not committed evil against you.

Proverbs 3:27–30

I walk in the way of righteousness,
in the midst of the paths of justice,

to cause those who love me to inherit property,
and I will fill their storehouses.

Proverbs 8:20–21

Deceitful balances are an abomination to Yahweh,
but a fair weight is his delight.

Proverbs 11:1

The field of the poor *produces* an abundance of food,
but it is carried away because of a lack of justice.

Proverbs 13:23

Better is a little with righteousness,
than great income without justice.

Proverbs 16:8

A verdict is on the lips of the king;
his mouth should not violate justice.
A just balance and scales are according to Yahweh;
all the weights in the bag are established by him.

Proverbs 16:10–11

The one who declares the wicked to be righteous, and the one
        who condemns the righteous;
indeed, both of them are an abomination to Yahweh.

Proverbs 17:15

A wicked person takes a secret bribe
to twist the paths of justice.

Proverbs 17:23

It is not good to issue a fine to a righteous person,
nor to beat nobles for *their* uprightness.

Proverbs 17:26

It is not good to show favoritism toward a wicked person,
nor to deprive a righteous person of justice.

Proverbs 18:5

An ungodly witness mocks justice,
and the mouth of criminals devours wickedness.

Proverbs 19:28

Unequal weights and unequal measures;
both of them are an abomination to Yahweh.

Proverbs 20:10

Unequal weights are an abomination to Yahweh,
and deceitful scales are not good.

Proverbs 20:23

To do righteousness and justice
is preferred by Yahweh rather than a sacrifice.

Proverbs 21:3

The violence of the wicked will drag them away
because they refused to act with justice.

Proverbs 21:7

To do justice is joyful for the righteous person,
but it is a terror to those doing wickedness.

Proverbs 21:15

The one who sows injustice will reap wickedness,
and the rod of his anger will fail.

Proverbs 22:8

The one who oppresses the poor for his own gain,
and the one who gives to the rich—both will come to poverty.

Proverbs 22:16

These *proverbs* also are for the wise:

To show favoritism in judgment is not good.

The one who says to the wicked person, "You are righteous,"—

peoples will curse him, *and* nations will be indignant with him.

But for those who offer rebuke, it will go well,

and upon them will come a good blessing.

Proverbs 24:23–25

Do not be a witness against your neighbor without cause;

would you deceive with your lips?

Do not say, "Just as he does to me, so I will do to him,

I will repay the man according to his *evil* work."

Proverbs 24:28–29

Evil people do not understand justice,

but those who are seeking Yahweh will come to understand it all.

Proverbs 28:5

To show favoritism is not good,

nevertheless, a person will do wrong for a piece of bread.

Proverbs 28:21

A king brings stability to the land by justice,

but a person who *demands* "contributions" will overthrow *the land*.

Proverbs 29:4

A king who judges the poor with faithfulness—

his throne will be established forever.

Proverbs 29:14

Many seek the attention of the one who rules,

but a person *receives* justice from Yahweh.

Proverbs 29:26

It is not for kings, O Lemuel,

not for kings to drink wine,

nor for those who rule *to drink* beer.

Otherwise, they will drink and forget what has been decreed,

and alter the legal claim of all the afflicted people.

Proverbs 31:4–5

Open your mouth for those who have no voice,

for the legal claim of all defenseless people.

Open your mouth, judge with righteousness,

and defend the cause of the afflicted and needy person.

Proverbs 31:8–9

KINDNESS/GENEROSITY

K indness and generosity are powerful virtues that enrich both the giver and the recipient. They stem from a heart that values compassion, fairness, and empathy. A kind person actively looks for ways to do good, whether through gentle words, treating others with respect, or offering financial or material help. Generosity is not measured by the quantity of what is given, but also by the willingness in one's heart—giving freely, even when resources are limited, demonstrates a noble and wise spirit.

The rewards for being kind and generous are many. Those who give generously receive blessing, prosperity, and favor. Their actions indicate goodwill toward others, foster trust, and build lasting influence with those around them. Kindness includes much more than giving generously; it is reflected in how one speaks, listens, shares, and responds to the needs of others. Even small acts of kindness are seeds that one plants which return to them in the form of peace, respect, and blessings, both physical and spiritual.

Generous people are aligned with the virtues of justice and truth, using what they have to support the poor, defend the vulnerable, and invest in others. Having a heart of generosity reflects a deep awareness of one's responsibility to their community and to God. It stands in contrast to selfishness, cruelty, or greed, which lead to abuse, isolation, distrust, and poverty. Stinginess and harshness may result in momentary gain or the appearance of benefit, but they render a high price in the end, often costing people their physical and spiritual well-being, contentment in life, and personal relationships.

Kindness is also a safeguard—it turns away people's wrath, heals emotional wounds, and diffuses anger and conflict. It invites honor rather than shame, peace instead of strife. A generous and kind person is not only wise, but will also be influential, creating ripples of blessing that touch lives far beyond the brief occasion of giving or helping. Kindness and generosity are virtues of strength and beauty, and the wise person will seek to adorn themselves with them.

The kind person benefits himself,
but the cruel person does himself harm.

Proverbs 11:17

There is one who generously scatters *wealth*, and it is
        continually added *to him,*
and one who is withholding *what is* right, *which* surely *will*
        end in poverty.
The person who blesses *others* will be made prosperous,
and the one who waters, indeed, he himself will be watered.

Proverbs 11:24–25

The righteous person cares for the life of his animal,
but the compassion of the wicked is cruel.

Proverbs 12:10

The one who shows contempt toward his neighbor is sinning,
but blessed are those who show favor to the poor.

Proverbs 14:21

The person who oppresses the poor taunts the one
     who created him,
but the person who shows favor to the needy glorifies him.

Proverbs 14:31

The one who shows favor to a poor person lends to Yahweh,
and he will repay him according to his *good* work.

Proverbs 19:17

The lazy person's desire will kill him
because his hands refuse to work.
All day *long* he craves *what he* desires,
but the righteous person gives and does not withhold
     his generosity.

Proverbs 21:25–26

The generous person will be blessed
because he gave some of his bread to the poor.

Proverbs 22:9

If the one who hates you is hungry, give him food to eat,
and if he is thirsty, give him water to drink,
for you will heap burning coals upon his head,
and Yahweh will reward you.

Proverbs 25:21–22

The person who increases his wealth by interest and
     by profiteering
collects it for the one who shows favor to the poor.

Proverbs 28:8

The person who gives to the poor will not *be in* need,
but the one who shuts his eyes *to them will receive* many curses.

Proverbs 28:27

She extends her hands to the afflicted,
and stretches out her hands to the needy.

Proverbs 31:20

KNOWLEDGE/
UNDERSTANDING

Knowledge and understanding are the foundation of living with wisdom. A person cannot make wise choices if they do not understand the choices they are making or have knowledge upon which they are informed and capable of seeing what is bad, good, and best in a situation. Having knowledge and understanding does not represent simply the accumulation of information, but the ability to perceive truth, discern right from wrong, and properly apply knowledge and insight in daily life. In Proverbs, the pursuit of knowledge begins with humility—recognizing one's need to learn—and with the fear of Yahweh as the foundation for all true understanding.

Those who seek knowledge are intentional about it and exhibit a teachable and disciplined heart. They listen more than they speak, ask profitable questions, value being corrected when they are wrong, and carefully consider the effect of their words and actions. This pursuit leads to sound judgment, peace, and success in life. Understanding gives a person the ability to navigate complex situations, avoid hidden danger, and solve problems with composure and clarity. It protects a person from deception, strengthens their relationships, and equips one to lead and influence others with wisdom.

Wise individuals surround themselves with others who can counsel well and do not assume they know it all. They embrace instruction from their parents, elders, and others who walk with integrity and demonstrate understanding. Rather than being led by emotion or impulsiveness, a person of understanding operates their decision-making through the lens of prudence and insight. As such, knowledge empowers them to speak words that heal, guide, and inspire others.

In contrast, those who reject knowledge—mockers, fools, and the arrogant—are blind to wisdom. To their own harm and destruction, they ignore advice, refuse correction, and often walk into trouble they could have avoided. Their pride prevents them from seeing what is true and good, and in their disdain for knowledge, they get caught in many pitfalls and end up bringing misery and suffering upon themselves and others.

The fear of Yahweh is the beginning of knowledge,

but fools show contempt for wisdom and *sound* teaching.

Proverbs 1:7

"How long, O naive ones, will you love naivety?

How long will mockers delight in mocking,

and fools hate knowledge?

Proverbs 1:22

My son, if you receive my words,

and store up my commandments with you,

making your ear attentive to Wisdom,

directing your heart to discernment,

for if you call out to understanding,

if you raise your voice to discernment,

if you seek her like silver,

and search for her like hidden treasure,

then you will understand the fear of Yahweh,

and you will find the knowledge of God.

Proverbs 2:1–5

Wisdom is the principal thing, *so* get wisdom;

and with all your purchases, purchase understanding.

Exalt her and she will lift you up;

she will honor you because you embrace her.

She will place on your head a wreath of grace;

she will present to you a beautiful crown."

Proverbs 4:7–9

My son, pay attention to my wisdom;

incline your ear to my discernment,

in order that you keep discretion,

and your lips guard knowledge.

Proverbs 5:1–2

Take my teaching, and not silver,

and knowledge rather than choice gold.

Proverbs 8:10

"I, Wisdom, dwell with prudence,

and I find knowledge and discretion.

Proverbs 8:12

The wise store up knowledge,

but the mouth of the fool *brings* destruction near.

Proverbs 10:14

The godless person ruins his neighbor with *his* mouth,

but the righteous will be delivered by knowledge.

Proverbs 11:9

A person will be praised for his insightful mouth,
but the one who has a twisted heart will be *viewed with* contempt.

Proverbs 12:8

Good judgment brings favor,
but the road of the unfaithful never changes.
Every prudent person acts with knowledge,
but a fool displays foolishness.

Proverbs 13:15–16

A mocker searches for wisdom but *finds* none,
but knowledge comes easily to the one who has understanding.
Walk away from the presence of a foolish person,
for *there* you will not know lips *that speak* knowledge.

Proverbs 14:6–7

The naive inherit foolishness,
but the prudent are crowned with knowledge.

Proverbs 14:18

The tongue of the wise produces good knowledge,
but the mouth of fools pours out foolishness.

Proverbs 15:2

The heart of the one who has understanding seeks knowledge,
but the mouth of fools feeds on foolishness.

Proverbs 15:14

Foolishness is a joy to the one who lacks *good* sense,
but a person with understanding walks with integrity.

Proverbs 15:21

How much better to get wisdom than gold!
And to get understanding is to be chosen rather than silver.

Proverbs 16:16

The one who holds back his words has *attained* knowledge,
and the one who has a cool spirit is a person of understanding.

Proverbs 17:27

A fool does not delight in understanding,
but only in expressing his own mind.

Proverbs 18:2

The heart of one who understands acquires knowledge,
and the ear of the wise seeks knowledge.

Proverbs 18:15

It is not good *to have* a desire without knowledge,
and one who makes haste with his feet commits sin.

Proverbs 19:2

The one who gets *good* sense loves his *own* soul;
the one who safeguards discernment will find good.

Proverbs 19:8

Strike a mocker and a naive person will act prudently,
and if you reprove the one who has understanding, he will
        discern knowledge.

Proverbs 19:25

My son, cease listening to teaching
and you will go astray from words of knowledge.

Proverbs 19:27

There is gold and a multitude of gems,
but lips bearing knowledge are a rare jewel.

Proverbs 20:15

When a mocker gets punished, the naive person becomes wise,
and when a wise person is instructed, he accepts knowledge.

Proverbs 21:11

The eyes of Yahweh guard knowledge,
but he overturns the words of the one acting unfaithfully.

Proverbs 22:12

Apply your heart to *sound* teaching,
and *apply* your ears to words of knowledge.

Proverbs 23:12

Get truth and do not sell it;
get wisdom and teaching and understanding.

Proverbs 23:23

By wisdom a house is built,
and by understanding it is established,
and by knowledge *its* rooms are filled
with all precious and pleasant wealth.
A wise man is strong,
and a person with knowledge grows in strength.
For with *wise* guidance you should wage your war,
and with a multitude of advisors there is deliverance.

Proverbs 24:3–6

On account of the transgression of the land, many are its rulers,
but by a person with understanding *and* knowledge order
        will be prolonged.

Proverbs 28:2

Evil people do not understand justice,
but those who are seeking Yahweh will come to understand it all.

Proverbs 28:5

LAZINESS

Laziness is a self-destructive quality that leads to poverty, disgrace, and missed opportunities. It is not merely a habit of inactivity, but more so a refusal to act in situations when wisdom and necessity call for it. The lazy person is often full of excuses, constantly delaying important work and choosing relaxation or distraction over responsibility. They crave rewards and other good things in life but are unwilling to do the work required to attain them, resulting in constant frustration, disappointment, and unmet needs.

This lack of initiative for the lazy person affects all areas of life—physical, mental, and spiritual, and certainly the areas of employment, finances, success, reputation, and relationships. Laziness is the opposite of discipline. It is the mark of weak character, and if left to spread, eventually it will take over all aspects of one's life and lead to utter ruin and brokenness. It can disguise itself as procrastination, unproductiveness, or vain talk, where grand ideas are announced or promises made, but its outcome is always the same: stagnation and failure to act or follow through. The lazy usually desire success or comfort, but they are devoid of personal initiative to pursue and exert the effort required to achieve it. This disconnect between desire and action results in failure to reach goals, and thus the loss of potential. The bottom line is that the lazy drift aimlessly and suffer the consequences of their selfish and neglectful tendency.

The diligent, on the other hand, plan and labor toward productive goals, and because of their willingness to apply themselves and not give up or allow themselves to be coaxed toward inaction, they receive abundance, honor, and security. Those who work hard, plan carefully, and follow through on their responsibilities are rewarded—not just reaping benefits financially or materially, but also by gaining the respect of others and a good reputation.

Proverbs declares that laziness reflects a heart that is resistant to training and discipline, and that disregards the value of time and opportunity. But wisdom calls a person to work hard, plan effectively, and persist until the job is done—not for the sake of busyness, but because a life of purpose and value is cultivated through steady, faithful labor.

Go to the ant, O lazy one,

watch its ways and become wise.

Because it has no leader,

overseer, or ruler,

yet it prepares its bread in summer;

it gathers its food in the harvest.

How long, O lazy one, will you lie *there*?

When will you rise up from your sleep?

"Just a little *more* sleep, a little *more* slumber,

a little *more* folding of the arms to lie *here*,"

and your poverty will come like a thief,

and your needs like an armed man.

Proverbs 6:6–11

The poor person works with an idle palm,

but a diligent hand makes *one* rich.

The one who gathers in the summer is an insightful son;

the one who is fast asleep at the harvest is a shameful son.

Proverbs 10:4–5

As vinegar is to the teeth and as smoke is to the eyes,

so *too* is the lazy one to those who send him.

Proverbs 10:26

The one who works his land will be satisfied with food,

but the one who pursues worthless things lacks sense.

Proverbs 12:11

The hand of the diligent will rule,

but the slack *hand* will become a forced laborer.

Proverbs 12:24

A lazy person will not catch his prey,

but the diligent *will obtain* precious wealth.

Proverbs 12:27

The appetite of the lazy person craves yet *gets* nothing,

but the desire of the diligent person will be fully satisfied.

Proverbs 13:4

The road of the lazy person is like a hedge of thorns,

but the path of the upright is an *open* highway.

Proverbs 15:19

The one who shows himself to be lax in his work

is a brother to the one who destroys.

Proverbs 18:9

Laziness causes one to fall into deep sleep,
and the idle person will go hungry.

Proverbs 19:15

The lazy person buries his hand in the dish;
indeed, he will not bring it back to his mouth.

Proverbs 19:24

A lazy person does not plow in the proper season,
so he looks *for grain* at the harvest but has nothing.

Proverbs 20:4

Do not love sleep, or you will become impoverished;
open your eyes *and* be satisfied with food.

Proverbs 20:13

The lazy person's desire will kill him
because his hands refuse to work.
All day *long* he craves *what he* desires,
but the righteous person gives and does not withhold *his*
        generosity.

Proverbs 21:25–26

The lazy person says, "There is a lion outside!
I will be killed in the public plaza."

Proverbs 22:13

I passed by the field of a lazy person,
and by the vineyard of a person lacking sense,
and behold, it was all overgrown with thistles;
its surface was covered with weeds,
and its stone wall had fallen down.
When I noticed, I paid attention;
I observed, *and* I learned *this* lesson:

"Just a little *more* sleep, a little *more* slumber,
a little *more* folding of the arms to lie *here*,"
and your poverty will come like a robber,
and your needs like an armed man.

Proverbs 24:30–34

A lazy person says, "*There is* a lion on the road!
A lion in the public plaza!"
As a door turns on its hinges,
so does a lazy person upon his bed.
A lazy person buries his hand in the dish,
but he is too tired to bring it back to his mouth.
A lazy person is wiser in his own eyes
than seven people who answer with good judgment.

Proverbs 26:13–16

The one who works his land will be satisfied with food,
but the one who pursues worthless things will be
        "satisfied" with poverty.

Proverbs 28:19

LIES/LYING

Lying is a deeply destructive behavior that undermines trust, damages relationships, and invites God's disapproval and judgment. It is closely associated with deceit, treachery, and injustice—traits that smear and tarnish the character of a person and bring harm to others. A lying tongue spreads conflict, conceals wicked intentions, and distorts reality, leading people astray and often having lasting effects and inflicting deep wounds. Whether through false testimony, flattery, or slander, dishonesty tears at the fabric of a community and destroys one's personal integrity.

Those who lie are called fools, not just morally but practically speaking, because their actions lead to serious consequences—betrayal, disgrace, ruin, and often retaliation by those being lied to. Lies may seem to bring an advantage in the moment, offering shortcuts to gain one's desires or escape from punishment, but they eventually catch up with the one who spoke them. Deception is short-lived, while truth endures. A liar may manipulate a situation temporarily and seem to get away with it, but a lie won't stay hidden forever. The liar will inevitably lose credibility and respect and be condemned by both people and God.

In contrast, being truthful when speaking is a mark of wisdom and righteousness. Honest people speak the truth and bring stability, healing, and peace. Their words can be trusted, their intentions are clear, and their presence results in bestowing life and light to those around them. Speaking the truth—especially when it's difficult—is an act of courage and faithfulness that builds strong character and relationships, inviting God's blessing in everything.

Proverbs emphasizes that God detests lying lips, especially when they are used to harm the innocent or pervert justice. Truth is not just a moral preference—it is a divine standard. A life committed to honesty and truth is a life full of wisdom, integrity, and the fear of Yahweh.

There are six things that Yahweh hates,

indeed, seven things are abominations to his soul:

prideful eyes, a lying tongue,

and hands shedding innocent blood;

a heart that devises wicked thoughts,

feet that are swift to run to *do* evil,

a false witness who breathes out lies,

and one who sows strife among brothers.

Proverbs 6:16–19

The one hiding *his* hatred *has* deceitful lips,

and the one spreading slander, he is a fool.

Proverbs 10:18

The one who speaks *what is* faithful declares an honest testimony,

but a false witness *utters* deceit.

Proverbs 12:17

Truthful lips will be established continually,

but a lying tongue will linger only for a moment.

Proverbs 12:19

Lying lips are an abomination to Yahweh,
but those who do *what is* faithful *obtain* his favor.

Proverbs 12:22

A righteous person hates a deceptive word,
but a wicked person will become a stench and display *his* shame.

Proverbs 13:5

A faithful witness will not lie,
but a deceptive witness breathes out lies.

Proverbs 14:5

A faithful witness rescues lives,
but the one who breathes out lies is treacherous.

Proverbs 14:25

An evildoer pays attention to wicked lips;
a liar listens to a destructive tongue.

Proverbs 17:4

Better is a poor person who walks in his integrity
than one who has twisted lips and is a fool.

Proverbs 19:1

A false witness will not go unpunished,
and the one who tells lies will not escape.

Proverbs 19:5

A false witness will not go unpunished,
and the one who tells lies will perish.

Proverbs 19:9

A person's delight is his loyalty,
and it is better to be poor than one who tells lies.

Proverbs 19:22

An ungodly witness mocks justice,
and the mouth of criminals devours wickedness.

Proverbs 19:28

Acquiring treasures by a lying tongue
is a fleeting vapor *of* those who seek death.

Proverbs 21:6

A false witness will perish,
but a person who listens will *be able to* continue speaking.

Proverbs 21:28

Do not be a witness against your neighbor without cause;
would you deceive with your lips?
Do not say, "Just as he does to me, so I will do to him,
I will repay the man according to his *evil* work."

Proverbs 24:28–29

Like clouds and wind but no rain
is a person who boasts of a gift never given.

Proverbs 25:14

Like a club or a sword or a sharp arrow
is a person bearing false witness against his neighbor.
Like a bad tooth or a foot that slips
is confidence in a person who acts unfaithfully in a
        time of distress.

Proverbs 25:18–19

A lying tongue hates those it oppresses,
and a flattering mouth creates a calamity.

Proverbs 26:28

A ruler who pays attention to deceptive words—
all his officials *become* wicked.

Proverbs 29:12

Two things I ask from you,
do not withhold *these* from me before I die:
remove deceitfulness and false speech far from me;
give me neither poverty nor wealth;
provide to me my portion of bread.

Proverbs 30:7–8

LIFE

Proverbs presents "life" as something more than simply being alive—life is not merely one's existence or breath. Rather, life refers to a rich and meaningful existence that is ultimately shaped by wisdom, righteousness, and the fear of Yahweh. True life is characterized by peace, purpose, and flourishing in every dimension: spiritually, physically, emotionally, relationally, and materially. It flows from wise choices, diligent work, moral integrity, and a heart that seeks understanding. Those who walk on the road that leads to life enjoy security, contentment, and honor; their days are full of joy, significance, and stability.

Living a true life is a gift that must be cultivated through discipline and guarded through discretion. True life is closely tied to listening—to others (especially parents), to instruction, to reproof, to sound counsel, and to God. Those who heed correction and embrace wisdom preserve their lives and avoid the snares of the adversary and wicked people. By contrast, the foolish reject counsel, act rashly, and chase vanity, and in doing so they shorten their days or waste their potential. Their paths are often marked by strife, regret, and ruin.

Proverbs highlights the fact that life is deeply relational. Peaceful, kind, and honest interactions nourish one's soul and prolong life, while bitterness, deceit, and anger sap its strength. The fear of Yahweh is foundational, giving direction and anchoring the heart in the reverence for God that leads to the fullness of life's deepest joys.

Life is not what you are given, but what you make of it. It is not random or solely physical—it is a spiritual journey with consequences and rewards shaped by one's choices. A well-lived life is marked by balance, understanding, righteousness, and a quiet trust in God's guidance through every season.

My son, do not forget my instruction,

and let your heart guard my commandments,

for they will add to you length of days,

years of life, and peace.

Proverbs 3:1–2

In her right hand is length of days,

in her left hand are riches and glory.

Proverbs 3:16

She is a tree of life to those taking hold of her,

and blessed are those *who are* holding her fast.

Proverbs 3:18

My son, do not let these depart from *before* your eyes:

guard sound advice and discretion,

so they will be life to your soul,

and grace for your neck.

Proverbs 3:21–22

When I was a son with my father,

a tender and only son in the sight of my mother,

he taught me and said to me, "Let your heart hold on to my words,
keep my commandments and live.

Proverbs 4:3–4

Listen, my son, and receive my words,
and the years of your life will be many.

Proverbs 4:10

Hold on to *my* teaching, do not let her go.
Guard her because she is your life.

Proverbs 4:13

My son, pay attention to my words,
incline your ear to my sayings.
Do not let them depart from *before* your eyes;
keep them in the midst of your heart.
For they are life to the ones who discover them,
and health to a person's whole body.

Proverbs 4:20–22

She will not consider the path of life;
her ways are unstable, *yet* she is not aware *of it*.

Proverbs 5:6

because the one who finds me finds life,
and he will obtain favor from Yahweh.
But the one who sins against me is doing violence to his *own* soul;
all those who hate me love death."

Proverbs 8:35–36

For by me your days will be multiplied,
and years of life will be added to you.

Proverbs 9:11

The mouth of a righteous person is a fountain of life,
but the mouth of the wicked conceals wrongdoing.

Proverbs 10:11

The wage of the righteous person is life;
the revenue of the wicked is sin.

Proverbs 10:16

The fear of Yahweh adds to *one's* days,
but the years of the wicked will be cut short.

Proverbs 10:27

...indeed, righteousness *leads* to life,
but the one who eagerly pursues evil is *heading* to his death.

Proverbs 11:19

The fruit of a righteous person is a tree of life,
and the wise person takes away souls *from death*.

Proverbs 11:30

In the path of righteousness is life,
and the journey of *that* road does not *lead to* death.

Proverbs 12:28

The one who guards his mouth watches over his life;
destruction will come to the one who opens his lips wide.

Proverbs 13:3

Hope delayed makes the heart sick,
but a desire that arrives is a tree of life.

Proverbs 13:12

The instruction of a wise person is a fountain of life,
that one may turn aside from the snares of death.

Proverbs 13:14

The fear of Yahweh is a fountain of life,
that one may turn aside from the snares of death.

Proverbs 14:27

A peaceful heart is the life of the flesh,
but envy is decay to the bones.

Proverbs 14:30

A healing tongue is a tree of life,
but perversion in it breaks *one's* spirit.

Proverbs 15:4

An ear that listens to life-giving reproof
will dwell among the wise.

Proverbs 15:31

In the light of a king's face there *is* life,
and his favor is like clouds *that bring* spring rain.

Proverbs 16:15

Good judgment is a fountain of life *for* its owner,
but the teaching of fools is foolishness.

Proverbs 16:22

Death and life are in the power of the tongue,
and those who love it will eat of its fruit.

Proverbs 18:21

The fear of Yahweh *leads* to life,
and the one *who has it* will sleep satisfied through the night *and*
    not be visited by evil.

Proverbs 19:23

The reward of humility—the fear of Yahweh—
is wealth, glory, and life.

Proverbs 22:4

A ruler who lacks understanding *commits* many extortions,
but the one who hates unjust gain will prolong *his* days.

Proverbs 28:16

LOVE

Love is a force of great strength and is an indispensable virtue that shapes relationships and restores peace. It is not a mere emotion or romantic attraction, but a choice to act with loyalty, patience, and grace—especially in the face of conflict or imperfection. Love covers offenses, promotes forgiveness, and seeks reconciliation. It builds trust and unity, holding relationships together through difficulties that would otherwise cause division.

True love is shown through acts of kindness, faithfulness, and a willingness to sacrifice one's own advantage or comfort for the good of others. It is expressed in both words and deeds, such as through encouragement, correction, loyalty, and generosity. Love does not spread gossip or stir up quarrels; instead, it silences strife and offers a safe place for others to grow, fail, and then begin again. Love is full of second chances, and it never runs dry.

In contrast, hatred is depicted as divisive and destructive. It fuels conflict, delights in wrongdoing, and brings about shame. Those who withhold love or act out of jealousy and contempt fracture relationships and erode the peace of a home or community.

This is because love is foundational in a family and community. A parent's loving discipline is essential for a child's growth, and the presence of love in the home—more than wealth or comfort—makes it a place of joy and safety. And in friendships and marriages, love is the glue that binds people through mutual respect, trust, and consistent care. And in a community, love is the fabric that weaves people's lives together and covers over their mistakes and imperfections.

Indeed, love is a mark of wisdom and godliness. It uplifts, heals, protects, and binds together. It is both the motive and the reward of righteous living—a virtue that gives life its warmth, its strength, and its deepest meaning.

My son, do not reject the discipline of Yahweh,
and do not abhor his reproof.
For the one whom Yahweh loves, he reproves,
like a father to his cherished son.

Proverbs 3:11–12

I love those who love me,
and those who desire me will find me.

Proverbs 8:17

Hatred stirs up strife,
but love covers over all transgressions.

Proverbs 10:12

The one who withholds his rod hates his son,
but the one who loves him desires discipline for him.

Proverbs 13:24

Better is a meal of vegetables when love is present,
than a fattened ox and hatred with it.

Proverbs 15:17

The one who covers over a transgression seeks love,
but the one who repeats the issue separates close friends.

Proverbs 17:9

A friend loves at all times,
and a brother is born for *times of* distress.

Proverbs 17:17

A person has many friends to socialize with,
but there is one who loves *him* who sticks closer than a brother.

Proverbs 18:24

Better is open reproof
than hidden love.
The wounds of a friend are faithful,
but an enemy multiplies kisses.

Proverbs 27:5–6

LUST/SEDUCTION

L ust and seduction are depicted as an enticement that lures people in, but it is a deadly trap designed to appeal to the senses while hiding the path to destruction. In Proverbs, the "strange" or "foreign" woman (which is a woman outside the marriage covenant) is used as a symbol of seduction. She is described as having lips that drip with honey, and her speech is smoother than oil. This imagery captures how enticing and pleasurable the lustful experience may initially seem. However, beneath the surface lies the real danger—what begins as sweet and smooth ends up as bitter as wormwood and as sharp as a double-edged sword. The path of lust leads not to love or fulfillment but descends to death and the grave—figuratively portraying lust as a power that will take the life of its victim.

The problem isn't solely with the desire that lust generates for physical beauty and sexual gratification, but also with the internal blindness it creates. Those who follow the path of lust lose sight of the road to life. The one who falls for the temptations of lust often doesn't realize the instability that it brings, nor do they recognize the ruin that lies ahead. The person who has been seduced by lust lacks awareness of their predicament and is unable to see the life-draining consequences.

Furthermore, Proverbs presents the seductive woman as being very persuasive, and her flattering words can overpower a person's sound judgment. Her influence is not forceful but subtle and strategic, catching her victims off guard. The young man who has been captivated by her does so without deliberation—without thinking—like an animal led blindly to the slaughter or a bird flying into a trap. There's a sense of inevitability once he is caught in her snare—his life is at stake, yet he is unaware of the cost until it is too late.

Giving in to lust isn't just a moral failing—it is a self-destructive act. It completely compromises one's mental clarity, overrides their discernment, leads them away from wisdom, and ultimately brings spiritual, emotional, and even physical injury, and potentially, utter ruin. However, the consequences are not often immediately felt or perceived, which is what makes the trap of lust so insidious. Regardless, the end result is the same: a loss of integrity, character, and even life.

Avoiding seduction and the power of lust requires foresight and wisdom. It is essential that a person remains grounded in godliness and virtue, not being swayed by charm or beauty, recognizing that temporary pleasure can never outweigh the irreversible damage and permanent effects it can cause. The wise guard their hearts and steer clear of what might seem pleasant and enticing but beneath is a road paved with regret and sorrow. Lust and seduction are not just trivial temptations of the flesh—they are powerful enemies at war with discernment, self-control, and commitment to wisdom and the path of life.

For the lips of the forbidden woman drip honey,

and her mouth is smoother than oil,

but in the end she is bitter as wormwood;

she is sharp as a two-edged sword.

Her feet go down to death;

her steps proceed toward Sheol.

She will not consider the path of life;

her ways are unstable, *yet* she is not aware *of it.*

Proverbs 5:3–6

By her great persuasion she seduces him,

by the seductiveness of her lips she leads him astray.

Suddenly he walks after her,

like an ox goes to the slaughter,

like a stag stepping into a snare,

until an arrow pierces his liver.

He is like a bird rushing into a trap;

and he does not know that it *will cost him* his life.

Proverbs 7:21–23

MAKING AGREEMENTS

Entering into financial agreements or pledges—especially with strangers or those who are not well known by the person—is a very risky and unwise decision. Making guarantees or acting as security for another person's debt is repeatedly warned against. These types of agreements can trap a person, leading to loss, humiliation, or even poverty. The urgency in these warnings reflects the seriousness of being legally or morally obligated in an agreement under stipulations and consequences that may turn out to be detrimental and unavoidable.

Such commitments, particularly when made impulsively or without careful judgment, are described as "snares." It is like being caught in a trap by a hunter from which there is likely no escape. Proverbs urges those who have entangled themselves in such deals to act quickly and humbly in order to free themselves, emphasizing the need for taking initiative to achieve a swift resolution. Even when motivated by kindness or loyalty, these pledges are seen as foolish if they put one's own stability or safety at risk (or that of family, friends, or the community).

There is a recurring call to exercise discernment and avoid impulsive or emotional decision-making when it comes to financial or legal guarantees. Wisdom means evaluating the risks, maintaining personal boundaries, and not allowing a spirit of generosity or excitement to override sound judgment. Agreements made without full understanding or a clear likelihood and ability to follow through can result in punishment as severe as losing one's own belongings, which are symbols of personal security and wealth.

What Proverbs advocates for is financial prudence, personal responsibility, and a cautious approach to making binding promises, especially on behalf of others. Such promises can entail unforeseen trouble that will cause regret and frustration. True wisdom is seen not only in being generous, but also in protecting oneself and household from exploitation and avoidable hardship.

My son, if you have put up security for your neighbor,

if you have entered into an agreement with a stranger,

then you have been ensnared by the words of your mouth,

you have been captured by the words of your mouth.

Do this now, my son, and be set free,

for you have put yourself into the hand of your neighbor.

Go! Humble yourself and pressure your neighbor.

Do not give *any* sleep to your eyes,

or slumber to your eyelids.

Be rescued like a gazelle from a hunter,

and like a bird from the hand of a fowler.

Proverbs 6:1–5

The one who puts up security *for* a stranger will suffer badly,

but the one who hates making *such* deals is secure.

Proverbs 11:15

A person lacking sense shakes hands on an agreement,
making a solemn pledge in the presence of his neighbor.

Proverbs 17:18

Take his garment since he has *agreed to* give security for a stranger;
hold it as security *when he has pledged* for a foreigner.

Proverbs 20:16

Do not be among those who shake hands *in a pledge*,
among those who put up security for loans.
If you have nothing with which to pay,
why should he take your bed out from under you?

Proverbs 22:26–27

Take his garment since he has *agreed to* give security for a stranger;
hold it as security *when he has pledged* for a foreign woman.

Proverbs 27:13

MEN/HUSBANDS

A man who seeks to live wisely and responsibly must begin by cultivating faithfulness, integrity, and honor in his life. Proverbs has much to say about men in the context of marriage as a husband. Rather than seeking fulfillment through chasing seductive women and unfaithfulness, a man is urged to be exhilarated by the love of his own wife. Wisdom declares that there is unparalleled joy and satisfaction in deeply valuing one's wife. A faithful and loving relationship brings physical and emotional satisfaction and spiritual blessing. On the other hand, infidelity is portrayed as an act of self-destruction, leading to disgrace and irreversible shame.

The home is both a reflection and a result of a man's character. A man who troubles his household, whether through foolishness or mistreatment, finds himself with nothing—he "inherits the wind." In contrast, a righteous man who walks in integrity becomes a lasting blessing to his children. His actions echo through generations, modeling a life of trustworthiness and strength. A man of faithfulness is rare and valuable; many men boast, but few truly live it out. When a man neglects or wanders from his responsibilities at home, and thus his marriage and family, he fails to protect his household and instead disrupts the balance and stability, bringing only trouble and strife.

To a husband, a prudent, noble wife is seen as a great treasure—a gift from God. She enhances her husband's life, even crowning him with honor. In contrast, a contentious or shameful wife can bring continual sorrow upon him, likened to a dripping roof or decay in one's bones. Yet these observations about women also reflect the responsibilities of husbands to foster peace, stability, and appreciation in the marriage relationship.

Before building a family, wisdom advises that a man should establish his livelihood and secure provision in order to properly care for his household. Responsible preparation ensures long-term success and stability. Furthermore, a man is to respect his parents, especially in matters of inheritance or provision. This is non-negotiable according to wisdom, for selfish disregard for them aligns a man with those who destroy rather than build.

Thus, a wise man lives with purpose, loyalty, and foresight. He values the quiet strength of a good home, understands the weight and significance of his choices, and seeks harmony with others (especially his wife) rather than stirring up strife. Such character and behavior in life brings lasting blessing—not just for the man himself, but for his entire household.

Let your fountain be continually blessed,
and rejoice because of the wife of your youth.
She is a loving doe and a graceful mountain goat;
let her breasts satisfy you at every *opportune* time—
going astray in her love.

Proverbs 5:18–19

The man committing adultery with a woman lacks sense;
he who does this is destroying his *own* soul.
He will find affliction and dishonor,
and his disgrace will not be blotted out.

Proverbs 6:32–33

The one who troubles his household will inherit wind,
and the fool will be a servant to one who is wise of heart.

Proverbs 11:29

An excellent wife is the crown of her husband,
but she who acts shamefully is like decay in his bones.

Proverbs 12:4

He who finds a wife finds a good thing,
and he obtains favor from Yahweh.

Proverbs 18:22

A foolish son *brings* destruction to his father,
and the contentions of a wife are *like* a constant drip.
A house and wealth are the inheritance from fathers,
but an insightful wife is from Yahweh.

Proverbs 19:13–14

Many people claim to be loyal,
but a faithful man, who can find?
A righteous person who walks in his integrity—
blessed are his children after him.

Proverbs 20:6–7

It is better to live on the corner of a rooftop
than in a house with a contentious wife.

Proverbs 21:9

It is better to live in a desolate land
than *with* a contentious and angry woman.

Proverbs 21:19

Prepare your outdoor work,
and carefully prepare it for yourself in the field;
afterwards, then, build your house.

Proverbs 24:27

Like a bird that wanders from her nest,
so is a person who wanders from his place.

Proverbs 27:8

A constant dripping on a day of steady rain
and a contentious wife are alike;
whoever can restrain her can *even* restrain the wind,
and can *even* grasp oil in his right hand.

Proverbs 27:15–16

The person who robs his father or his mother and says, "It is not
        a transgression,"
he is a friend of a person *who causes* destruction.

Proverbs 28:24

MARRIAGE

Marriage is a sacred and godly union that has the power to bring one of two experiences in life: joy, stability, and honor—or conflict, frustration, and heartache. A faithful and wise spouse is a profound blessing, a source of lifelong strength, security, and favor from Yahweh. Proverbs says that a good wife is more valuable than jewels; she strengthens her household, contributes diligently, and earns the trust and praise of her husband and children. Her character is marked by strength, wisdom, and kindness, and she demonstrates what it means to live with the fear of Yahweh.

Marital intimacy is encouraged and celebrated strictly within the covenant of marriage. The imagery of drinking from one's own cistern highlights the importance of marital fidelity and the delight that comes from absolute devotion to one's spouse. As such, men are urged to find satisfaction and delight in their wife, cherishing her with tenderness and joy.

However, Proverbs also presents a realistic view of the challenges in marriage. Some marriages do not result in positive outcomes and happiness. A contentious or quarrelsome spouse is likened to a constant dripping—they are an endless nuisance, unsettling, and wearisome. This type of tension and interaction is so disruptive in a marriage that it is said to be better to live in isolation on the roof of the house than in a home filled with strife. Such descriptions serve as both warnings and insights into the emotional toll of unresolved conflict within marriage, and the importance of carefully choosing a spouse who exhibits the characteristics of godliness and wisdom.

Ultimately, a successful marriage is rooted in mutual respect, emotional and spiritual strength, and a shared commitment to living with the fear of Yahweh, forming a three-fold cord that is strong and enduring. The fruit of such a union is not only personal companionship and fulfillment, but also a thriving household that is blessed by Yahweh and abounding with joy and peace.

Drink water from your own cistern,

and fresh water from the midst of your own well.

Should your springs overflow outside,

streams of water in the public plazas?

Let them be for you alone,

and not for strangers with you.

Let your fountain be continually blessed,

and rejoice because of the wife of your youth.

She is a loving doe and a graceful mountain goat;

let her breasts satisfy you at every *opportune* time—

going astray in her love.

So why go astray, my son, with a forbidden woman,

and *why* do you embrace the bosom of a foreign woman?

Proverbs 5:15–20

An excellent wife is the crown of her husband,

but she who acts shamefully is like decay in his bones.

Proverbs 12:4

He who finds a wife finds a good thing,
and he obtains favor from Yahweh.

Proverbs 18:22

A foolish son *brings* destruction to his father,
and the contentions of a wife are *like* a constant drip.
A house and wealth are the inheritance from fathers,
but an insightful wife is from Yahweh.

Proverbs 19:13–14

It is better to live on the corner of a rooftop
than in a house with a contentious wife.

Proverbs 21:9

It is better to live in a desolate land
than *with* a contentious and angry woman.

Proverbs 21:19

It is better to sit on the corner of a rooftop
than in a house with a contentious wife.

Proverbs 25:24

A constant dripping on a day of steady rain
and a contentious wife are alike;
whoever can restrain her can *even* restrain the wind,
and can *even* grasp oil in his right hand.

Proverbs 27:15–16

MONEY/WEALTH/RICHES

oney, wealth, and riches are viewed one of two ways in Proverbs: either they are the product of a life of wisdom and prudence where God blesses and prospers the one who lives righteously and submits to his authority, or they are a snare and a trap for those who trust in them and will lead the person yearning for more to his own destruction and peril.

But wealth is not condemned in itself; it certainly is a reward for diligence, planning, and righteous living. It provides security, influence, and the ability to bless others. However, the pursuit of wealth for its own sake—or through dishonest means or because of greed—brings only misery, turmoil, and, in some cases, even poverty.

Proverbs praises hard work, discipline, and generosity as the paths to sustainable prosperity. Wealth gained slowly and honestly is seen as enduring, while riches that are gained quickly or through unethical tactics will soon vanish. Laziness, over-indulgence, and poor stewardship will lead to financial ruin. Thus, wisdom, rather than riches, is to be prized above all as the greatest treasure and wealth—offering long-lasting value, protection, and security that money alone cannot provide.

There is also a clear recognition of wealth's limitations. It cannot save anyone in the day of judgment, it can fade or disappear quickly, and it can be a cause of isolation or a corrupting influence if not handled with humility and discernment. Riches must be paired with righteousness, generosity to the poor, and a heart that trusts in God rather than material possessions. The wise person understands the fleeting nature of money and uses it for godly purposes, but does not rely on it for their self-worth or use it to oppress or manipulate others.

Additionally, Proverbs emphasizes the responsibility of those who have wealth. Oppressing the poor or ignoring cries for justice brings God's judgment and anger. Instead, the one who gives generously will be blessed, and giving to those in need is seen as lending to God himself. Moreover, true success is measured not in financial abundance but in a person's integrity, generosity, and lasting influence.

Overall, money is portrayed not as an end to be sought after for itself, but as a means to do good to others. However, wealth must be managed with wisdom, guided by righteousness, and held with humility of heart, knowing that all wealth is ultimately from God who blesses those who walk upright before Him.

Honor Yahweh from your wealth,

and from the firstfruits of all your revenue,

and your storehouses will be completely filled,

and your wine vats will overflow with new wine.

Proverbs 3:9–10

Riches and glory are with me,

enduring prosperity and righteousness.

My fruit is better than gold, even *better than* refined gold,

and my gain *is better* than silver.

I walk in the way of righteousness,

in the midst of the paths of justice,

to cause those who love me to inherit property,
and I will fill their storehouses.

Proverbs 8:18–21

Treasures *gained* by wickedness profit nothing,
but righteousness will deliver from death.

Proverbs 10:2

The rich person's wealth is his fortified city;
the destruction of the poor is their poverty.

Proverbs 10:15

The blessing from Yahweh is what makes one rich,
and he does not combine pain with *the blessing*.

Proverbs 10:22

Riches will not profit on the day of wrath,
but righteousness will deliver from death.

Proverbs 11:4

When a wicked person dies, his hope perishes,
and *his* hope of wealth perishes.

Proverbs 11:7

There is one who generously scatters *wealth*, and it is
        continually added *to him,*
and one who is withholding *what is* right, *which* surely *will*
        end in poverty.
The person who blesses *others* will be made prosperous,
and the one who waters, indeed, he himself will be watered.
The people will curse the one who withholds grain,
but a blessing *will be* upon the head of the one who sells grain.
The one who is on the lookout for *what is* good seeks favor,
but the one who is intent on evil, it will come to him.

The one who trusts in his wealth, he will fall,
but the righteous will bud like a leaf.

Proverbs 11:24–28

A lazy person will not catch his prey,
but the diligent *will obtain* precious wealth.

Proverbs 12:27

There is one who pretends to be rich, but *has* nothing;
another pretends to be poor *but has* great wealth.
The ransom for a person's soul is his wealth,
but the poor does not hear a *threatening* rebuke.

Proverbs 13:7–8

Wealth *obtained* by fraud will dwindle away,
but the one who gathers little by little increases *his wealth*.

Proverbs 13:11

The one who ignores discipline *will get* poverty and dishonor,
but the one who heeds reproof will be honored.

Proverbs 13:18

A good person will provide an inheritance for his
        children's children,
but the wealth of the sinner is being stored up for the
        righteous person.
The field of the poor *produces* an abundance of food,
but it is carried away because of a lack of justice.

Proverbs 13:22–23

A poor person is hated even by his neighbor,
but there are many who love the rich.

Proverbs 14:20

In all hard work there is profit,

but *mere* words from the lips surely *lead* to poverty.

The crown of the wise is *their* wealth,

but the foolishness of fools is *still* foolishness.

Proverbs 14:23–24

The house of the righteous person *has* great treasure,

but trouble is stirred up by the revenue of the wicked person.

Proverbs 15:6

Better is a little with the fear of Yahweh

than great treasure and turmoil with it.

Proverbs 15:16

Better is a little with righteousness,

than great income without justice.

Proverbs 16:8

How much better to get wisdom than gold!

And to get understanding is to be chosen rather than silver.

Proverbs 16:16

Better to be humble in spirit with the poor

than to share the plunder with the proud.

Proverbs 16:19

Better is a dry *piece of* bread and peace with it,

than a household full of feasting with strife.

Proverbs 17:1

Why is there payment in the hand of a fool to buy wisdom

when *he has* no sense?

Proverbs 17:16

A rich person's wealth is his strong city,
indeed, *it is* like a high wall in his imagination.

Proverbs 18:11

The poor person speaks *with gentle* pleas,
but the rich person answers forcefully.

Proverbs 18:23

Wealth will add many friends,
but a poor person will be separated from his friend.

Proverbs 19:4

All the brothers of a poor person hate him;
indeed, how much more do his friends distance
        themselves from him.
He pursues *them with* words, *but* they do not *respond.*

Proverbs 19:7

A house and wealth are the inheritance from fathers,
but an insightful wife is from Yahweh.

Proverbs 19:14

Do not love sleep, or you will become impoverished;
open your eyes *and* be satisfied with food.

Proverbs 20:13

An inheritance *gained* quickly at the beginning
will not be blessed in the end.

Proverbs 20:21

Acquiring treasures by a lying tongue
is a fleeting vapor *of* those who seek death.

Proverbs 21:6

The one who closes his ear to the cry of the poor,
he will also cry out and not be answered.

Proverbs 21:13

The one who loves pleasure *will become* a poor person;
the one who loves wine and oil will not become rich.

Proverbs 21:17

Desirable treasure and oil are in the dwelling place of
        the wise person,
but the foolish person consumes it.

Proverbs 21:20

The rich and the poor have this in common:
Yahweh is the one who creates them all.

Proverbs 22:2

The reward of humility—the fear of Yahweh—
is wealth, glory, and life.

Proverbs 22:4

The rich person rules over the poor,
and the borrower is a slave to the lender.

Proverbs 22:7

The one who oppresses the poor for his own gain,
and the one who gives to the rich—both will come to poverty.

Proverbs 22:16

Do not rob a poor person because he is poor,
and do not crush the needy at the *city* gate,
for Yahweh will defend their case,
and he will rob the life of those who robbed them.

Proverbs 22:22–23

Do not wear yourself out by attempting to get rich;
cease from *relying upon* your *own* understanding.
If your eyes fly to it, then it is gone,
for it surely makes wings for itself like an eagle,
and it flies *into* the sky.

Proverbs 23:4–5

By wisdom a house is built,
and by understanding it is established,
and by knowledge *its* rooms are filled
with all precious and pleasant wealth.

Proverbs 24:3–4

I passed by the field of a lazy person,
and by the vineyard of a person lacking sense,
and behold, it was all overgrown with thistles;
its surface was covered with weeds,
and its stone wall had fallen down.
When I noticed, I paid attention;
I observed, *and* I learned *this* lesson:
"Just a little *more* sleep, a little *more* slumber,
a little *more* folding of the arms to lie *here*,"
and your poverty will come like a robber,
and your needs like an armed man.

Proverbs 24:30–34

Know well the condition of your flock;
pay attention to your herds,
for treasure will not last,
nor does a crown *last* for multiple generations.

Proverbs 27:23–24

Better is a poor person who walks in his integrity
than a person who is crooked in his ways, even though he is rich.

Proverbs 28:6

The person who increases his wealth by interest and
      by profiteering
collects it for the one who shows favor to the poor.

Proverbs 28:8

A rich person is wise in his own eyes,
but the poor person with understanding sees right through him.

Proverbs 28:11

A ruler who lacks understanding *commits* many extortions,
but the one who hates unjust gain will prolong *his* days.

Proverbs 28:16

The one who works his land will be satisfied with food,
but the one who pursues worthless things will be
      "satisfied" with poverty.
A faithful person *will have* many blessings,
but the one who makes haste to get rich will not go unpunished.
To show favoritism is not good,
nevertheless, a person will do wrong for a piece of bread.
A stingy person makes haste toward wealth,
but he does not know that poverty will come to him.

Proverbs 28:19–22

A greedy soul stirs up strife,
but the person who trusts in Yahweh will be made prosperous.

Proverbs 28:25

A person who loves wisdom makes his father glad,
but the man who gets involved with prostitutes
     destroys his wealth.

Proverbs 29:3

Two things I ask from you,
do not withhold *these* from me before I die:
remove deceitfulness and false speech far from me;
give me neither poverty nor wealth;
provide to me my portion of bread.
Otherwise, I might become satisfied and deny *you* and say,
"Who is Yahweh?"
Or, in the other case, I might become impoverished and steal
and desecrate the name of my God.

Proverbs 30:7–9

NAIVETY/INEXPERIENCE

N aivety and inexperience are conditions where a person is deficient in knowledge or understanding, which produces a detrimental vulnerability that, while not inherently sinful, places the individual at significant risk if it is not addressed through the pursuit of wisdom. The naive are open to and swayed by external influences—easily led astray by temptation, deception, or the allure of pleasure and flattery—simply because they lack discernment and fortitude. Their openness and gullibility are not inherently malicious or sin-oriented, but their failure to have wisdom and understanding leaves them unguarded and prey to following the road of foolishness that leads to wickedness and death.

The naive are contrasted with the wise, who actively seek knowledge, listen to instruction, and recognize danger in advance. While the inexperienced wander blindly into trouble, the prudent see the consequences that lie ahead and take precautions to avoid encountering them. Proverbs frequently depicts the naive as being easily seduced by persuasive voices around them—whether the suggestions of immoral people, peer pressure, or the flattery of others. Without being aware of outcomes or effects, they make rash and ignorant choices that lead to shame, regret, and their own destruction.

However, naivety is not a permanent condition; it is correctable. Wisdom calls out publicly to the simple and naive, inviting them to turn toward her and then learn and grow. The young and inexperienced are encouraged to seek wise counsel, receive reproof, and treasure instruction like a valuable inheritance. Those who do so can transition from naive to discerning, gaining vital tools and the ability to navigate life wisely and avoid the snares that catch those who remain in their naive condition.

Naivety is the starting point of every person, but it must not be the place one dwells for long—one must move forward by embracing discipline, training through instruction, and walking on the road of wisdom. The cost of remaining naive is high, but the reward of pursuing understanding is a life of protection, prosperity, and purposeful direction.

To know wisdom and teaching,

to understand words *that give* understanding,

to receive wise teaching

in righteousness, justice, and integrity;

to give prudence to the naive,

knowledge and discretion to the youth.

Proverbs 1:2–4

"How long, O naive ones, will you love naivety?

How long will mockers delight in mocking,

and fools hate knowledge?

Proverbs 1:22

For the turning away of the naive will kill them,

and the *false* security of fools will destroy them.

Proverbs 1:32

For at the window of my house,

I looked down through my lattice,

and I saw among the naive,

and I discerned among the youths a young man lacking sense.

He was passing along the street near her corner,

and he was taking steps on the road to her house,

at dusk, in the evening of the day,

in the middle of the night and the *gloomy* darkness,

And look! A woman *comes* to meet him,

dressed as a prostitute and with a cunning heart.

Proverbs 7:6–10

Understand prudence, O naive ones,

and understand *good* sense, O foolish ones.

Proverbs 8:5

Lady Wisdom has built her house;

she has carved out her seven pillars.

She has slaughtered her meat;

she has mixed her wine;

indeed, she has prepared her table.

She has sent out her female servants;

she calls out from the tops of the heights of the town,

"Whoever is naive, let him turn in here."

To the one lacking sense, she says,

"Come! Eat my food,

and drink the wine that I have mixed.

Leave *your* naive ways and live.

And go straight *ahead* on the road of understanding."

Proverbs 9:1–6

A naive person will believe any word,
but the prudent person carefully considers his steps.

Proverbs 14:15

The naive inherit foolishness,
but the prudent are crowned with knowledge.

Proverbs 14:18

Strike a mocker and a naive person will act prudently,
and if you reprove the one who has understanding, he will
        discern knowledge.

Proverbs 19:25

When a mocker gets punished, the naive person becomes wise,
and when a wise person is instructed, he accepts knowledge.

Proverbs 21:11

A prudent person sees evil and hides,
but the naive continue on and are punished.

Proverbs 22:3

A prudent person sees evil *and* hides,
but the naive continue on and are punished.

Proverbs 27:12

NEIGHBORS

Proverbs offers rich guidance on how to live wisely and honorably with neighbors, recognizing that close proximity, regular
interaction, and social influence can either foster a mutual-
ly enjoyable relationship or provoke tension and conflict. Personal integrity is at the heart of wisdom—speaking truthfully, acting
with fairness, and respecting boundaries. Moreover, trust is central
to good relationships, but it can be quickly damaged by gossip or
disrespect. A quick way to sabotage a neighborly relationship is to
speak falsely or in a flattering way with hidden motives, as disin-
genuousness creates suspicion and distrust.

A wise neighbor is considerate, avoiding both overfamiliarity and
unnecessary intrusion. Bothering your neighbor too often can wear
out a welcome, while thoughtful distance maintains personal space,
respect, and peace. When a neighbor is in need, showing kindness,
discretion, and empathy are helpful in strengthening the relationship, especially when a neighbor is in a vulnerable predicament. At
those times, helping them by being generous, withholding criticism
through emotional restraint, or being patient with understanding
builds a trustworthy and enduring bond.

Strong relationships take time and effort to build, but they can be
torn down quickly. False accusations, deceitful speech, or crude
jokes under the pretense of playfulness can undermine a relationship, destroy credibility, and sow strife. Those who plot or stir up

trouble for their neighbors are seen as dangerous and foolish. Conversely, withholding help or acting with cold indifference when a neighbor could use a hand violates the moral duty one has to those who live nearby. Wisdom demands that a person not withhold good if they are able to provide it to their neighbor.

Discernment and restraint in dealing with neighborly disputes can be overlooked as a critical aspect of wisdom. Jumping to conclusions or spreading misinformation damages reputations and relationships. The wise person considers all sides and seeks peaceful resolution, upholding justice rather than fueling contention. Wisdom advises that it is better to be wronged than to wrong your neighbor in return, as revenge never settles a dispute but instead increases bitterness, anger, and resentment.

A good neighbor embodies reliability, discretion, and genuine concern—traits that bring peace and stability between people. Therefore, relations with neighbors, when nurtured with wisdom, become sources of mutual support, refuge, and strength. This brings blessing to you and all those who live near you.

Do not tell your neighbors, "Go, and come back,
and tomorrow I will give *it*," when it is with you.
Do not devise evil against your neighbor;
he lives near you and trusts *you*.

Proverbs 3:28–29

The godless person ruins his neighbor with *his* mouth,
but the righteous will be delivered by knowledge.

Proverbs 11:9

The one who shows contempt for his neighbor lacks sense,
but a person with understanding remains silent.

Proverbs 11:12

A righteous person shows the way for his neighbor,
but the road of the wicked causes them to wander astray.

Proverbs 12:26

A poor person is hated even by his neighbor,
but there are many who love the rich.
The one who shows contempt toward his neighbor is sinning,
but blessed are those who show favor to the poor.

Proverbs 14:20–21

A violent person entices his neighbor,
and he leads him on a road that is not good.

Proverbs 16:29

The first person to present his case in a dispute *seems* right
until a neighbor comes and questions him.

Proverbs 18:17

The soul of the wicked person desires evil;
his neighbor finds no favor in his eyes.

Proverbs 21:10

Do not be a witness against your neighbor without cause;
would you deceive with your lips?
Do not say, "Just as he does to me, so I will do to him,
I will repay the man according to his *evil* work."

Proverbs 24:28–29

for it is better that it be said to you, "Come up here,"
than to be placed lower in the presence of a noble.
What your eyes have seen,

do not go out to argue *your dispute* too hastily;

otherwise, what will you do in the end

when your neighbor humiliates you?

Argue your dispute with your neighbor,

but do not reveal another person's secret,

or the one who hears *it* might put you to shame,

and your bad reputation will not go away.

Proverbs 25:7–10

Let your foot visit your neighbor's house sparingly,

so that he does not have too much of you and hate you.

Like a club or a sword or a sharp arrow

is a person bearing false witness against his neighbor.

Proverbs 25:17–18

Like a maniac shooting flaming arrows,

arrows, and death,

so is a person who deceives his neighbor,

then says, "Was I not simply joking?"

Proverbs 26:18–19

Do not forsake your friend or your father's friend,

and do not enter into your brother's house on the day

of your distress;

better is a neighbor nearby than a brother far away.

Proverbs 27:10

The one who blesses his friend with a loud voice in

the early morning,

it will be regarded as a curse to him.

Proverbs 27:14

A person who flatters his neighbor

spreads a net for his feet.

Proverbs 29:5

OBEDIENCE

O bedience is another foundational virtue that leads to life, wisdom, and blessing. It begins with a willing heart that listens carefully to instruction—especially from parents and wise mentors—and treasures their knowledge and teaching as a most valuable possession. Obedience is not merely compliance, but rather an active choice to submit to Yahweh's authority, value wise guidance, seek truth, and align one's life with godly principles.

The obedient person guards their heart, watches their speech, and considers their actions carefully, trusting that the words of the wise serve as a lamp and light along their path to help them not stumble and fall. Proverbs asserts that obedience brings health, long life, peace, and God's favor. It is how knowledge is put into right action and how wisdom moves from the mind and into everyday life. Those who take instruction seriously and obey it are protected from danger, temptation, and suffering.

In contrast, disobedience is the way of the foolish. They reject correction, scorn discipline, and disregard authority, all of which lead to disgrace and ruin. A stubborn person or one who mocks others reveals a heart that resists learning and invites destruction. Such a person loses their way, is harmful to others, and ultimately undermines their own well-being. The consequences of rebelling against wisdom have deep personal effects—corrupting relationships, reputations, and one's own soul.

Obedience requires reverence for God. To obey wise instruction is to walk in the fear of Yahweh, acknowledging his authority and trusting in his care. An obedient heart reflects humility, teachability, and a desire to live rightly. In this sense, obedience is not oppressive but rather liberating. It isn't a taskmaster of dos and don'ts, but a way of life that leads to goodness, stability, and safety. However, it is a daily choice to follow the voice of wisdom and remain on the path that leads to life.

Listen, my son, to your father's teaching,

and do not ignore the instruction of your mother,

because they are a wreath of grace for your head,

and a necklace for your neck.

Proverbs 1:8–9

My son, if you receive my words,

and store up my commandments with you,

making your ear attentive to Wisdom,

directing your heart to discernment,

for if you call out to understanding,

if you raise your voice to discernment,

if you seek her like silver,

and search for her like hidden treasure,

then you will understand the fear of Yahweh,

and you will find the knowledge of God.

Proverbs 2:1–5

My son, do not forget my instruction,

and let your heart guard my commandments,

for they will add to you length of days,
years of life, and peace.

Proverbs 3:1–2

My son, do not reject the discipline of Yahweh,
and do not abhor his reproof.
For the one whom Yahweh loves, he reproves,
like a father to his cherished son.

Proverbs 3:11–12

Listen, O sons, to the teaching of a father,
and pay attention in order to learn understanding,
for I give good teaching to you all;
do not abandon my instruction.
When I was a son with my father,
a tender and only son in the sight of my mother,
he taught me and said to me, "Let your heart hold on to my words,
keep my commandments and live.

Proverbs 4:1–4

Listen, my son, and receive my words,
and the years of your life will be many.

Proverbs 4:10

My son, pay attention to my words,
incline your ear to my sayings.
Do not let them depart from *before* your eyes;
keep them in the midst of your heart.
For they are life to the ones who discover them,
and health to a person's whole body.

Proverbs 4:20–22

My son, pay attention to my wisdom;
incline your ear to my discernment,
so that you keep discretion,
and your lips guard knowledge.

Proverbs 5:1–2

But now, *my* sons, listen to me,
and do not depart from the words of my mouth.
Keep your road far from her,
and do not go near to the door of her house,
otherwise you might give your honor to others,
and your years to a cruel person;
otherwise strangers might eat their fill from your strength,
and your hard-earned goods *end up* in the house of a foreigner,

Proverbs 5:7–10

My son, keep your father's commandments,
and do not ignore the instruction of your mother.
Bind them upon your heart always,
tie them around your neck.
As you walk here and there, she will lead you;
when you lie down, she will watch over you,
and *when* you wake up, she will speak with you.

Proverbs 6:20–22

My son, keep my words,
and store up my commandments with you.
Keep my commandments and live,
and my instruction as the pupil of your eye.
Bind them upon your fingers;
write them upon the tablet of your heart.

Proverbs 7:1–3

The wise heart accepts commandments,
but the one who is foolish with his lips will come to ruin.

Proverbs 10:8

A wise son *listens to his* father's discipline,
but a mocker does not listen to rebuke.

Proverbs 13:1

The one who despises a word *of instruction* will come to ruin,
but the one who fears the commandment will be rewarded.

Proverbs 13:13

A fool spurns discipline from his father,
but the one who heeds reproof acts prudently.

Proverbs 15:5

The one who ignores discipline despises his *own* soul,
but the one who listens to reproof acquires *good* sense.
The fear of Yahweh is what wisdom teaches,
and humility goes before glory.

Proverbs 15:32–33

The one who keeps the commandment watches over his life,
but the one who has contempt for his road will die.

Proverbs 19:16

Listen to your father who begot you,
and do not show contempt for your mother when she is old.

Proverbs 23:22

Those who abandon the Law praise the wicked,
but those who keep the Law contend against them.

Proverbs 28:4

He who keeps the Law is a discerning son,
but he who associates with those who lack restraint brings shame
　　　upon his father.

Proverbs 28:7

An eye that mocks at his father
and despises obedience to his mother—
ravens of the valley will peck it out,
and the offspring of a vulture will eat it.

Proverbs 30:17

OPPRESSION

As a violation of justice, compassion, and living with the fear of Yahweh, oppression makes a mockery of God's rule and authority. It reveals a corrupt heart that misuses power to exploit, silence, or trample the poor and vulnerable. Whether through economic injustice, legal manipulation, or disregard for the needs of others, oppression brings moral corruption to individuals and society as a whole. Those who gain wealth or position by using or pushing down others are warned of divine judgment—God sees the plight of the oppressed and promises to defend them. Make no mistake: one day, those who oppress others will receive retribution for what they have done.

Proverbs consistently call for empathy and fairness in all matters, urging those in positions of influence—especially rulers and judges—to advocate for those who cannot stand up for themselves and protect the rights of the needy. Ignoring the cries of the poor is portrayed not only as heartless, but as self-destructive—those who turn a deaf ear to the needy will themselves be ignored in their time of need. In contrast, the righteous care about justice for the poor and act as protectors, not predators.

Even more alarming is the portrayal of poor people who become oppressors themselves. When those who have suffered turn around and exploit others, their injustice is seen as especially heinous and destructive, since they know what it is like to be oppressed. Such behavior magnifies the damage that oppression can cause and reveals the depth of corruption that can take root when power is abused.

Proverbs advocates that positions of power—such as leadership, wealth, and influence—come with responsibility. Those who rule justly and with compassion establish peace and security, while those who use their position for personal gain at others' expense sow unrest and rebellion. The wise use their voice to defend the defenseless, knowing that integrity and mercy are the true marks of strength. In the end, God is the defender of the oppressed, and those who act with justice align themselves with God's heart and desire.

The person who oppresses the poor taunts the one
        who created him,
but the person who shows favor to the needy glorifies him.

Proverbs 14:31

All the days of the afflicted person are bad,
but a merry heart *has* a lasting banquet.

Proverbs 15:15

The one who mocks the poor taunts the one who created him;
the one who is joyful at a calamity will not go unpunished.

Proverbs 17:5

The one who closes his ear to the cry of the poor,
he will also cry out and not be answered.

Proverbs 21:13

The one who oppresses the poor for his own gain,
and the one who gives to the rich—both will come to poverty.

Proverbs 22:16

Do not rob a poor person because he is poor,
and do not crush the needy at the *city* gate,
for Yahweh will defend their case,
and he will rob the life of those who robbed them.

Proverbs 22:22–23

A poor man who oppresses the weak
is *like* a beating rain that does not *leave* food.

Proverbs 28:3

Like a roaring lion and a charging bear,
so is a wicked person ruling over a poor people.
A ruler who lacks understanding *commits* many extortions,
but the one who hates unjust gain will prolong *his* days.

Proverbs 28:15–16

A king brings stability to the land by justice,
but a person who *demands* "contributions" will overthrow *the land.*

Proverbs 29:4

A righteous person knows the legal claim of the poor;
a wicked person does not understand *this* knowledge.

Proverbs 29:7

The poor person and the one who oppresses *others* have
this in common:
Yahweh gives light to the eyes of them both.

Proverbs 29:13

It is not for kings, O Lemuel,
not for kings to drink wine,
nor for those who rule *to drink* beer.

Otherwise, they will drink and forget what has been decreed,
and alter the legal claim of all the afflicted people.

Proverbs 31:4–5

Open your mouth for those who have no voice,
for the legal claim of all defenseless people.
Open your mouth, judge with righteousness,
and defend the cause of the afflicted and needy person.

Proverbs 31:8–9

PATIENCE

Patience is celebrated as a mark of wisdom, strength, and self-control. It reflects a calm and discerning spirit that chooses thoughtful responses over impulsive reactions. A patient person does not allow anger or offense to dictate their behavior. Instead, they delay judgment, overlook minor wrongs, and act with calculated self-restraint, especially in emotionally volatile situations. This ability to remain composed, especially under tense and difficult circumstances, yields peace, diffuses conflict, and earns the respect of others.

Patience is not weakness—it is power under control. It is considered greater than physical might or conquest because governing oneself well is often harder than conquering external challenges. A patient person brings stability to relationships, promotes understanding, and helps maintain harmony in the community. Through quiet perseverance, a patient person can persuade and influence others more effectively than through force or harsh argumentation.

In contrast, impatience exposes a lack of understanding and often leads to foolishness or strife. Quick-tempered reactions reveal immaturity and invite unnecessary trouble and quarrels. Those who lack patience are easily provoked, creating division and escalating conflict where remaining calm and composed could have brought about a beneficial resolution.

The power of patience lies in its ability to serve as a protective force that guards against rash decision making. It also can preserve relationships—especially during times of tension or frustration. But most importantly, it opens the way for wisdom to flourish in one's life by being willing to take the long journey of transformation. It is a core virtue that strengthens one's character, brings honor and a good name, and trains a person to align themselves with the gentle, steady rhythm of wise living.

The anger of a fool is known at once,
but a prudent person conceals dishonor.

Proverbs 12:16

The one who is slow to get angry *possesses* great understanding,
but the one who is easily angered displays foolishness.

Proverbs 14:29

A hot-tempered person incites strife,
but one who is slow to get angry peacefully settles a dispute.

Proverbs 15:18

The one who is slow to get angry is better than a mighty person,
and one who rules his spirit is *better* than one who captures a city.

Proverbs 16:32

A person's good judgment makes him slow to anger,
and it is his honor to overlook an offense.

Proverbs 19:11

With patience a ruler can be persuaded,
and a gentle tongue can break a bone.

Proverbs 25:15

PEACE

Peace is one of the richest treasures that one obtains from wise, righteous living. It is both a personal state of inner tranquility and a social condition of living harmoniously with others. A peaceful heart brings life to the body, promoting well-being and contentment that transcends happiness from external circumstances. This true peace flows from integrity, gentleness, and trust in God's wisdom, offering an inner state of calmness even in the midst of difficult trials.

In addition to inner peace, relational peace is also highly valued. It is better to live modestly with love and peace with others than with abundance marked by strife and tension. A gentle response and a calm spirit have the power to de-escalate conflict, while a hot temper and contentious attitude fuel division. Furthermore, peacekeepers are praised for their ability to create an environment where trust, respect, and unity can thrive.

Peace comes not by passivity, but through deliberate choices—loving others instead of one's ego and pride, having patience instead of provoking others, and living with righteousness rather than retaliating and getting even. When a person's ways please God, even their enemies are at peace with them. Discipline, especially in the family setting, is also shown as a pathway to peace, bringing rest and joy to both parents and children when handled with wisdom and love.

Peace is more than the absence of conflict—it is the fruit of a heart rooted in wisdom, humility, and compassion. A life aimed at peace brings stability and rest, since lives filled with turmoil and strife bring nothing but heartache and pain. Peacefulness also strengthens relationships and reflects the heart of God. Peace is not only a reward for wise living but is also a testimony to its great power.

My son, do not forget my instruction,
and let your heart guard my commandments,
for they will add to you length of days,
years of life, and peace.

Proverbs 3:1–2

Her ways are pleasant ways,
and all her pathways are peace.

Proverbs 3:17

Deceit *is* in the heart of those who devise evil,
but those who counsel peace *have* joy.

Proverbs 12:20

A peaceful heart is the life of the flesh,
but envy is decay to the bones.

Proverbs 14:30

Better is a meal of vegetables when love is present,
than a fattened ox and hatred with it.
A hot-tempered person incites strife,
but one who is slow to get angry peacefully settles a dispute.

Proverbs 15:17–18

When Yahweh takes pleasure in a person's ways,
even his enemies will make peace with him.

Proverbs 16:7

Better is a dry *piece of* bread and peace with it,
than a household full of feasting with strife.

Proverbs 17:1

Correct your son, and he will give you rest,
and he will give delight to your soul.

Proverbs 29:17

PLANNING/ PREPARATION/COUNSEL

S uccess in life isn't just about having ambition—it requires wisdom, careful planning, and seeking sound advice. Those who rely solely on their own understanding and cleverness are more likely to stumble, while those who seek counsel from others increase their chances of success. Thoughtful preparation is crucial, but ultimately, it is God who directs a person's steps toward success.

Without careful planning, a person is bound to rush into decisions, which will lead to failure. But those who take the time to seek wisdom and guidance will flourish. Wisdom is often buried deep within the heart, and it takes discernment to draw it out. A truly wise person values the insight of others, understanding that multiple perspectives provide insight and will lead to better choices.

Committing one's plans to God provides stability, as divine wisdom surpasses all human understanding. Though people may make many plans, it is God's purpose that ultimately prevails. Success is not just about strategy—it requires humility, a willingness to learn, and alignment with God's will. Those who lack vision and discipline live recklessly, leading to foolish and careless actions that bring hardship and suffering. In contrast, pursuing a life of wisdom will result in flourishing and fulfillment.

Before taking on major commitments, a person should ensure they have laid a solid foundation. Just as a wise leader seeks counsel before going into battle, those who prepare diligently set themselves up for success. The truly wise recognize this and commit their efforts to God, ensuring their plans align with His will.

Preparation also involves responsibility and foresight. A wise person does not neglect their duties but works to secure the future. Even so, no one should boast about tomorrow, for the future is uncertain. True wisdom strikes a balance—careful planning paired with unwavering trust in God's direction.

A wise person will listen and increase in learning,
and a discerning person will get wise guidance,

Proverbs 1:5

Without wise guidance people will fall,
but with a multitude of advisors there is deliverance.

Proverbs 11:14

The thoughts of the righteous are just,
but the guidance of the wicked is deceitful.

Proverbs 12:5

Do not those who plan evil go astray?
But loyalty and faithfulness *are with* those who plan good.

Proverbs 14:22

By a lack of counsel, plans are shattered,
but with a multitude of advisors *a plan* will stand.

Proverbs 15:22

The plans of the heart *belong* to the person,
but the answer of the tongue *comes* from Yahweh.

All a person's ways are pure in his own eyes,
but Yahweh examines the motives.
Commit your works to Yahweh,
and your plans will be established.

Proverbs 16:1–3

A person's heart devises his way,
but Yahweh prepares his steps.

Proverbs 16:9

The lot is cast into the lap,
but each of its judgments is from Yahweh.

Proverbs 16:33

Many plans are in a person's heart,
but Yahweh's counsel will stand.

Proverbs 19:21

Plans are established by counsel,
so make war by wise guidance.

Proverbs 20:18

A person's steps are *directed* by Yahweh;
how then can a person understand his road?

Proverbs 20:24

The plans of a diligent person surely *will lead* to abundance,
but everyone who acts hastily surely *will come to* poverty.

Proverbs 21:5

For with *wise* guidance you should wage your war,
and with a multitude of advisors there is deliverance.

Proverbs 24:6

Prepare your outdoor work,
and carefully prepare it for yourself in the field;
afterwards, then, build your house.

Proverbs 24:27

Do not boast about tomorrow,
for you do not know what the day will bring forth.

Proverbs 27:1

When there is no vision, people are unrestrained,
but blessed is the one who keeps the Law.

Proverbs 29:18

Strength and majesty are her clothing,
and she laughs at the days to come.

Proverbs 31:25

PRAYER/VOWS/ SACRIFICES

Prayer, vows, and sacrifices are treated in Proverbs not as mere words, promises, and rituals, but as expressions of the heart measured by sincerity, obedience, and alignment with righteous living. True devotion to God is not about religious performance but about honoring God with a life of integrity, justice, and deep reverence for him.

Prayer, when it flows from a pure heart and a life submitted to God's ways, is powerful—and God hears and listens to it. But when it comes from the wicked—those who reject God's instruction or live deceitfully—it is detestable, and God disregards their words.

Sacrifices offered with wrong motives, especially in covering sinful behavior or in an attempt to manipulate God, are condemned. Such offerings may appear holy on the outside, but without genuine repentance and moral re-alignment, they are offensive to God. What pleases him far more than external rituals is a life of righteousness and obedience. Devotion must be rooted in godly behavior, not just performing religious duties or rituals.

Vows, likewise, are to be made with careful thought and follow-through. Making a rash promise to God and then reconsidering it is not how one makes a genuine vow; rather, it is a sign of impulsiveness and disrespect, revealing immaturity and insincerity.

Words spoken to God carry weight and must reflect a heart that understands the seriousness of one's commitment in making a vow.

What God desires is authenticity in one's worship and devotion to him. Prayer, sacrifices, and vows are deeply meaningful only when they arise from a humble, obedient heart. The focus must not be on outward actions but on the inward truth of genuine worship, showing that a life that honors God in even the smallest ways is more powerful than an impressive sacrifice and offering brought to the altar.

Honor Yahweh from your wealth,
and from the firstfruits of all your revenue,

Proverbs 3:9

"I *made* peace offerings;
today I fulfilled my vows.
So I came out to meet you,
to diligently seek your face, and I have found you.

Proverbs 7:14–15

A sacrifice *made by* the wicked is an abomination to Yahweh,
but the prayer of the upright *brings* his favor.

Proverbs 15:8

Yahweh is far from the wicked,
but he hears the prayer of the righteous.

Proverbs 15:29

It is a snare for a person to carelessly declare, "It is holy!"
and *then* to inquire *about it* after making his vows.

Proverbs 20:25

To do righteousness and justice
is preferred by Yahweh rather than a sacrifice.

Proverbs 21:3

A sacrifice *offered by* the wicked is an abomination;
how much more when he brings it with deceitful intent.

Proverbs 21:27

The person who turns his ear away from listening to the Law,
even his prayer is an abomination.

Proverbs 28:9

PRIDE

Pride is a dangerous and self-deceiving force that leads to disgrace and destruction in life. Moreover, it is an attitude of the heart that sets a person in opposition to God. Pride arises from an inflated sense of self—arrogance, entitlement, or a stubborn refusal to listen or comply with others. It blinds a person to their flaws, limits, and need for correction. Resisting all influence of wisdom, the proud mock others and show disdain for humility, creating conflict by seeing themselves as better than others. Pride is especially offensive to God, who detests a heart that is puffed up, and Proverbs considers it one of the foremost evils.

The proud person trusts in their own opinions, refuses instruction, and seeks recognition, often exalting themselves at the expense of others. Though the proud may seem strong or impressive outwardly to others, their pride breeds a hidden trap and sets them up for a downfall. Destruction often follows closely behind pride, not only through direct consequences but through the erosion of character, relationships, and trust. Furthermore, even boasting about the future is criticized as presumptuous, revealing a heart that lacks prudence and wisdom.

In contrast, humility is consistently exalted as a prized virtue of the wise. Those who lower themselves are then lifted up, honored, and respected. True wisdom and honor are found in modesty and self-control—not in self-promotion or trying to get ahead of others.

Letting others speak well of you rather than praising yourself is a mark of maturity and self-confidence.

Pride can be found in the heart of anyone, from the most powerful individuals to the weakest; those who demonstrate a rebellious and disrespectful attitude, or those who despise others and criticize them to make themselves look good. An inflated sense of self distorts one's judgment and thus fuels injustice. Proverbs makes clear that while pride may cause a person to elevate themselves in their own eyes or even temporarily before others, it ultimately will lead to their downfall. Instead, a humble, teachable heart will receive favor, grow in wisdom, and walk a path that results in glory, respect, and lasting honor.

There are six things that Yahweh hates,

indeed, seven things are abominations to his soul:

prideful eyes, a lying tongue,

and hands shedding innocent blood;

a heart that devises wicked thoughts,

feet that are swift to run to *do* evil,

a false witness who breathes out lies,

and one who sows strife among brothers.

Proverbs 6:16–19

The fear of Yahweh is to hate evil—

pride and arrogance and the path of evil

and a perverse mouth, I hate.

Proverbs 8:13

Arrogance comes, then dishonor comes,

but wisdom is with the modest.

Proverbs 11:2

Arrogance only causes strife,
but wisdom is with those who accept advice.

Proverbs 13:10

Yahweh will tear down the house of the proud,
but he will cause the territory of the widow to stand.

Proverbs 15:25

Every arrogant heart is an abomination to Yahweh;
be assured, he will not go unpunished.

Proverbs 16:5

Pride goes before disaster,
and a puffed-up spirit before stumbling.
Better to be humble in spirit with the poor
than to share the plunder with the proud.

Proverbs 16:18–19

A fool does not delight in understanding,
but only in expressing his own mind.

Proverbs 18:2

Before disaster the heart of a person is puffed up,
but humility goes before glory.

Proverbs 18:12

Haughty eyes and an arrogant heart—
the lamp of the wicked—is sin.

Proverbs 21:4

The presumptuous *and* proud person—"Mocker" is his name—
acts with arrogant presumptuousness.

Proverbs 21:24

Do not rejoice when your enemy falls,
and let not your heart celebrate when he stumbles,
otherwise Yahweh will see *it*, and it is evil in his eyes,
and he might turn away his anger from him.

Proverbs 24:17–18

Do not honor yourself in the presence of the king,
and do not stand among great people;
for it is better that it be said to you, "Come up here,"
than to be placed lower in the presence of a noble.
What your eyes have seen,

Proverbs 25:6–7

Do you see a person who is wise in his own eyes?
There is more hope for a fool than for him.

Proverbs 26:12

Do not boast about tomorrow,
for you do not know what the day will bring forth.
Let another praise you and not your *own* mouth—
a stranger—and not your *own* lips.

Proverbs 27:1–2

The one who spoils his servant from childhood—
in the end he will become rebellious.

Proverbs 29:21

A person's pride will bring him low,
but a humble spirit will obtain glory.

Proverbs 29:23

There is a generation that curses its father
and that does not bless its mother.
A generation that is pure in its own eyes

A generation—how haughty are its eyes,
and *how high* its eyelids are lifted up!
A generation whose teeth are swords
and fangs are knives,
to devour the poor from the land
and the needy from humankind.

Proverbs 30:11–14

PROSPERITY/SUCCESS

Prosperity and success are the fruit of wisdom, diligence, generosity, and a life of obedience to God. True success is not defined by wealth or status, but by safety, stability, honor, and other enduring qualities—both materially and relationally. Those who work steadily, plan wisely, seek the counsel of others, and live righteously are positioned to gain abundance in life, and with it, peace of mind. Their efforts yield fruit because they act with foresight, patience, and integrity.

It might seem like common sense that hard work is the foundation to living prosperously, but the benefit is only achieved in applying the wisdom. A hard work ethic is contrasted with idle talk and laziness, which lead to poverty and a person's unmet potential. While anyone can earn money, lasting wealth comes through continuous, productive labor and careful financial stewardship, not through taking shortcuts or pursuing reckless endeavors for quick money. Examples of working wisely include: farmers who tend their fields faithfully, diligent workers who focus on completing their tasks, and builders who plan carefully how to construct. These all demonstrate the path to sustainable success in actively pursuing their goals and not trying to skip out on the work required to get the job done right.

Generosity also plays a key role in prosperity. Those who give freely, without fear, find themselves replenished, while those who hoard or act greedily often experience lack. Furthermore, while it might seem counterintuitive, prosperity is multiplied when it is shared, and a person's joy increases when the blessings of their success benefit others.

Wise speech, moral integrity, and attentiveness to instruction also contribute to flourishing in life. A person who guards their words, listens to advice, and honors God with their resources positions themselves to receive both the favor of God and others, and the fruitfulness that comes from being humble and wise. Prosperity is thus not random or a matter of "luck," but it is the result of godly character-driven choices and faithful living.

Thus, prosperity and success in Proverbs are not just about riches, fame, or easy living. Rather, it is about a life that produces good in every area: financial, relational, and spiritual. It reflects a heart aligned with God's wisdom, hands and feet committed to working hard, and a desire to honor God first and give generously to others.

Honor Yahweh from your wealth,

and from the firstfruits of all your revenue,

and your storehouses will be completely filled,

and your wine vats will overflow with new wine.

Proverbs 3:9–10

Riches and glory are with me,

enduring prosperity and righteousness.

My fruit is better than gold, even *better than* refined gold,

and my gain *is better* than silver.

I walk in the way of righteousness,

in the midst of the paths of justice,

to cause those who love me to inherit property,
and I will fill their storehouses.

Proverbs 8:18–21

A town rejoices at the prosperity of the righteous,
and there is joyful shouting at the death of the wicked.

Proverbs 11:10

There is one who generously scatters *wealth*, and it is
    continually added *to him,*
and one who is withholding *what is* right, *which* surely *will*
    end in poverty.
The person who blesses *others* will be made prosperous,
and the one who waters, indeed, he himself will be watered.
The people will curse the one who withholds grain,
but a blessing *will be* upon the head of the one who sells grain.
The one who is on the lookout for *what is* good seeks favor,
but the one who is intent on evil, it will come to him.
The one who trusts in his wealth, he will fall,
but the righteous will bud like a leaf.

Proverbs 11:24–28

The one who works his land will be satisfied with food,
but the one who pursues worthless things lacks sense.

Proverbs 12:11

From the fruit of his mouth a person is satisfied with good,
and the accomplishments of a person's hands will return to him.

Proverbs 12:14

With no oxen, the feeding trough is clean,
but abundant revenue *comes* by the strength of an ox.

Proverbs 14:4

A poor person is hated even by his neighbor,
but there are many who love the rich.

Proverbs 14:20

In all hard work there is profit,
but *mere* words from the lips surely *lead* to poverty.

Proverbs 14:23

By a lack of counsel, plans are shattered,
but with a multitude of advisors *a plan* will stand.

Proverbs 15:22

The one who comprehends a *wise* saying will find good,
and blessed is the one who trusts in Yahweh.

Proverbs 16:20

A twisted heart will not find good,
and the one who has a double tongue will fall into evil.

Proverbs 17:20

The one who gets *good* sense loves his *own* soul;
the one who safeguards discernment will find good.

Proverbs 19:8

The plans of a diligent person surely *will lead* to abundance,
but everyone who acts hastily surely *will come to* poverty.

Proverbs 21:5

Know well the condition of your flock;
pay attention to your herds,
for treasure will not last,
nor does a crown *last* for multiple generations.
When the grass is removed and *new* growth appears,
and the plants of the mountains are gathered together,

lambs *will provide* your clothing,

and male goats *will cover* the price of a field,

and *there will be* enough milk from the female goats for your food,

for the food of your house,

and the care of your female servants.

Proverbs 27:23–27

A greedy soul stirs up strife,

but the person who trusts in Yahweh will be made prosperous.

Proverbs 28:25

PRUDENCE

P rudence is a hallmark of the wise who demonstrate foresight, discretion, and thoughtful decision-making. It is the ability to discern what is appropriate in any given situation, avoid potential danger, and act with deliberate caution rather than on impulse or haphazardly. The prudent person is attentive to the path ahead of them, considering both the necessary steps that need to be taken immediately and the best long-term course of action to prevent unwanted consequences. This careful approach provides protection, preserves reputation, and fosters peace.

A prudent person has an alert mind and a disciplined heart, demonstrating self-restraint—especially in speech by avoiding saying rash words or foolish boasts. In addition, a prudent person stores knowledge and speaks with calculated wisdom, unlike the fool who blurts out everything and exposes their ignorance and shame. Prudence also manifests itself in managing resources wisely, planning well, and recognizing the value of the right timing and need for personal restraint, knowing the potential harm in blindly following one's feelings and emotions.

Moreover, prudence involves reading people and situations accurately, steering clear of traps that snare the careless and unthinking. The prudent are cautious without being fearful; they are not naive, but are circumspect and grounded in reality. They avoid certain entanglements with mockers or fools, knowing that some people and conversations are simply not worth the cost and won't result in a positive outcome. They also value personal correction, learning from instruction, and navigating life with moral clarity and emotional control.

Leaders and servants alike are judged by their prudence. A prudent life is not flashy, but it is vastly powerful, marked by stability, success, and enduring wisdom. Essentially, prudence is living with one's eyes wide open: guided by careful insight, anchored in truth, and aimed at a life of safety, honor, and good stewardship.

The proverbs of Solomon, the son of David, king of Israel:

...to give prudence to the naive,

knowledge and discretion to the youth.

Proverbs 1:1, 4

Focus your eyes in front of you,

and let your eyelids *look* straight ahead of you.

Carefully weigh the path of your feet,

and let all your roads be established.

Do not turn to the right or to the left;

keep your foot away from evil.

Proverbs 4:25–27

Understand prudence, O naive ones,

and understand *good* sense, O foolish ones.

Proverbs 8:5

"I, Wisdom, dwell with prudence,

and I find knowledge and discretion.

Proverbs 8:12

The one who gathers in the summer is an insightful son;
the one who is fast asleep at the harvest is a shameful son.

Proverbs 10:5

By an abundance of words transgression will not cease,
but the one who restrains his lips is insightful.

Proverbs 10:19

The one who shows contempt for his neighbor lacks sense,
but a person with understanding remains silent.

Proverbs 11:12

A prudent person conceals knowledge,
but the heart of fools proclaims foolishness.

Proverbs 12:23

Every prudent person acts with knowledge,
but a fool displays foolishness.

Proverbs 13:16

The wisdom of a prudent person is to understand his road,
but the foolishness of fools is deceit.

Proverbs 14:8

A naive person will believe any word,
but the prudent person carefully considers his steps.
A wise person is cautious and turns away from evil,
but a fool is angry and is overconfident.

Proverbs 14:15–16

The naive inherit foolishness,
but the prudent are crowned with knowledge.

Proverbs 14:18

The king's favor is toward an insightful servant,
but his anger will be *upon* the one who acts shamefully.

Proverbs 14:35

The path of life leads upward for the one who has insight
in order to turn him away from Sheol below.

Proverbs 15:24

The heart of a righteous person considers how to answer,
but the mouth of the wicked pours out evil things.

Proverbs 15:28

An insightful servant will rule over a shameful son,
and he will share the inheritance among brothers.

Proverbs 17:2

A house and wealth are the inheritance from fathers,
but an insightful wife is from Yahweh.

Proverbs 19:14

The person who wanders from the road of understanding
will rest in the assembly of the dead.

Proverbs 21:16

A wicked person hardens his face,
but an upright person, he gives thought to his ways.

Proverbs 21:29

A prudent person sees evil and hides,
but the naive continue on and are punished.

Proverbs 22:3

Do not speak into the ears of a fool,
for he will have contempt for the prudence of your words.

Proverbs 23:9

A prudent person sees evil *and* hides,
but the naive continue on and are punished.

Proverbs 27:12

REPUTATION/
CHARACTER

Reputation and character are deeply intertwined concepts in Proverbs. An honorable reputation is not built on a person's appearances or charm, but on their integrity, wisdom, and godly conduct. Proverbs declares that a good name is more desirable than great riches, for it reflects the essence of who a person truly is and how they are known by others, whereas money says nothing about who a person truly is and what is inside them. Reputation is established by a person's character—the inner moral compass that shapes their decisions, relationships, and daily behavior.

A person's character isn't revealed through a single incident or action; it reveals itself consistently over time through behavior more than words. The person who lives honorably earns respect and trust, while one who acts deceitfully or foolishly invites disgrace. Boasting is discouraged; praise is most meaningful when it comes from others, not from self-promotion. Inner strength, humility, and faithfulness build a reputation that stands firm even under intense scrutiny by others.

Protecting one's reputation means guarding both behavior and speech. Reckless or slanderous talk can damage a reputation—both theirs and others'—beyond repair. To safeguard one's reputation, wisdom calls for discretion in conflict, respect for others, and a careful handling of interpersonal matters. What one reveals or conceals will affect others' perception of them and can either elevate or destroy their standing in the eyes of the community.

A person of noble character with good reputation is a stabilizing force in a family, among friends, and in society. Their reputation not only benefits them personally but also brings honor to those connected to them. In the end, a good reputation is the fruit of a life lived with wisdom, prudence, and integrity, which results in a legacy that outlives even the greatest of wealth and leaves behind a name that inspires trust and respect.

The memory of a righteous person is a blessing,
but the name of the wicked will rot.

Proverbs 10:7

A person will be praised for his insightful mouth,
but the one who has a twisted heart will be *viewed with* contempt.

Proverbs 12:8

Even a young boy is known by his actions,
whether *or not* his conduct is pure and upright.

Proverbs 20:11

A *good* name is to be chosen over great wealth;
favor is better than silver and gold.

Proverbs 22:1

Argue your dispute with your neighbor,
but do not reveal another person's secret,
or the one who hears *it* might put you to shame,
and your bad reputation will not go away.

Proverbs 25:9–10

Let another praise you and not your *own* mouth—
a stranger—and not your *own* lips.

Proverbs 27:2

Her husband is known at the *city* gates,
when he sits with the elders of the land.

Proverbs 31:23

REWARDS AND CONSEQUENCES

P roverbs draws a vivid picture of life as a large tapestry constructed from cause and effect, where every action results in an outcome—either blessings and rewards for the wise and righteous, or hardship and suffering for the foolish and wicked. This principle is woven throughout every practical and moral dimension of life, underscoring the reality that choices are not isolated—they carry lasting effects and impact on oneself and others.

Those who pursue wisdom, integrity, diligence, and reverence for God are promised blessings: long life, peace, prosperity, favor, and security. Their paths are stable and directed toward good; they enjoy the fruits of honest labor, trustworthy relationships, and divine protection. Even in difficult times, the righteous can rise again, because their foundation is firmly established upon God and their discipline and character sustain them. The rewards of such a life extend beyond the individual, benefiting families, friends, communities, and future generations.

In contrast, those who reject wisdom, indulge in deceit, or follow wickedness set themselves on a path toward destruction. Their lives are marked by instability, fear, broken relationships, and ruin. They may seem to prosper for a time, but their success is often shallow and short-lived. Hidden sins, careless words, and unjust actions all bring consequences—sometimes it happens immediately, but at other times, it is a gradual decay. The prosperity of the wicked may fall suddenly, or they are ensnared by their own actions, or they experience the harm they caused others as it returns to them.

Proverbs also places strong emphasis on divine justice in its description of rewards and consequences. God watches over the upright and resists the proud and unjust. Even secret choices and attitudes of the heart play a factor, since nothing escapes God's notice. Acts of mercy and generosity are rewarded, while exploitation and cruelty bring harsh judgment. Proverbs makes it clear that reward and punishment are not arbitrary—they reflect the nature of God's moral order in the world (i.e., doing good is rewarded, and doing evil is punished).

The main point comes down to seeing that every decision shapes the outcome of a situation. Wisdom calls for thoughtful, righteous living, not merely for immediate gain and benefit, but because it aligns with what is good, true, and profitable. Furthermore, the rewards are not just external, physical blessings, but also inner peace and stability, a clear conscience, and an honorable legacy that others respect and admire. Conversely, the consequences of ignoring wisdom are real, often irreversible, bringing trouble and pain into life. They serve as warnings for all who would oppose God's authority and rule regarding how he commands people to live.

But since you refused me when I called,

I stretched out my hand but no one paid attention,

and you neglected all my counsel,

and you did not want my reproof—

I also will laugh at your distress;

I will mock when what you dread comes,

when your terror comes like a violent storm,

and your calamity like a whirlwind,
and trouble and distress come upon you all.

Proverbs 1:24–27

Because they hated knowledge,
and they did not choose the fear of Yahweh;
they were not interested in my counsel,
and they spurned all my reproof,
so they will eat from the fruit of their *own* way,
and from their *own* schemes they will have *their* fill.
For the turning away of the naive will kill them,
and the *false* security of fools will destroy them.
But the one who listens to me will live in safety,
and will be at ease from the dread of evil."

Proverbs 1:29–33

For the upright will live in the land,
and the blameless will remain in it.
But the wicked will be cut off from the land,
and the unfaithful will be uprooted from it.

Proverbs 2:21–22

My son, do not forget my instruction,
and let your heart guard my commandments,
for they will add to you length of days,
years of life, and peace.

Proverbs 3:1–2

Honor Yahweh from your wealth,
and from the firstfruits of all your revenue,
and your storehouses will be completely filled,
and your wine vats will overflow with new wine.

Proverbs 3:9–10

Yahweh's curse is upon the house of the wicked person,

but he blesses the dwelling of the righteous person.

He mocks at the mockers,

but he gives grace to the humble.

The wise will inherit glory,

but fools exalt shame.

Proverbs 3:33–35

But now, *my* sons, listen to me,

and do not depart from the words of my mouth.

Keep your road far from her,

and do not go near to the door of her house,

otherwise you might give your honor to others,

and your years to a cruel person;

otherwise strangers might eat their fill from your strength,

and your hard-earned goods *end up* in the house of a foreigner,

Proverbs 5:7–10

The one acting wickedly—his *own* iniquities will capture him,

and he will be seized by the cords of his *own* sin.

He will die because of lack of discipline,

and in the abundance of his foolishness he goes astray.

Proverbs 5:22–23

With perversions in his heart he devises evil,

at every moment he sows strife.

Therefore, his calamity will come suddenly,

in an instant he will be broken and there will be no remedy.

Proverbs 6:14–15

Can a man snatch up fire against his chest

and his clothes not be burnt?

Or can a man walk upon hot coals

and his feet not get burned?

So is the one who goes into his neighbor's wife;

all who touch her will not go unpunished.

People do not despise a thief when he steals

to feed himself when he is hungry.

But when he is caught, he will repay seven times;

he will repay with all the wealth of his house.

The man committing adultery with a woman lacks sense;

he who does this is destroying his *own* soul.

He will find affliction and dishonor,

and his disgrace will not be blotted out.

For jealousy enrages a husband,

and he will not spare *him* in the day of *his* vengeance.

He will not be persuaded by any ransom,

nor will he be satisfied when you make many bribes.

Proverbs 6:27–35

I love those who love me,

and those who desire me will find me.

Riches and glory are with me,

enduring prosperity and righteousness.

My fruit is better than gold, even *better than* refined gold,

and my gain *is better* than silver.

I walk in the way of righteousness,

in the midst of the paths of justice,

to cause those who love me to inherit property,

and I will fill their storehouses.

Proverbs 8:17–21

because the one finding me finds life,
and he will obtain favor from Yahweh.
But the one sinning against me is doing violence to his *own* soul;
all those who hate me love death."

Proverbs 8:35–36

If you are wise, you are wise for your own *benefit*;
and if you mock, you will bear *the consequence* by yourself.

Proverbs 9:12

Yahweh does not cause the righteous soul to go hungry,
but he will push away what the wicked desire.

Proverbs 10:3

The one who walks blamelessly walks securely,
but the one who perverts his ways will be made known.

Proverbs 10:9

The wage of the righteous person is life;
the revenue of the wicked is sin.

Proverbs 10:16

The wicked person's horror will come upon him,
but the desire of the righteous will be given *to them*.
When the storm passes through, then the wicked
        person is no more,
but the righteous person *has* a foundation that endures.
As vinegar is to the teeth and as smoke is to the eyes,
so *too* is the lazy one to those who send him.
The fear of Yahweh adds to *one's* days,
but the years of the wicked will be cut short.
The hope of the righteous is joy,
but the expectation of the wicked will perish.

The road of Yahweh is a place of refuge for the blameless person,
but it is destruction for those who act wickedly.
The righteous person will not ever be moved,
but the wicked will not live in the land.

Proverbs 10:24–30

The integrity of the upright will lead them,
but the perversity of the unfaithful will destroy them.

Proverbs 11:3

The righteousness of the blameless person will make
     his road straight,
but the wicked person will fall by his wickedness.
The righteousness of the upright will deliver them,
but the unfaithful will be taken captive by their desire.
When a wicked person dies, his hope perishes,
and *his* hope of wealth perishes.
A righteous person is delivered from trouble,
but a wicked person takes his place.

Proverbs 11:5–8

The kind person benefits himself,
but the cruel person does himself harm.
The wicked person makes a deceptive wage,
but the one who sows righteousness *receives* a true reward;
indeed, righteousness *leads* to life,
but the one who eagerly pursues evil is *heading* to his death.

Proverbs 11:17–19

Be assured: an evil person will not go unpunished,
but the offspring of the righteous will escape.

Proverbs 11:21

The desire of the righteous *ends* only *in* good,

but the hope of the wicked *ends in* wrath.

There is one who generously scatters *wealth*, and it is

      continually added *to him,*

and one who is withholding *what is* right, *which* surely *will*

      end in poverty.

The person who blesses *others* will be made prosperous,

and the one who waters, indeed, he himself will be watered.

The people will curse the one who withholds grain,

but a blessing *will be* upon the head of the one who sells grain.

The one who is on the lookout for *what is* good seeks favor,

but the one who is intent on evil, it will come to him.

The one who trusts in his wealth, he will fall,

but the righteous will bud like a leaf.

The one who troubles his household will inherit wind,

and the fool will be a servant to one who is wise of heart.

The fruit of a righteous person is a tree of life,

and the wise person takes away souls *from death.*

Behold! The righteous person will be repaid on the earth;

indeed, how much more the wicked person who sins!

Proverbs 11:23–31

The wicked will be overthrown and will be no more,

but the house of the righteous will stand.

Proverbs 12:7

The one who works his land will be satisfied with food,

but the one who pursues worthless things lacks sense.

Proverbs 12:11

From the fruit of his mouth a person is satisfied with good,

and the accomplishments of a person's hands will return to him.

Proverbs 12:14

No disaster will come upon the righteous person,
but the wicked are filled *with* misfortune.

Proverbs 12:21

The one who guards his mouth watches over his life;
destruction will come to the one who opens his lips wide.
The appetite of the lazy person craves yet *gets* nothing,
but the desire of the diligent person will be fully satisfied.

Proverbs 13:3–4

Wealth *obtained* by fraud will dwindle away,
but the one who gathers little by little increases *his wealth*.

Proverbs 13:11

The one who despises a word *of instruction* will come to ruin,
but the one who fears the commandment will be rewarded.

Proverbs 13:13

A wicked messenger will fall into evil,
but a faithful messenger *brings* healing.

Proverbs 13:17

Evil pursues sinners,
but goodness will reward the righteous.
A good person will provide an inheritance for his
    children's children,
but the wealth of the sinner is being stored up for the
    righteous person.

Proverbs 13:21–22

The righteous person eats to the satisfaction of his appetite,
but the belly of the wicked lacks *food*.

Proverbs 13:25

The house of the wicked will be destroyed,
but the tent of the upright will sprout forth.

Proverbs 14:11

The one who is disloyal in *his* heart will be satisfied
        from his *own* ways,
but a good person *will be satisfied* from his deeds.

Proverbs 14:14

Do not those who plan evil go astray?
But loyalty and faithfulness *are with* those who plan good.

Proverbs 14:22

A wicked person will be cast down by his *own* evil,
but the righteous person takes refuge in his *own* blamelessness.

Proverbs 14:32

The house of the righteous person *has* great treasure,
but trouble is stirred up by the revenue of the wicked person.

Proverbs 15:6

The one who pursues unjust gain troubles his household,
but the one who hates gifts *that influence* will live.

Proverbs 15:27

The one who mocks the poor taunts the one who created him;
the one who is joyful at a calamity will not go unpunished.

Proverbs 17:5

As for the one who repays good with evil,
evil will not depart from his house.

Proverbs 17:13

A twisted heart will not find good,
and the one who has a double tongue will fall into evil.

Proverbs 17:20

A false witness will not go unpunished,
and the one who tells lies will not escape.

Proverbs 19:5

A false witness will not go unpunished,
and the one who tells lies will perish.

Proverbs 19:9

The one who shows favor to a poor person lends to Yahweh,
and he will repay him according to his *good* work.

Proverbs 19:17

Bread *gained* by deceit is sweet to a person,
but afterwards his mouth will be filled with gravel.

Proverbs 20:17

The one who closes his ear to the cry of the poor,
he will also cry out and not be answered.

Proverbs 21:13

Thorns and traps are on the road of the twisted person;
the one who watches over his life will stay far from them.

Proverbs 22:5

The one who sows injustice will reap wickedness,
and the rod of his anger will fail.

Proverbs 22:8

Do not rob a poor person because he is poor,
and do not crush the needy at the *city* gate,
for Yahweh will defend their case,
and he will rob the life of those who robbed them.

Proverbs 22:22–23

If you show yourself to be lax on a day of trouble,
your strength is limited.

Deliver those who are being dragged off to death,
and do not hold back from *helping* those who are stumbling
         to the slaughter.
If you say, "Behold, we did not know this,"
doesn't he who examines the hearts discern it?
Doesn't he who guards your soul know it?
Will he not repay a person according to his work?

Proverbs 24:10–12

Do not lie in wait like the wicked against the dwelling place
         of the righteous;
do not assault his place of rest.
For a righteous person will fall seven times, and he stands back up,
but the wicked stumble in *times of* distress.

Proverbs 24:15–16

Do not be agitated because of those who do evil;
do not be envious of the wicked.
For there will be no future for the evil person;
the lamp of the wicked will go out.

Proverbs 24:19–20

The person who digs a pit will fall into it,
and the person rolling a stone, it will come back upon him.

Proverbs 26:27

The one who guards a fig tree will eat of its fruit,
and the one who watches over his master will be honored.

Proverbs 27:18

The person who increases his wealth by interest and
         by profiteering
collects it for the one who shows favor to the poor.

Proverbs 28:8

The person who leads the upright astray onto an evil road
will fall into his *own* pit,
but the blameless will inherit what is good.

Proverbs 28:10

The one who walks blamelessly will be delivered,
but the one who is crooked in his ways will fall suddenly.
The one who works his land will be satisfied with food,
but the one who pursues worthless things will be
"satisfied" with poverty.

Proverbs 28:18–19

The person who gives to the poor will not *be in* need,
but the one who shuts his eyes *to them will receive* many curses.

Proverbs 28:27

An eye that mocks at his father
and despises obedience to his mother—
ravens of the valley will peck it out,
and the offspring of a vulture will eat it.

Proverbs 30:17

RIGHTEOUSNESS

Righteousness is a central theme in Proverbs, portrayed as the guiding virtue of a life that submits to God, pursues God's will, and does what is good, just, and true. It is not just moral behavior for self-righteousness, but a way of living that honors God and brings blessings to oneself and others. The righteous are described as upright, honest, and generous. They care about justice and compassion, and they are deeply committed to living with wisdom. Their lives reflect integrity in both private and public spheres, and their character brings joy to their family, strength to the community, and stability to society at large.

The benefits of righteousness are many! It leads to a secure and enduring legacy—protection from harm, joy in times of adversity, and confidence even when trouble comes. The path of the righteous is bright and illuminated, growing even clearer and stronger over time. Their prayers are heard, their words bring healing and life, and their influence extends far beyond their own lives, like a tree that bears lasting fruit. Even their children benefit from their life and are seen as part of the blessing that righteousness brings.

In contrast, the wicked live on unstable ground that can be quickly swept away from under them. Their actions may yield temporary prosperity and gain, but their foundation is weak and faulty, and they are susceptible to destruction coming swiftly and unexpectedly. Wickedness invites trouble, silences moral virtue, corrupts one's character, and ultimately leads to ruin—socially, spiritually, and often physically as well. The wicked are a source of fear, injustice, and instability in their families and communities, but their influence is short-lived compared to the enduring impact of the righteous.

God's favor rests on the righteous; he delights in them and their road and upholds them through trials. They walk with courage, speak with discernment, and act with compassion. Even in adversity, the righteous will rise again if they fall, because their lives are built on trust in God and are anchored in his truth. Their righteousness not only shapes their destiny but serves as a light and refuge to others.

Righteousness is both a shield and a compass: it directs the wise in how to live, protects them from harm, and leads them toward a life of honor, peace, and lasting joy. It is the defining mark of a person who lives with God's wisdom and who contributes meaningfully to the world around them according to God's will.

Yahweh's curse is upon the house of the wicked person,
but he blesses the dwelling of the righteous person.

Proverbs 3:33

But the path of the righteous is like the light of dawn,
shining ever brighter until the full *light of* day.
The road of the wicked is like the *gloomy* darkness;
they do not know what they are stumbling over.

Proverbs 4:18–19

Treasures *gained* by wickedness profit nothing,
but righteousness will deliver from death.

Proverbs 10:2

Blessings are upon the head of a righteous person,
but the mouth of the wicked conceals wrongdoing.
The memory of a righteous person is a blessing,
but the name of the wicked will rot.

Proverbs 10:6–7

The mouth of a righteous person is a fountain of life,
but the mouth of the wicked conceals wrongdoing.

Proverbs 10:11

The wage of the righteous person is life;
the revenue of the wicked is sin.

Proverbs 10:16

The lips of a righteous person will shepherd many people,
but fools will die for a lack of sense.

Proverbs 10:21

The wicked person's horror will come upon him,
but the desire of the righteous will be given *to them.*
When the storm passes through, then the wicked
        person is no more,
but the righteous person *has* a foundation that endures.

Proverbs 10:24–25

The hope of the righteous is joy,
but the expectation of the wicked will perish.

Proverbs 10:28

The righteous person will not ever be moved,
but the wicked will not live in the land.
The mouth of a righteous person will bring forth the
        fruit of wisdom,
but the tongue *speaking* perversions will be cut off.

The lips of a righteous person know *what is* acceptable,

but the mouth of the wicked *knows* perversions.

Proverbs 10:30–32

The integrity of the upright will lead them,

but the perversity of the unfaithful will destroy them.

Riches will not profit on the day of wrath,

but righteousness will deliver from death.

The righteousness of the blameless person will make

       his road straight,

but the wicked person will fall by his wickedness.

The righteousness of the upright will deliver them,

but the unfaithful will be taken captive by their desire.

When a wicked person dies, his hope perishes,

and *his* hope of wealth perishes.

A righteous person is delivered from trouble,

but a wicked person takes his place.

Proverbs 11:3–8

A town rejoices at the prosperity of the righteous,

and there is joyful shouting at the death of the wicked.

By the blessing of the upright a town will be exalted,

but it will be thrown down by the mouth of the wicked.

Proverbs 11:10–11

The wicked person makes a deceptive wage,

but the one who sows righteousness *receives* a true reward;

indeed, righteousness *leads* to life,

but the one who eagerly pursues evil is *heading* to his death.

A twisted heart is an abomination to Yahweh,

but the road of the blameless is his delight.

Be assured: an evil person will not go unpunished,
but the offspring of the righteous will escape.

Proverbs 11:18–21

The desire of the righteous *ends* only *in* good,
but the hope of the wicked *ends in* wrath.

Proverbs 11:23

The one who trusts in his wealth, he will fall,
but the righteous will bud like a leaf.

Proverbs 11:28

The fruit of a righteous person is a tree of life,
and the wise person takes away souls *from death*.
Behold! The righteous person will be repaid on the earth;
indeed, how much more the wicked person who sins!

Proverbs 11:30–31

A person will not be established by wickedness,
but the root of the righteous will not be moved.

Proverbs 12:3

The thoughts of the righteous are just,
but the guidance of the wicked is deceitful.
The words of the wicked lie in wait for blood,
but the mouth of the upright will deliver them.
The wicked will be overthrown and will be no more,
but the house of the righteous will stand.

Proverbs 12:5–7

The righteous person cares for the life of his animal,
but the compassion of the wicked is cruel.

Proverbs 12:10

The wicked person desires the spoils of evil people,
but the root of the righteous produces *its own fruit.*
By the transgression of *his* lips an evil person *will fall into* a snare,
but the righteous person will escape from trouble.

Proverbs 12:12–13

No disaster will come upon the righteous person,
but the wicked are filled *with* misfortune.

Proverbs 12:21

A righteous person shows the way for his neighbor,
but the road of the wicked causes them to wander astray.

Proverbs 12:26

In the path of righteousness is life,
and the journey of *that* road does not *lead to* death.

Proverbs 12:28

A righteous person hates a deceptive word,
but a wicked person will become a stench and display *his* shame.
Righteousness guards the one whose way is blameless,
but wickedness overthrows a sinner.

Proverbs 13:5–6

The light of the righteous shines *brightly,*
but the lamp of the wicked will go out.

Proverbs 13:9

Evil pursues sinners,
but goodness will reward the righteous.
A good person will provide an inheritance for his
        children's children,
but the wealth of the sinner is being stored up for the
        righteous person.

Proverbs 13:21–22

The righteous person eats to the satisfaction of his appetite,
but the belly of the wicked lacks *food*.

Proverbs 13:25

The house of the wicked will be destroyed,
but the tent of the upright will sprout forth.

Proverbs 14:11

An evil person will bow down in the presence of good people,
and the wicked *will bow* at the gates of a righteous person.

Proverbs 14:19

Do not those who plan evil go astray?
But loyalty and faithfulness *are with* those who plan good.

Proverbs 14:22

A wicked person will be cast down by his *own* evil,
but the righteous person takes refuge in his *own* blamelessness.

Proverbs 14:32

Righteousness exalts a nation,
but sin is a disgrace to any people.

Proverbs 14:34

The house of the righteous person *has* great treasure,
but trouble is stirred up by the revenue of the wicked person.

Proverbs 15:6

A sacrifice *made by* the wicked is an abomination to Yahweh,
but the prayer of the upright *brings* his favor.
The road of the wicked person is an abomination to Yahweh,
but he loves the one who eagerly pursues righteousness.

Proverbs 15:8–9

The road of the lazy person is like a hedge of thorns,
but the path of the upright is an *open* highway.

Proverbs 15:19

The heart of a righteous person considers how to answer,
but the mouth of the wicked pours out evil things.
Yahweh is far from the wicked,
but he hears the prayer of the righteous.

Proverbs 15:28–29

Better is a little with righteousness,
than great income without justice.

Proverbs 16:8

It is an abomination for kings to commit wickedness,
because the throne is established in righteousness.
Righteous lips are the delight of kings,
and the one who speaks with integrity will be loved.

Proverbs 16:12–13

The highway of the upright is to turn away from evil;
the one who guards his road is keeping watch over his life .

Proverbs 16:17

Gray hair is a crown of splendor;
it is found on the road of righteousness.

Proverbs 16:31

Yahweh's name is a strong tower;
the righteous person runs to it and is secure.

Proverbs 18:10

A righteous person who walks in his integrity—
blessed are his children after him.

Proverbs 20:7

To do righteousness and justice
is preferred by Yahweh rather than a sacrifice.

Proverbs 21:3

The road of a guilty person is crooked,
but *as for* the pure person, his works are upright.

Proverbs 21:8

A wicked person is a ransom for a righteous person,
and the one acting unfaithfully is *a ransom* in place of the upright.

Proverbs 21:18

The one who pursues righteousness and loyalty
will find life, righteousness, and glory.

Proverbs 21:21

The lazy person's desire will kill him
because his hands refuse to work.
All day *long* he craves *what he* desires,
but the righteous person gives and does not withhold *his*
        generosity.

Proverbs 21:25–26

A wicked person hardens his face,
but an upright person, he gives thought to his ways.

Proverbs 21:29

The father of a righteous person will rejoice exceedingly,
and the man who fathers a wise *son* will delight in him;
may your father and your mother be glad,
and may she who gave birth to you rejoice.

Proverbs 23:24–25

Do not lie in wait like the wicked against the dwelling place
        of the righteous;
do not assault his place of rest.
For a righteous person will fall seven times, and he stands back up,
but the wicked stumble in *times of* distress.

Proverbs 24:15–16

A wicked person flees when no one is pursuing,
but the righteous are confident like a lion.

Proverbs 28:1

When the righteous triumph, there is great glory,
but when the wicked rise up, people conceal themselves.

Proverbs 28:12

When the righteous increase, the people rejoice,
but when a wicked person rules, the people groan.

Proverbs 29:2

An evil person is ensnared by transgression,
but a righteous person sings aloud and rejoices.
A righteous person knows the legal claim of the poor;
a wicked person does not understand *this* knowledge.

Proverbs 29:6–7

When the wicked increase, transgression increases,
but the righteous will see their ruin.

Proverbs 29:16

A dishonest person is an abomination to the righteous,
and the one whose road is upright is an abomination to
        a wicked person.

Proverbs 29:27

RULERS/AUTHORITY

Rulers and authority figures are held to a high standard where leadership is viewed as both a powerful force and a sacred responsibility. True authority is rooted in wisdom, justice, and the fear of Yahweh. Good rulers promote stability and justice, acting as protectors of the weak and innocent. Their decisions affect not only individuals but the direction of entire nations, and their character shapes the moral climate of the society they rule over.

A righteous leader brings joy and flourishing to the people. When those in power rule with fairness and uphold truth, society thrives and people prosper. Such rulers and leaders value honesty, seek wise counsel, and surround themselves with people of integrity. Mercy and faithfulness to God are key virtues for those in authority, sustaining their reign and earning the loyalty and respect of their subjects. Wisdom enables them to discern rightly, uphold justice, and administer discipline when necessary.

However, Proverbs also gives a sobering warning about the dangers of corrupt and foolish leaders. When rulers are wicked, deceitful, or easily influenced by lies or prone to manipulation, the people suffer and groan under oppression and abuse. Bribery, arrogance, and mishandling of power unravel the foundation of their authority. Rash judgments, over-indulgence, over-confidence, and showing prejudice and favoritism weaken and destroy leaders. This has a fallout effect on society and results in hardship and suffering for the people. Furthermore, those who oppress the poor or exploit their position are especially condemned as wicked leaders.

Rulers are called to be discerning, self-controlled, and careful in their speech and decisions. They must not be swayed by flattery or be quick to get angry, nor should they live a plush life and neglect the needs of the powerless and vulnerable. A wise ruler values truth and justice over public opinion, and building long-term stability over short-term gain and popularity.

Leadership is ultimately an authority entrusted to a person by God. Proverbs states that the hearts of rulers are in God's hand, and their success is tied to their willingness to act with humility, righteousness, and understanding. Whether a king or house-manager, authority is best exercised through wisdom, proper restraint and discipline, and a deep commitment to justice and the well-being of those under one's care.

By me kings reign,

and *by me* rulers decree righteousness.

By me rulers govern;

even nobles—all who judge *with* righteousness.

Proverbs 8:15–16

A town rejoices at the prosperity of the righteous,

and there is joyful shouting at the death of the wicked.

Proverbs 11:10

The king's glory is in the abundance of people,

but a ruler's ruin is in the lack of people.

Proverbs 14:28

The king's favor is toward an insightful servant,
but his anger will be *upon* the one who acts shamefully.

Proverbs 14:35

A verdict is on the lips of the king;
his mouth should not violate justice.

Proverbs 16:10

It is an abomination for kings to commit wickedness,
because the throne is established in righteousness.
Righteous lips are the delight of kings,
and the one who speaks with integrity will be loved.
A king's rage *is like* messengers of death,
but a wise person will pacify *the anger*.
In the light of a king's face there *is* life,
and his favor is like clouds *that bring* spring rain.

Proverbs 16:12–15

Eloquent speech is not fitting for a godless person,
how much less *fitting* are deceptive lips for a nobleman?

Proverbs 17:7

Many will entreat the favor of a generous person,
and everyone is a friend to a person who gives gifts.

Proverbs 19:6

Luxury is not fitting for a fool;
how much less *fitting* for a servant to rule over princes.

Proverbs 19:10

The king's rage is like the growl of a lion,
but his favor is like the dew upon the grass.

Proverbs 19:12

The terror of a king is like the growl of a lion;
the one who infuriates him does wrong to his *own* life.

Proverbs 20:2

A king sitting upon the throne of justice
scatters every evil with his eyes.

Proverbs 20:8

A wise king separates out the wicked,
and he rolls the *threshing* wheel over them again *and again.*

Proverbs 20:26

Covenant loyalty and faithfulness guard the king,
yes, he upholds his throne by covenant loyalty.

Proverbs 20:28

The heart of a king is *like* water canals in Yahweh's hand;
he turns it wherever he delights.

Proverbs 21:1

The person who loves a pure heart,
whose lips are gracious—a king is his friend.

Proverbs 22:11

Do you see a man skilled in his occupation?
He will stand in the presence of kings;
he will not stand in the presence of obscure people.

Proverbs 22:29

When you sit to eat with a ruler,
carefully discern who is before you,
and put a knife in your throat
if you *have* a greedy appetite.

Do not crave his tasty foods,

for it is deceptive bread.

Proverbs 23:1–3

My son, fear Yahweh and the king;

do not get involved with those who think otherwise,

for disaster will suddenly arise from them,

and who knows the ruin *that can come* from the two of them?

Proverbs 24:21–22

It is the glory of God to conceal a matter,

but it is the glory of kings to search out a matter.

As the heavens are high and the earth is deep,

so the hearts of kings are unsearchable.

Remove the dross from silver,

and a vessel comes out for the refiner;

remove the wicked person from the presence of the king,

and his throne will be established in righteousness.

Do not honor yourself in the presence of the king,

and do not stand among great people;

for it is better that it be said to you, "Come up here,"

than to be placed lower in the presence of a noble.

What your eyes have seen,

Proverbs 25:2–7

With patience a ruler can be persuaded,

and a gentle tongue can break a bone.

Proverbs 25:15

As cold water is to a weary soul,

so is good news from a distant land.

Proverbs 25:25

The one who guards a fig tree will eat of its fruit,
and the one who watches over his master will be honored.

Proverbs 27:18

On account of the transgression of the land, many are its rulers,
but by a person with understanding *and* knowledge order
      will be prolonged.
A poor man who oppresses the weak
is *like* a beating rain that does not *leave* food.

Proverbs 28:2–3

When the righteous triumph, there is great glory,
but when the wicked rise up, people conceal themselves.

Proverbs 28:12

Like a roaring lion and a charging bear,
so is a wicked person ruling over a poor people.
A ruler who lacks understanding *commits* many extortions,
but the one who hates unjust gain will prolong *his* days.

Proverbs 28:15–16

When the wicked rise up, people hide themselves,
but when they perish, the righteous increase.

Proverbs 28:28

When the righteous increase, the people rejoice,
but when a wicked person rules, the people groan.

Proverbs 29:2

A king brings stability to the land by justice,
but a person who *demands* "contributions" will overthrow *the land.*

Proverbs 29:4

A ruler who pays attention to deceptive words—
all his officials *become* wicked.

Proverbs 29:12

A king who judges the poor with faithfulness—
his throne will be established forever.

Proverbs 29:14

Many seek the attention of the one who rules,
but a person *receives* justice from Yahweh.

Proverbs 29:26

The land trembles under three things,
and under four it cannot bear up:
under a servant when he becomes king,
and a godless person when he is satisfied with food,
under a hated woman when she gets married,
and a servant when she displaces her mistress.

Proverbs 30:21–23

The words of King Lemuel,
an inspired utterance that his mother taught him:
What, O my son? And what, O son of my womb?
And what, O son of my vows?
Do not give your strength to women,
or your ways to those who destroy kings.
It is not for kings, O Lemuel,
not for kings to drink wine,
nor for those who rule *to drink* beer.
Otherwise, they will drink and forget what has been decreed,
and alter the legal claim of all the afflicted people.
Give beer to the person who is disheartened,

and wine to the bitter soul.

Let him drink and forget his poverty,

and no longer remember his troubles.

Open your mouth for those who have no voice,

for the legal claim of all defenseless people.

Open your mouth, judge with righteousness,

and defend the cause of the afflicted and needy person.

Proverbs 31:1–9

SECURITY/SAFETY

Security and safety are the natural outcomes of living with wisdom, righteousness, and trust in God. A life grounded in discernment and integrity creates a clear and steady path free from fear and impediments. Wise living protects a person from harm—guarding their steps, guiding their decisions, and shielding them from traps that ensnare the foolish and reckless. It provides not only physical protection but also creates a safe harbor of emotional and spiritual peace.

Those who walk in integrity are described as walking securely, where they have no need to fear being exposed or overthrown since their lives are stable and transparent. They are not hiding a secret sin that they fear will someday be found out. In addition, righteousness serves as a safeguard, delivering people from trouble and anchoring them when storms arise. Even in adversity, the righteous find refuge and rescue in their godly character and in God's protection and provision for them. In contrast, the wicked, though they may seem strong for a time or secure in their ways, will be ultimately uprooted, undone by their own corruption, and their wickedness will come back upon them like a stone that they rolled to crush others.

One of the most vivid images of safety is the name of God (Yahweh) being a strong tower—the righteous run to it and are protected. This underscores the role of trust in God as a core part of wisdom that brings true security. Human cleverness or physical strength offers little in times of real trouble compared to the power of God toward those who revere him and rely upon his strength. Those who lean upon God's strength dwell in peace and sleep without fear, knowing their protection rests on someone who is unshakable and undefeatable.

The fear of people is another threat to one's safety, often leading to compromise or instability, because trusting in people is never secure. People are weak, imperfect, and prone to foolishness, and they will let one another down; but trusting in God brings confidence and safety. Wisdom guards not only actions but also emotions, keeping anxiety at bay and providing calmness and peace in times of uncertainty.

Those who seek security in wealth, status, or control will be disappointed. But those who put their trust in Yahweh, allowing His wisdom to govern their daily life, will find safety and security that is deep, lasting, and resilient—anchored in truth, protected by prudence, and sustained by the power of God.

For the turning away of the naive will kill them,

and the *false* security of fools will destroy them.

But the one who listens to me will live in safety,

and will be at ease from the dread of evil."

Proverbs 1:32–33

For wisdom will come into your heart,

and knowledge will be pleasant to your soul;

discretion will watch over you,

and discernment will guard you,

to deliver you from the way of evil,

from the one speaking perverse things,

Proverbs 2:10–12

My son, do not let these depart from *before* your eyes:

guard sound advice and discretion,

so they will be life to your soul,

and grace for your neck.

Then you will walk on your way in safety,

and your foot will not stumble.

Proverbs 3:21–23

When you lie down, you will not be afraid;

when you fall asleep, your sleep will be sweet.

Do not be afraid of sudden terror,

and of the devastation of the wicked when it comes,

for Yahweh will be your confidence,

and he will keep your foot from being caught.

Proverbs 3:24–26

Do not abandon her and she will watch over you,

love her and she will guard you.

Proverbs 4:6

The one who walks blamelessly walks securely,

but the one who perverts his ways will be made known.

Proverbs 10:9

When the storm passes through, then the wicked

person is no more,

but the righteous person *has* a foundation that endures.

Proverbs 10:25

The road of Yahweh is a place of refuge for the blameless person,
but it is destruction for those who act wickedly.
The righteous person will not ever be moved,
but the wicked will not live in the land.

Proverbs 10:29–30

Riches will not profit on the day of wrath,
but righteousness will deliver from death.
The righteousness of the blameless person will make
        his road straight,
but the wicked person will fall by his wickedness.
The righteousness of the upright will deliver them,
but the unfaithful will be taken captive by their desire.

Proverbs 11:4–6

A righteous person is delivered from trouble,
but a wicked person takes his place.

Proverbs 11:8

A person will not be established by wickedness,
but the root of the righteous will not be moved.

Proverbs 12:3

No disaster will come upon the righteous person,
but the wicked are filled *with* misfortune.

Proverbs 12:21

In the mouth of a fool is a prideful rod,
but the lips of the wise will watch over them.

Proverbs 14:3

In the fear of Yahweh there is strong confidence,
and he will be a shelter for his children.

Proverbs 14:26

A wicked person will be cast down by his *own* evil,

but the righteous person takes refuge in his *own* blamelessness.

Proverbs 14:32

Yahweh's name is a strong tower;

the righteous person runs to it and is secure.

Proverbs 18:10

The fear of Yahweh *leads* to life,

and the one *who has it* will sleep satisfied through the night *and*
not be visited by evil.

Proverbs 19:23

The person who digs a pit will fall into it,

and the person rolling a stone, it will come back upon him.

Proverbs 26:27

A wicked person flees when no one is pursuing,

but the righteous are confident like a lion.

Proverbs 28:1

The person who trusts in his own heart—he is a fool;

but the one who walks in wisdom—he will be delivered.

Proverbs 28:26

The fear of people will bring a snare,

but the one who trusts in Yahweh will be protected.

Proverbs 29:25

SELF-CONTROL

Having the discipline of self-control is esteemed as a core virtue of wisdom. It is the ability to govern one's impulses—whether in speech, emotion, desire, or appetite—and to act with restraint and dignity rather than immediate gratification and indulgence. A person with self-control protects themselves from shame, conflict, and ruin, while those who lack it are vulnerable to attack, like a city with broken-down walls that is open to chaos and being easily conquered.

In speaking to others, self-control is crucial. The wise limit their words, think before speaking, and avoid outbursts and foolish jests. By contrast, those who speak rashly or too much are often ensnared by their own words, stirring up strife or revealing their own foolishness. The disciplined person who controls their mouth listens more than they talk and knows the power of silence and when best to speak.

Regarding emotions, self-control is seen in a calm demeanor and measured responses. A person who restrains their anger demonstrates deep understanding, while one who vents all their feelings is a fool. To have restraint over your emotions displays true strength of character and brings peace to relationships and steadiness to life. Particularly, the ability to control one's temper is of great importance and value, and such a person is said to be stronger than one who conquers a city.

Desires and appetites are also areas where self-control is vital. Overindulgence—whether in food, drink, or pleasure—inevitably leads to one's harm. Wisdom teaches moderation in all things, cautioning against giving in to every craving or pursuing gratification without proper boundaries. By not living a life of excess, a person preserves their health, reputation, and dignity.

The principle of self-control is all about mastering the self rather than being mastered by yourself. Whether one is mastering their emotions, desires, pride, or other motivating factors, a mind that is shaped by wisdom and a heart that submits to discipline and training will prove invaluable for work, relationships, and every other endeavor. By exhibiting self-control, one gains respect, stability, and long-term well-being, building a life that is prosperous, honorable, and free from the regrets of foolish indulgences.

Then you will say, "O how I have hated discipline,

and my heart has spurned reproof.

I did not listen to the voice of my teachers,

nor did I incline my ear to those instructing me.

I was soon in all sorts of trouble

in the midst of the assembly and congregation."

Proverbs 5:12–14

By an abundance of words transgression will not cease,

but the one who restrains his lips is insightful.

Proverbs 10:19

The one who shows contempt for his neighbor lacks sense,

but a person with understanding remains silent.

Proverbs 11:12

The one who guards his mouth watches over his life;
destruction will come to the one who opens his lips wide.

Proverbs 13:3

The one who is slow to get angry is better than a mighty person,
and one who rules his spirit is *better* than one who captures a city.

Proverbs 16:32

The one who holds back his words has *attained* knowledge,
and the one who has a cool spirit is a person of understanding.

Proverbs 17:27

The one who watches over his mouth and his tongue
guards his life from trouble.

Proverbs 21:23

When you sit to eat with a ruler,
carefully discern whoa is before you,
and put a knife in your throat
if you *have* a greedy appetite.

Proverbs 23:1–2

Did you find some honey? Eat just enough for you,
so that you do not have too much of it and then vomit it up.

Proverbs 25:16

It is not good to eat much honey,
nor *for people* to seek glory *on top of* glory.
Like a city broken into, *one* without a wall,
is a person who has no self-control over his emotions.

Proverbs 25:27–28

A fool lets out all of his emotions,
but a wise person keeps them calm within.

Proverbs 29:11

SHAME/DISGRACE/ DISHONOR

S hame, disgrace, and dishonor are the natural consequences of foolishness. When one rejects wisdom, the outcome most certainly will contain these. But these outcomes are not merely social embarrassments a person can shrug off; they are reflections of a deeper failure in character and judgment. Those who act dishonorably bring trouble not only on themselves, but also on their families, friends, and communities, tarnishing their reputation and weakening—if not destroying—trust with others.

Fools, mockers, and those who resist correction are frequent recipients of shame. Their words and actions display a lack of understanding, often exposing them to public disgrace. A person who refuses to listen, learn, or control their impulses ultimately suffers the natural fallout of damaged relationships, lost opportunities, or downright raw humiliation. Moreover, children who are rebellious or act foolishly bring grief and dishonor to their parents, becoming a source of sorrow rather than pride.

Conducting oneself with moral purity and honor brings blessing and life, while sexual immorality is a sure path to disgrace, bringing injury to one's name and reputation that is not easily forgotten. Those who engage in sexual immorality show a lack of self-control and wisdom, and its consequences often include both personal regret and public scorn. Furthermore, disloyalty, slander, and betrayal—especially in close relationships—results in dishonor and ruin, as they violate the ethical foundation of wise living.

Honor comes to those who live with integrity, humility, and understanding, while disgrace follows the one who despises counsel and truth. Those who pursue righteousness and wisdom are lifted up in honor and respect, whereas those who seek selfish glory and honor for themselves ironically lose it and cannot find it. In addition, avoiding quarrels, respecting others, and welcoming instruction and correction builds a strong reputation of good character and dignity. Even in conflict, a wise person guards their reputation by acting with discretion and fairness, not letting their emotions, opinions, or biases interfere.

What shame, dishonor, and disgrace come down to is not just how others view a person or regard them with suspicion or contempt, but about the distance they create for themselves from the road of wisdom. The humble will be honored and exalted, but the proud and arrogant will be brought low and disgraced. Wisdom doesn't seek its own glory but waits to be praised and commended by others through humility and patience.

The wise will inherit glory,
but fools exalt shame.

Proverbs 3:35

The man committing adultery with a woman lacks sense;
he who does this is destroying his *own* soul.
He will find affliction and dishonor,
and his disgrace will not be blotted out.

Proverbs 6:32–33

The one who rebukes a mocker brings shame upon himself,
and the one who reproves a wicked person *brings*
      injury upon himself.

Proverbs 9:7

The one who gathers in the summer is an insightful son;
the one who is fast asleep at the harvest is a shameful son.

Proverbs 10:5

Wisdom is found upon the lips of the discerning,
but a rod *will strike* the back of the one lacking sense.

Proverbs 10:13

Arrogance comes, then dishonor comes,
but wisdom is with the modest.

Proverbs 11:2

The one who shows contempt for his neighbor lacks sense,
but a person with understanding remains silent.

Proverbs 11:12

An excellent wife is the crown of her husband,
but she who acts shamefully is like decay in his bones.

Proverbs 12:4

A righteous person hates a deceptive word,
but a wicked person will become a stench and display *his* shame.

Proverbs 13:5

The one who ignores discipline *will get* poverty and dishonor,
but the one who heeds reproof will be honored.

Proverbs 13:18

Righteousness exalts a nation,
but sin is a disgrace to any people.

The king's favor is toward an insightful servant,
but his anger will be *upon* the one who acts shamefully.

Proverbs 14:34–35

A fool spurns discipline from his father,
but the one who heeds reproof acts prudently.

Proverbs 15:5

A wise son makes a father glad,
but a foolish person shows contempt for his mother.

Proverbs 15:20

An insightful servant will rule over a shameful son,
and he will share the inheritance among brothers.

Proverbs 17:2

He who fathers a fool *does so* to his own grief,
and the father of a godless person will have no joy.

Proverbs 17:21

A foolish son is grief to his father
and bitterness to the woman who bore him.

Proverbs 17:25

When a wicked person enters, contempt also enters,
and with dishonor *comes* scorn.

Proverbs 18:3

He who assaults *his* father and drives *his* mother away
is a shameful and disgraceful son.

Proverbs 19:26

It is an honor for a person to cease from strife,
but every fool will quarrel.

Proverbs 20:3

do not go out to argue *your dispute* too hastily;

otherwise, what will you do in the end

when your neighbor humiliates you?

Argue your dispute with your neighbor,

but do not reveal another person's secret,

or the one who hears *it* might put you to shame,

and your bad reputation will not go away.

Proverbs 25:8–10

SPEECH/WORDS

T he importance of being careful with one's words is made explicitly clear in Proverbs, as speech and words are powerful and have the capacity to heal or harm, build up or tear down, and guide or deceive. The way a person speaks reveals their character and greatly influences their relationships, reputation, and opportunities. Wise speech is thoughtful, honest, and timely, bringing life, resolution, and blessing. The right words spoken at the right time are like purified silver, nourishing fruit, and elegant ornaments, symbolizing their immense value and beauty when used properly.

Words have real consequences, and their effects are felt by all who receive them. They can lift a heavy heart, diffuse anger, and bring clarity and joy. But they can also inflame conflict, spread lies, and inflict lasting damage. The effect of words is pronounced: a gentle answer turns away wrath, while harsh words provoke anger; flattery and gossip are dangerous, enticing the simple and creating division; and the fool is known for their excessive or reckless speech, while the wise person exercises restraint, speaking with care and thoughtfulness by weighing the impact of words before speaking them.

When speaking, being truthful is essential. Honest words bring justice and stability, while lying lips are detestable to God and lead to the ruin of oneself and others. The person who guards their mouth preserves their life, whereas those who speak without censoring

themselves invite trouble. Listening before speaking and thinking
before responding are hallmarks of wisdom, allowing one's speech
to become a source of good and blessing rather than evil and harm.

Receiving and sharing wise counsel are of great benefit to both the
speaker and the listener, bringing safety and soundness to one's decisions and actions. Words formed by wisdom are persuasive, healing, and enduring. No one's words are neutral; every word carries
power, either toward oneself or others. Furthermore, the words
that a person speaks reflect their heart and shape the world around
them. Thus, those who speak with integrity, kindness, and understanding show that they walk in the fear of Yahweh, and they contribute to peace, justice, and flourishing.

Listen, O sons, to the teaching of a father,

and pay attention in order to learn understanding,

for I give good teaching to you all;

do not abandon my instruction.

Proverbs 4:1–2

My son, if you have put up security for your neighbor,

if you have entered into an agreement with a stranger,

then you have been ensnared by the words of your mouth,

you have been captured by the words of your mouth.

Proverbs 6:1–2

By her great persuasion she seduces him,

by the seductiveness of her lips she leads him astray.

Proverbs 7:21

Listen, for I speak of things that are correct,

and the opening of my lips *brings forth* upright *words.*

For my mouth will utter truth,

and wickedness *is* an abomination to my lips.

All the words of my mouth *are spoken* in righteousness;

nothing in them *is* twisted or perverted.

All of them *are* straightforward to the one who understands,

and they are right to those finding knowledge."

Proverbs 8:6–9

Blessings are upon the head of a righteous person,

but the mouth of the wicked conceals wrongdoing.

Proverbs 10:6

The wise heart accepts commandments,

but the one who is foolish with his lips will come to ruin.

Proverbs 10:8

The one winking *his* eye causes pain,

and the one who is foolish with his lips will come to ruin.

The mouth of a righteous person is a fountain of life,

but the mouth of the wicked conceals wrongdoing.

Proverbs 10:10–11

Wisdom is found upon the lips of the discerning,

but a rod *will strike* the back of the one lacking sense.

The wise store up knowledge,

but the mouth of the fool *brings* destruction near.

Proverbs 10:13–14

The one hiding *his* hatred *has* deceitful lips,

and the one spreading slander, he is a fool.

By an abundance of words transgression will not cease,

but the one who restrains his lips is insightful.

The tongue of a righteous person is choice silver;
the heart of the wicked is *worth* little.

Proverbs 10:18–20

The mouth of a righteous person will bring forth the
        fruit of wisdom,
but the tongue *speaking* perversions will be cut off.
The lips of a righteous person know *what is* acceptable,
but the mouth of the wicked *knows* perversions.

Proverbs 10:31–32

The godless person ruins his neighbor with *his* mouth,
but the righteous will be delivered by knowledge.

Proverbs 11:9

By the blessing of the upright a town will be exalted,
but it will be thrown down by the mouth of the wicked.

Proverbs 11:11

The words of the wicked lie in wait for blood,
but the mouth of the upright will deliver them.

Proverbs 12:6

By the transgression of *his* lips an evil person *will fall into* a snare,
but the righteous person will escape from trouble.
From the fruit of his mouth a person is satisfied with good,
and the accomplishments of a person's hands will return to him.

Proverbs 12:13–14

The one who speaks *what is* faithful declares an honest testimony,
but a false witness *utters* deceit.
There is one who speaks recklessly, like the stabbings of a sword,
but the tongue of the wise is healing.

Truthful lips will be established continually,
but a lying tongue will linger only for a moment.

Proverbs 12:17–19

Lying lips are an abomination to Yahweh,
but those who do *what is* faithful *obtain* his favor.

Proverbs 12:22

Anxiety in a person's heart weighs it down,
but a good word makes it glad.

Proverbs 12:25

From the fruit of his mouth a person enjoys *what* is good,
but the desire of unfaithful people is violence.
The one who guards his mouth watches over his life;
destruction will come to the one who opens his lips wide.

Proverbs 13:2–3

In the mouth of a fool is a prideful rod,
but the lips of the wise will watch over them.

Proverbs 14:3

An easily angered person acts foolishly,
and a schemer will be hated.

Proverbs 14:17

In all hard work there is profit,
but *mere* words from the lips surely *lead* to poverty.

Proverbs 14:23

A gentle response turns away rage,
but a hurtful word increases anger.
The tongue of the wise produces good knowledge,
but the mouth of fools pours out foolishness.

Proverbs 15:1–2

The heart of the one who has understanding seeks knowledge,
but the mouth of fools feeds on foolishness.

Proverbs 15:14

Better is a meal of vegetables when love is present,
than a fattened ox and hatred with it.

Proverbs 15:17

A person *gets* joy from the answer of his mouth,
and how good is a word in its *proper* time!

Proverbs 15:23

Evil thoughts are an abomination to Yahweh,
but pleasant words are pure.

Proverbs 15:26

The heart of a righteous person considers how to answer,
but the mouth of the wicked pours out evil things.

Proverbs 15:28

The plans of the heart *belong* to the person,
but the answer of the tongue *comes* from Yahweh.

Proverbs 16:1

Righteous lips are the delight of kings,
and the one who speaks with integrity will be loved.

Proverbs 16:13

A person with a wise heart will be called "one who understands,"
and the sweetness of *his* lips will increase persuasiveness.

Proverbs 16:21

The heart of a wise person gives insight to his mouth,
and it increases the persuasiveness of his lips.

Pleasant words are a honeycomb,
sweet to the soul and healing to the bones.

Proverbs 16:23–24

A person of Belial digs up evil,
and *the words* upon his lips are like a burning fire.

Proverbs 16:27

An evildoer pays attention to wicked lips;
a liar listens to a destructive tongue.

Proverbs 17:4

Eloquent speech is not fitting for a godless person,
how much less *fitting* are deceptive lips for a nobleman?

Proverbs 17:7

The one who holds back his words has *attained* knowledge,
and the one who has a cool spirit is a person of understanding.
Even a fool who remains silent is thought to be wise;
when he shuts his lips, he is *considered* to be discerning.

Proverbs 17:27–28

The words of a person's mouth *are* deep waters,
a flowing stream, a fountain of wisdom.

Proverbs 18:4

The lips of a fool bring strife,
and his mouth calls for beatings.
The mouth of a fool *will bring* destruction to him,
and his lips are a snare to his soul.
The words of a gossip are like delicacies,
and they go down into one's innermost being.

Proverbs 18:6–8

A person's stomach will be satisfied from the fruit of his mouth;
he will be satisfied *from* the revenue of his lips.
Death and life are in the power of the tongue,
and those who love it will eat of its fruit.

Proverbs 18:20–21

There is gold and a multitude of gems,
but lips bearing knowledge are a rare jewel.

Proverbs 20:15

A gossip walks around revealing secrets,
so do not get involved with a person who speaks
        loosely with his lips.

Proverbs 20:19

The one who watches over his mouth and his tongue
guards his life from trouble.

Proverbs 21:23

The eyes of Yahweh guard knowledge,
but he overturns the words of the one acting unfaithfully.

Proverbs 22:12

The mouth of the forbidden women is a deep pit;
the person with whom Yahweh is angry will fall in there.

Proverbs 22:14

Incline your ear and listen to the words of the wise,
and apply your heart to my knowledge,
for it is delightful when you keep them within you,
then they will be established together upon your lips.

Proverbs 22:17–18

My son, if your heart is wise,
my own heart will indeed rejoice.
My inward parts will rejoice
when your lips speak with great integrity.

Proverbs 23:15–16

Like apples of gold in settings of silver
is a word spoken at the *proper* moment.

Proverbs 25:11

With patience a ruler can be persuaded,
and a gentle tongue can break a bone.

Proverbs 25:15

The north wind brings rain,
and a tongue *telling* secrets brings an angry face.

Proverbs 25:23

When the wood is gone, a fire will go out,
and when there is no gossip, contentions will grow quiet.
Like charcoal for hot coals and wood for fire,
so is a contentious person for kindling strife.
The words of a gossip are like delicacies,
and they go down into one's innermost being.

Proverbs 26:20–22

Like a clay vessel covered with silver dross
are smooth lips and a wicked heart.
A person who hates disguises himself with his lips,
but he harbors deceit in his inner being;
when his speech is gracious, do not believe him,
for in his heart are seven abominations.
Though his hatred is covered by deception,

his evil will be exposed in *the midst of* the congregation.

The person who digs a pit will fall into it,

and the person rolling a stone, it will come back upon him.

A lying tongue hates those it oppresses,

and a flattering mouth creates a calamity.

Proverbs 26:23–28

Let another praise you and not your *own* mouth—

a stranger—and not your *own* lips.

Proverbs 27:2

One who reproves a person will afterward find more favor

than the person who flatters with the tongue.

Proverbs 28:23

A person who flatters his neighbor

spreads a net for his feet.

Proverbs 29:5

A servant cannot be corrected *simply* with words,

for he understands, but he does not respond.

Proverbs 29:19

Every word of God is refined;

he is a shield for those who take refuge in him.

Do not add to his words or else he will reprove you,

and you will be found *to be* a liar.

Proverbs 30:5–6

She opens her mouth with wisdom,

and instruction about covenant faithfulness is upon her tongue.

Proverbs 31:26

STEALING/THEFT

Stealing is strongly condemned as an act of moral corruption that leads to personal ruin and condemnation. While the temptation to gain wealth quickly or through dishonest means may be strong, and some may seem to have succeeded and prospered through it, the long-term consequences far outweigh any short-lived benefit. Stolen bread seems sweet in the moment, but it turns to gravel in the mouth—leaving the thief with guilt, emptiness, and broken relationships. The path of the thief is marked by deceit, violence, betrayal, and ultimately destruction.

Those who steal, whether by force, deception, or exploitation, not only harm others but undermine their own integrity and security. Even if theft seems justified or goes unnoticed at first, it sabotages one's character and invites shame, conflict, and punishment.

Theft is also portrayed as a betrayal of trust, especially when committed within one's family. A child who robs or dishonors their parents brings disgrace and causes deep relational damage, and a person who associates with thieves will become complicit and will bring a curse upon themselves. Thus, a friend of thieves will suffer. Justice, whether human or divine, will not ignore such wrongdoing.

Even petty or survival-based theft is not excusable. Though there may be understanding for a starving person who steals food or other life necessities, nevertheless, restitution is still required—sometimes several times over—showing that integrity matters even in hardship and adversity.

Hard work, honesty, and generosity are the path to lasting fulfillment and honor. Taking what belongs to someone else, or taking a dishonest shortcut to wealth, may seem to get a person where they want to go, but it leads to a painful dead end. True gain in life comes from righteousness, wisdom, and trust in God's provision, not from the deceptive and destructive allure of wealth and possessions.

My son, if sinners entice you,

do not consent.

If they say, "Come with us, let's lie in wait to *shed* blood,

let's ambush an innocent person for no *good* reason.

We will swallow them alive, just as Sheol does,

and whole, just as those who go down into the pit.

We will find all sorts of valuable things;

we will fill our houses with plunder.

Throw your lot in with us;

we will all share the loot."

My son, do not walk on *that* road with them;

keep your feet from their pathway,

for their feet run to *do* evil,

and they make haste to shed blood.

Proverbs 1:10–16

For in vain the net is spread

in the sight of a bird,

but these lie in wait for their own blood;

they set an ambush for their *own* souls!
This is the way of everyone who pursues unjust gain;
it takes away the life of its owners.

Proverbs 1:17–19

People do not despise a thief when he steals
to feed himself when he is hungry.
But when he is caught, he will repay seven times;
he will repay with all the wealth of his house.

Proverbs 6:30–31

Treasures *gained* by wickedness profit nothing,
but righteousness will deliver from death.

Proverbs 10:2

The one who pursues unjust gain troubles his household,
but the one who hates gifts *that influence* will live.

Proverbs 15:27

He who assaults *his* father and drives *his* mother away
is a shameful and disgraceful son.

Proverbs 19:26

Bread *gained* by deceit is sweet to a person,
but afterwards his mouth will be filled with gravel.

Proverbs 20:17

Do not rob a poor person because he is poor,
and do not crush the needy at the *city* gate,
for Yahweh will defend their case,
and he will rob the life of those who robbed them.

Proverbs 22:22–23

The person who robs his father or his mother and says, "It is not a
        transgression,"
he is a friend of a person *who causes* destruction.

Proverbs 28:24

The person who partners with a thief hates his *own* soul;
he is put under oath *to testify*, but discloses nothing.

Proverbs 29:24

TEMPTATION

T emptation is a seductive and destructive force that lures a person and makes promises of pleasure, gain, or excitement, but ultimately leads to pain and downfall. It often appears attractive—cloaked in persuasive words, charming appearances, or enticing offers—but its end is filled with regret, loss, and even death. Proverbs repeatedly warns against the allure of sinful companions, sexual immorality, and deceptive invitations that mask danger behind a veil of excitement and delight.

Temptation targets the inexperienced and the unguarded—those who lack wisdom, discipline, or vigilance. The enticement of sin often begins with flattering speech, appealing to desire, pride, or curiosity. Whether it's the offer to join in a dishonest plot to make a profit, or the seduction of sexual immorality promising secret thrills and pleasure, the result is the same: moral compromise, personal disgrace, erosion of character, and often irreversible consequences. What begins as a moment of weakness and indulgence can quickly end in poverty, dishonor, or destruction of one's life and legacy.

The antidote for temptation is a proactive pursuit of wisdom and understanding to protect and guard against the powerful seduction of sin. Wisdom enters the heart and acts as a shield, preserving discretion and delivering one from the road of wickedness and darkness. Staying away from paths of temptation, resisting the invitation of others to sin, and keeping one's heart aligned with what is right are repeated themes in Proverbs to defend against temptation and evil.

Even though many temptations are fueled by things we encounter around us, temptation is a battle of the heart and mind. The wise are alert, grounded in godly instruction, and guarded by understanding and discernment. They avoid not just the act, but the path that leads to it—choosing discipline, self-control, and fear of Yahweh over the fleeting satisfaction of sin. The message of Proverbs is clear: temptation can be strong, but wisdom is stronger, and those who listen to her dwell in safety; meanwhile, those who yield to sin walk the road of destruction.

My son, if sinners entice you,
do not consent.

Proverbs 1:10

For wisdom will come into your heart,
and knowledge will be pleasant to your soul;
discretion will watch over you,
and discernment will guard you,
to deliver you from the way of evil,
from the one speaking perverse things,
from the ones who forsake the upright paths
to walk on the roads of darkness;
from the ones who are glad in doing evil,
who rejoice in the perverseness of evil;
from those whose paths are twisted,
and *from* the devious in their ways;
and to deliver you from the forbidden woman,

from the foreign woman *who is* flattering *with* her words,

who leaves the mate of her youth,

and has forgotten the covenant she made before her God,

for her house sinks down to death,

and her paths *lead* to the dead.

Proverbs 2:10–18

For the lips of the forbidden woman drip honey,

and her mouth is smoother than oil,

but in the end she is bitter as wormwood;

she is sharp as a two-edged sword.

Her feet go down to death;

her steps proceed toward Sheol.

She will not consider the path of life;

her ways are unstable, *yet* she is not aware *of it*.

Proverbs 5:3–6

But now, *my* sons, listen to me,

and do not depart from the words of my mouth.

Keep your road far from her,

and do not go near to the door of her house,

otherwise you might give your honor to others,

and your years to a cruel person;

otherwise strangers might eat their fill from your strength,

and your hard-earned goods *end up* in the house of a foreigner,

and in the end you groan

when your flesh—even your body—are used up.

Proverbs 5:7–11

For the commandment is a lamp and the instruction is a light,

and reproofs *that offer* correction are a road *leading to* life,

to keep you from the evil woman,

from the flattering tongue of the foreign woman.

Do not desire her beauty in your heart,

and do not allow her to capture you with her eyes.

For on account of a prostitute *a man is reduced to* a piece of bread,

and an adulteress hunts for a precious life.

Can a man snatch up fire against his chest

and his clothes not be burnt?

Or can a man walk upon hot coals

and his feet not get burned?

So is the one who goes into his neighbor's wife;

all who touch her will not go unpunished.

                                                              Proverbs 6:23–29

For at the window of my house,

I looked down through my lattice,

and I saw among the naive,

and I discerned among the youths a young man lacking sense.

He was passing along the street near her corner,

and he was taking steps on the road to her house,

at dusk, in the evening of the day,

in the middle of the night and the *gloomy* darkness,

And look! A woman *comes* to meet him,

dressed as a prostitute and with a cunning heart.

She is boisterous and rebellious;

her feet do not stay in her house.

She is now on the street, now in the public plazas;

she lies in wait at every corner.

So she seizes him and kisses him,

and shamelessly she says to him,

"I *made* peace offerings;

today I fulfilled my vows.

So I came out to meet you,

to diligently seek your face, and I have found you.

I have spread covers on my couch;

embroidered fabrics from Egypt.

I have perfumed my bed

with myrrh, aloes, and cinnamon.

Come, let's drink our fill of lovemaking until the morning;

let's delight ourselves with much love.

For *my* husband is not home;

he has gone on a long journey.

He took a bag of silver in his hand;

he will come home at the full moon."

By her great persuasion she seduces him,

by the seductiveness of her lips she leads him astray.

Suddenly he walks after her,

like an ox goes to the slaughter,

like a stag stepping into a snare,

until an arrow pierces his liver.

He is like a bird rushing into a trap;

and he does not know that it *will cost him* his life.

Proverbs 7:6–23

And now, O sons, listen to me,

and pay attention to the words of my mouth.

Do not allow your heart to turn aside to her ways;

do not wander off onto her paths,

for she has brought down many victims,

and numerous are all her slain.

Her house *has many* paths to Sheol,

descending to the chambers of death.

Proverbs 7:24–27

Lady Wisdom has built her house;

she has carved out her seven pillars.

She has slaughtered her meat;

she has mixed her wine;

indeed, she has prepared her table.

She has sent out her female servants;

she calls out from the tops of the heights of the town,

"Whoever is naive, let him turn in here."

To the one lacking sense, she says,

"Come! Eat my food,

and drink the wine that I have mixed.

Leave *your* naive ways and live.

And go straight *ahead* on the road of understanding."

The one who rebukes a mocker brings shame upon himself,

and the one who reproves a wicked person *brings*

injury upon himself.

Do not reprove a mocker or he will hate you;

reprove a wise man and he will love you.

Give *instruction* to a wise person and he will become even wiser;

teach a righteous person and he will increase in learning.

The fear of Yahweh is the starting point of wisdom,

and the knowledge of the Holy One is *the starting point*

of understanding.

For by me your days will be multiplied,

and years of life will be added to you.

If you are wise, you are wise for your own *benefit*;

and if you mock, you will bear *the consequence* by yourself.

Lady Folly is boisterous,

lacking in understanding, and does not know anything.

And she sits at the entrance of her house,

on a throne at the heights of the city,

calling out to those passing by *on* the road,

to the ones making their paths straight,

"Whoever is naive, let him turn in here."

And she says to the one lacking sense,

"Stolen waters are sweet,

and food *eaten in* secret is pleasant."

But he does not know that the dead are there;

the ones who have accepted her *invitation* are in the
> depths of Sheol.

Proverbs 9:1–18

The mouth of the forbidden women is a deep pit;

the person with whom Yahweh is angry will fall in there.

Proverbs 22:14

VIOLENCE

Violence is never condoned in Proverbs but is described as both a product and a path of wickedness associated with cruelty, oppression, injustice, and destruction. It arises in hearts that plot evil, delight in wrongdoing, and reject the ways of peace. Those who use violence to achieve power, wealth, or revenge are not only a danger to others, but set themselves on a course toward personal ruin and divine condemnation.

Violent people often exhibit deceit, manipulation, and corrupt speech. Their influence is contagious and dangerous, especially to the naive and gullible. Proverbs warns against joining with those who entice others into violence for profit or revenge, exposing the foolishness and evil involved in shedding innocent blood. Such alliances ultimately ensnare the participants, leading to their own demise and destruction.

God detests those who stir up conflict, inflict injury, and prey upon others, or devise schemes of harm. Their actions are not only morally reprehensible but also disruptive to the peace and security of a community. Even the words of violent people are used as weapons, filled with animosity and hate; they are like arrows that wound and instill fear in all those around them.

In contrast, the wise pursue peace, kindness, and safety. They avoid the path of the violent, choosing instead to build others up, acting with compassion and empathy and seeking to heal and speak life. While those who are merciful and gentle are a blessing and do good to others, they also strengthen their own soul and enrich their life through their godly demeanor and conduct.

Violence only leads down the road of darkness to restlessness, suffering, and moral decay. It may yield quick results or worldly gain, but it leads to internal torment, social collapse, and civil and divine punishment. Even if the violent think they can get away with their crime, there is always a price to be paid, and they won't escape without being harmed. Violence breeds violence, and those who are violent toward others receive violence in return. Thus, wisdom calls people to refuse participation in acts of violence in all its forms, and urges the pursuit of peace, justice, and righteousness.

My son, if sinners entice you,

do not consent.

If they say, "Come with us, let's lie in wait to *shed* blood,

let's ambush an innocent person for no *good* reason.

We will swallow them alive, just as Sheol does,

and whole, just as those who go down into the pit.

We will find all sorts of valuable things;

we will fill our houses with plunder.

Throw your lot in with us;

we will all share the loot."

My son, do not walk on *that* road with them;

keep your feet from their pathway,

for their feet run to *do* evil,

and they make haste to shed blood.

Proverbs 1:10–16

Do not envy a violent person,

and do not choose any of his ways.

For devious people are an abomination to Yahweh,

but his counsel is with the upright.

Proverbs 3:31–32

Do not enter the path of the wicked,

and do not proceed on the road of the evil ones.

Disregard it; do not pass upon it.

Turn away from it and pass on by.

For they cannot sleep unless they do evil,

and their sleep is stolen unless they cause *another* to stumble.

For they eat the bread of wickedness,

and they drink the wine of violence.

Proverbs 4:14–17

There are six things that Yahweh hates,

indeed, seven things are abominations to his soul:

prideful eyes, a lying tongue,

and hands shedding innocent blood;

a heart that devises wicked thoughts,

feet that are swift to run to *do* evil,

a false witness who breathes out lies,

and one who sows strife among brothers.

Proverbs 6:16–19

Blessings are upon the head of a righteous person,

but the mouth of the wicked conceals wrongdoing.

Proverbs 10:6

The mouth of a righteous person is a fountain of life,

but the mouth of the wicked conceals wrongdoing.

Proverbs 10:11

A gracious woman will attain glory,
but ruthless men will attain riches.
The kind person benefits himself,
but the cruel person does himself harm.

Proverbs 11:16–17

From the fruit of his mouth a person enjoys *what* is good,
but the desire of unfaithful people is violence.

Proverbs 13:2

A violent person entices his neighbor,
and he leads him on a road that is not good.

Proverbs 16:29

The violence of the wicked will drag them away
because they refused to act with justice.

Proverbs 21:7

Do not envy evil people,
and do not desire to be with them.
For their hearts plot violence,
and their lips speak trouble.

Proverbs 24:1–2

A person who is burdened by *shedding* the blood of another will
        flee until death;
do not let anyone support him.

Proverbs 28:17

People who cause bloodshed hate a blameless person,
but the upright show concern for his life.

Proverbs 29:10

WICKED/WICKEDNESS

Wickedness is characterized in many ways, but they all stem from disobedience and rebellion against God and his commandments. Wickedness consists of deceit, violence, arrogance, oppression, immorality, and a rejection of wisdom. The path of the wicked is marked by darkness, instability, and turmoil. Though the wicked may appear to prosper for a time, their foundation is weak and faulty, and their downfall and destruction is certain.

Ultimately, the behavior of the wicked springs from a corrupt heart, and from that darkened heart they lie and deceive, stir up strife and conflicts, exploit the weak and innocent, and resist teaching and correction. Their words are harmful, their motives are selfish and greedy, and their influence spreads chaos and suffering. They actively plot evil and take pleasure in wrongdoing, and they are not content to just do evil themselves; they seek to draw others into their wicked and destructive ways, too. Keeping company with the wicked is dangerous, especially for the naive and immature who can be easily ensnared by their schemes and corrupted into following their road of darkness.

God's attitude toward the wicked is clear: he opposes and despises them, detests their sacrifices and plans, and ensures that justice eventually catches up with them. The wicked may evade human judgment (perhaps for a season or longer), but divine retribution is inevitable. Their lamp will be snuffed out, their name forgotten, and their place upon the earth removed.

In opposition to wickedness, the righteous are stable, joyful, and secure. They flourish like a well-rooted tree near water, while the wicked are uprooted and swept away. The difference in outcomes cannot be starker: the righteous find life and peace and create an enduring legacy; the wicked inherit fear, ruin, and disgrace. When disaster strikes, the righteous will persevere, but the wicked are overthrown and destroyed.

Isolation, unrest, and shame are outcomes of wickedness, as it poisons the soul and fractures families and communities. Wickedness is a path of self-destruction, while the fear of Yahweh and a life of integrity lead to enduring peace and honor. The wise are urged not to envy the wicked or be drawn into their ways, but to avoid their road and stand firm in righteousness, trusting Yahweh that justice, in due time, will ultimately prevail.

For the upright will live in the land,

and the blameless will remain in it.

But the wicked will be cut off from the land,

and the unfaithful will be uprooted from it.

Proverbs 2:21–22

Yahweh's curse is upon the house of the wicked person,

but he blesses the dwelling of the righteous person.

Proverbs 3:33

Do not enter the path of the wicked,

and do not proceed on the road of the evil ones.

Disregard it; do not pass upon it.

Turn away from it and pass on by.

For they cannot sleep unless they do evil,

and their sleep is stolen unless they cause *another* to stumble.

For they eat the bread of wickedness,

and they drink the wine of violence.

Proverbs 4:14–17

But the path of the righteous is like the light of dawn,

shining ever brighter until the full *light of* day.

The road of the wicked is like the *gloomy* darkness;

they do not know what they are stumbling over.

Proverbs 4:18–19

A person of Belial, a man of wickedness,

is the one walking *with* a crooked mouth,

winking with his eyes, signaling with his foot,

instructing with his fingers.

With perversions in his heart he devises evil,

at every moment he sows strife.

Therefore, his calamity will come suddenly,

in an instant he will be broken and there will be no remedy.

Proverbs 6:12–15

The memory of a righteous person is a blessing,

but the name of the wicked will rot.

Proverbs 10:7

The one winking *his* eye causes pain,

and the one who is foolish with his lips will come to ruin.

The mouth of a righteous person is a fountain of life,

but the mouth of the wicked conceals wrongdoing.

Proverbs 10:10–11

The wicked person's horror will come upon him,
but the desire of the righteous will be given *to them*.
When the storm passes through, then the wicked
        person is no more,
but the righteous person *has* a foundation that endures.

Proverbs 10:24–25

The fear of Yahweh adds to *one's* days,
but the years of the wicked will be cut short.
The hope of the righteous is joy,
but the expectation of the wicked will perish.

Proverbs 10:27–28

The righteous person will not ever be moved,
but the wicked will not live in the land.

Proverbs 10:30

The righteousness of the blameless person will make
        his road straight,
but the wicked person will fall by his wickedness.
The righteousness of the upright will deliver them,
but the unfaithful will be taken captive by their desire.
When a wicked person dies, his hope perishes,
and *his* hope of wealth perishes.
A righteous person is delivered from trouble,
but a wicked person takes his place.

Proverbs 11:5–8

A town rejoices at the prosperity of the righteous,
and there is joyful shouting at the death of the wicked.
By the blessing of the upright a town will be exalted,
but it will be thrown down by the mouth of the wicked.

Proverbs 11:10–11

The wicked person makes a deceptive wage,

but the one who sows righteousness *receives* a true reward;

indeed, righteousness *leads* to life,

but the one who eagerly pursues evil is *heading* to his death.

A twisted heart is an abomination to Yahweh,

but the road of the blameless is his delight.

Be assured: an evil person will not go unpunished,

but the offspring of the righteous will escape.

Proverbs 11:18–21

The desire of the righteous *ends* only *in* good,

but the hope of the wicked *ends in* wrath.

Proverbs 11:23

Behold! The righteous person will be repaid on the earth;

indeed, how much more the wicked person who sins!

Proverbs 11:31

A good person will obtain favor from Yahweh,

but a person with wicked schemes, he will condemn.

A person will not be established by wickedness,

but the root of the righteous will not be moved.

Proverbs 12:2–3

The thoughts of the righteous are just,

but the guidance of the wicked is deceitful.

The words of the wicked lie in wait for blood,

but the mouth of the upright will deliver them.

The wicked will be overthrown and will be no more,

but the house of the righteous will stand.

Proverbs 12:5–7

The righteous person cares for the life of his animal,
but the compassion of the wicked is cruel.

Proverbs 12:10

The wicked person desires the spoils of evil people,
but the root of the righteous produces *its own fruit*.
By the transgression of *his* lips an evil person *will fall into* a snare,
but the righteous person will escape from trouble.

Proverbs 12:12–13

Deceit *is* in the heart of those who devise evil,
but those who counsel peace *have* joy.
No disaster will come upon the righteous person,
but the wicked are filled *with* misfortune.

Proverbs 12:20–21

A righteous person shows the way for his neighbor,
but the road of the wicked causes them to wander astray.

Proverbs 12:26

From the fruit of his mouth a person enjoys *what* is good,
but the desire of unfaithful people is violence.

Proverbs 13:2

A righteous person hates a deceptive word,
but a wicked person will become a stench and display *his* shame.
Righteousness guards the one whose way is blameless,
but wickedness overthrows a sinner.

Proverbs 13:5–6

The light of the righteous shines *brightly*,
but the lamp of the wicked will go out.

Proverbs 13:9

A wicked messenger will fall into evil,
but a faithful messenger *brings* healing.

Proverbs 13:17

Evil pursues sinners,
but goodness will reward the righteous.

Proverbs 13:21

The righteous person eats to the satisfaction of his appetite,
but the belly of the wicked lacks *food*.

Proverbs 13:25

The house of the wicked will be destroyed,
but the tent of the upright will sprout forth.

Proverbs 14:11

An evil person will bow down in the presence of good people,
and the wicked *will bow* at the gates of a righteous person.

Proverbs 14:19

A wicked person will be cast down by his *own* evil,
but the righteous person takes refuge in his *own* blamelessness.

Proverbs 14:32

A sacrifice *made by* the wicked is an abomination to Yahweh,
but the prayer of the upright *brings* his favor.
The road of the wicked person is an abomination to Yahweh,
but he loves the one who eagerly pursues righteousness.

Proverbs 15:8–9

Evil thoughts are an abomination to Yahweh,
but pleasant words are pure.

Proverbs 15:26

Yahweh is far from the wicked,
but he hears the prayer of the righteous.

Proverbs 15:29

Yahweh made everything with an answer to it,
and even the wicked person on a day of evil.

Proverbs 16:4

A person of Belial digs up evil,
and *the words* upon his lips are like a burning fire.

Proverbs 16:27

The one who winks his eyes devises perversions;
the one who purses his lips brings evil to pass.

Proverbs 16:30

An evildoer pays attention to wicked lips;
a liar listens to a destructive tongue.

Proverbs 17:4

Surely a rebellious person seeks evil,
so a cruel messenger will be sent against him.

Proverbs 17:11

A wicked person takes a secret bribe
to twist the paths of justice.

Proverbs 17:23

When a wicked person enters, contempt also enters,
and with dishonor *comes* scorn.

Proverbs 18:3

An ungodly witness mocks justice,
and the mouth of criminals devours wickedness.

Proverbs 19:28

The one who curses his father or his mother,
his lamp will go out in a time of darkness.

Proverbs 20:20

The violence of the wicked will drag them away
because they refused to act with justice.
The road of a guilty person is crooked,
but *as for* the pure person, his works are upright.

Proverbs 21:7–8

The soul of the wicked person desires evil;
his neighbor finds no favor in his eyes.

Proverbs 21:10

A righteous person keeps an eye on the house of
        the wicked person,
bringing the wicked to ruin.

Proverbs 21:12

A wicked person is a ransom for a righteous person,
and the one acting unfaithfully is *a ransom* in place of the upright.

Proverbs 21:18

A sacrifice *offered by* the wicked is an abomination;
how much more when he brings it with deceitful intent.

Proverbs 21:27

A wicked person hardens his face,
but an upright person, he gives thought to his ways.

Proverbs 21:29

Do not lie in wait like the wicked against the dwelling place
        of the righteous;
do not assault his place of rest.

For a righteous person will fall seven times, and he stands back up,
but the wicked stumble in *times of* distress.

Proverbs 24:15–16

Do not be agitated because of those who do evil;
do not be envious of the wicked.
For there will be no future for the evil person;
the lamp of the wicked will go out.

Proverbs 24:19–20

Like a spring *that has been* trampled *in* and *like* a ruined fountain
is a righteous person who wavers in the presence of
    a wicked person.

Proverbs 25:26

A wicked person flees when no one is pursuing,
but the righteous are confident like a lion.

Proverbs 28:1

Those who abandon the Law praise the wicked,
but those who keep the Law contend against them.

Proverbs 28:4

The person who turns his ear away from listening to the Law,
even his prayer is an abomination.

Proverbs 28:9

When the righteous triumph, there is great glory,
but when the wicked rise up, people conceal themselves.

Proverbs 28:12

When the righteous increase, the people rejoice,
but when a wicked person rules, the people groan.

Proverbs 29:2

An evil person is ensnared by transgression,

but a righteous person sings aloud and rejoices.

A righteous person knows the legal claim of the poor;

a wicked person does not understand *this* knowledge.

Proverbs 29:6–7

When the wicked increase, transgression increases,

but the righteous will see their ruin.

Proverbs 29:16

A dishonest person is an abomination to the righteous,

and the one whose road is upright is an abomination to

  a wicked person.

Proverbs 29:27

There is a generation that curses its father

and that does not bless its mother.

A generation that is pure in its own eyes

but has not been washed from its excrement.

A generation—how haughty are its eyes,

and *how high* its eyelids are lifted up!

A generation whose teeth are swords

and fangs are knives,

to devour the poor from the land

and the needy from humankind.

Proverbs 30:11–14

This is the way of the woman who commits adultery:

she eats and wipes her mouth,

and says, "I have not committed *any* wickedness."

Proverbs 30:20

WISDOM

isdom is the central and most important virtue in Proverbs and is portrayed as more precious than silver or gold and more desirable than any worldly success or other treasure one might obtain. It is the foundation for a life of righteousness, peace, and lasting prosperity. Wisdom begins with the fear of Yahweh—an attitude of reverence, humility, and obedience to God and his authority—and it shapes every aspect of life and every choice a person makes: everything they say and do.

Wisdom is not an intellectual matter, but it is highly practical, guiding how one is to speak, work, spend or save money, make plans, achieve goals, and interact with others. It guards against temptation, protects a person from ruin, and leads to inner peace and outward success. Those who seek wisdom diligently—by treasuring instruction, listening to counsel, and becoming disciplined—gain understanding, discernment, and confidence. They are able to avoid evil traps, the road of foolishness, and harmful relationships. Furthermore, the wise make sound decisions, are a source of life and well-being, and enjoy stability and favor from God and people.

In Proverbs, wisdom is personified as a woman calling out to the simple-minded and inexperienced, inviting them to live and walk in her ways. Her voice offers life, truth, and protection, and she is available to anyone who will listen. But those who reject her do so at their own peril. Ignoring wisdom leads to confusion, suffering, and destruction, as wisdom watches over one's life against the influence of evil and wickedness.

Living wisely means embracing teaching and discipline, guarding one's heart, and pursuing truth even when it's difficult or seemingly disadvantageous. Wisdom equips people to build strong homes and families, form healthy relationships, raise children with integrity and good character, and promote justice and compassion. A wise person brings joy to parents, honor and stability to communities, and strength and sound advice to their family and friends. However, the wise do not know all there is to know, but rather understand their limits and their need for more understanding and counsel. Therefore, they are teachable, prudent, and self-controlled, while fools mock instruction and correction—and in their over-confidence, wander into trouble and harm.

True wisdom only comes from God and must be sought with fervor and frequency. Even if one obtains wisdom, it can be lost if careless or if distraction arise. Obtaining wisdom requires a heart that genuinely desires it and a mind that is open to learning and growing. Those who embrace wisdom will find life, security, and blessing—not just for themselves, but for all those around them. A life rooted in wisdom is a life of godly purpose, peace, and enduring significance. Wisdom is the principal thing in life; so get wisdom!

The proverbs of Solomon, the son of David, king of Israel:

To know wisdom and teaching,

to understand words *that give* understanding,

to receive wise teaching

in righteousness, justice, and integrity;

to give prudence to the naive,

knowledge and discretion to the youth.

A wise person will listen and increase in learning,

and a discerning person will get wise guidance,

to understand a proverb and an obscure expression,

words of the wise and their riddles.

The fear of Yahweh is the beginning of knowledge,

but fools show contempt for wisdom and *sound* teaching.

Proverbs 1:1–7

Lady Wisdom shouts aloud in the street,

in the public plazas she raises her voice;

at the head of noisy *streets* she calls out,

where the city gates open she speaks her words:

"How long, O naive ones, will you love naivety?

How long will mockers delight in mocking,

and fools hate knowledge?

If you turn back *to me* at my reproof,

look, I will pour out my spirit upon you all,

I will make known my words to you all.

But since you refused me when I called,

I stretched out my hand but no one paid attention,

and you neglected all my counsel,

and you did not want my reproof—

I also will laugh at your distress;

I will mock when what you dread comes,

when your terror comes like a violent storm,

and your calamity like a whirlwind,

and trouble and distress come upon you all.

Then they will call upon me, but I will not answer;

they will diligently seek me, but will not find me.

Because they hated knowledge,

and they did not choose the fear of Yahweh;

they were not interested in my counsel,

and they spurned all my reproof,

so they will eat from the fruit of their *own* way,

and from their *own* schemes they will have *their* fill.

For the turning away of the naive will kill them,

and the *false* security of fools will destroy them.

But the one who listens to me will live in safety,

and will be at ease from the dread of evil."

Proverbs 1:20–33

My son, if you receive my words,

and store up my commandments with you,

making your ear attentive to wisdom,

directing your heart to discernment,

for if you call out to understanding,

if you raise your voice to discernment,

if you seek her like silver,

and search for her like hidden treasure,

then you will understand the fear of Yahweh,

and you will find the knowledge of God.

For Yahweh gives Wisdom,

from his mouth *comes forth* knowledge and discernment.

Proverbs 2:1–6

Then you will understand righteousness and justice

and integrity—every good path.

For wisdom will come into your heart,

and knowledge will be pleasant to your soul;

Proverbs 2:9–10

Do not be wise in your own eyes;

fear Yahweh and turn away from evil.

It will be healing for your flesh,

and a refreshing drink to your bones.

Proverbs 3:7–8

Blessed is the person who finds wisdom,

and the one who obtains discernment,

for the gain from her is better than the gain from silver,

and her revenue *is better* than gold.

She is more precious than gems,

and nothing you desire can compare with her.

In her right hand is length of days,

in her left hand are riches and glory.

Her ways are pleasant ways,

and all her pathways are peace.

She is a tree of life to those taking hold of her,

and blessed are those *who are* holding her fast.

Proverbs 3:13–18

Yahweh founded the earth by wisdom;

he established the heavens by discernment,

the depths *of the ocean* were split open by his knowledge,

and the clouds drip dew.

Proverbs 3:19–20

My son, do not let these depart from *before* your eyes:

guard sound advice and discretion,

so they will be life to your soul,

and grace for your neck.

Then you will walk on your way in safety,

and your foot will not stumble.

When you lie down, you will not be afraid;

when you fall asleep, your sleep will be sweet.

Proverbs 3:21–24

Get wisdom! Get understanding!

Do not forget and do not turn away from the words of my mouth.

Do not abandon her and she will watch over you,

love her and she will guard you.

Wisdom is the principal thing, *so* get wisdom;

and with all your purchases, purchase understanding.

Proverbs 4:5–7

On the road of wisdom I teach you;

I lead you on the upright paths.

When you walk, your steps will not be hampered,

and if you run, you will not stumble.

Hold on to *my* teaching, do not let her go.

Guard her because she is your life.

Proverbs 4:11–13

My son, pay attention to my wisdom;

incline your ear to my discernment,

in order that you keep discretion,

and your lips guard knowledge.

Proverbs 5:1–2

Say to wisdom, "You are my sister,"

and call understanding, "*my* relative,"

in order to keep you from the forbidden woman,

from the foreign woman *who* flatters with her words.

Proverbs 7:4–5

Doesn't wisdom call out,

and discernment raise her voice?

At the top of the heights overlooking the road,

at the crossroads she takes her stand.

Beside the gates at the opening to the city,

at the entrance of the gateways, she shouts aloud:

"To you, O men, I call out,

and my voice *is* to all humankind.

Understand prudence, O naive ones,

and understand *good* sense, O foolish ones.

Listen, for I speak of things that are correct,

and the opening of my lips *brings forth* upright *words*.

For my mouth will utter truth,

and wickedness *is* an abomination to my lips.

All the words of my mouth *are spoken* in righteousness;

nothing in them *is* twisted or perverted.

All of them *are* straightforward to the one who understands,

and they are right to those finding knowledge."

Take my teaching, and not silver,

and knowledge rather than choice gold.

Because wisdom is better than gems,

and all delightful things cannot be compared with her.

"I, Wisdom, dwell with prudence,

and I find knowledge and discretion.

The fear of Yahweh is to hate evil—

pride and arrogance and the path of evil

and a perverse mouth, I hate.

I possess counsel and sound advice.

I have understanding; I possess strength.

By me kings reign,

and *by me* rulers decree righteousness.

By me rulers govern;

even nobles—all who judge *with* righteousness.

I love those who love me,

and those who desire me will find me.

Riches and glory are with me,

enduring prosperity and righteousness.

My fruit is better than gold, even *better than* refined gold,

and my gain *is better* than silver.

I walk in the way of righteousness,

in the midst of the paths of justice,

to cause those who love me to inherit property,

and I will fill their storehouses.

Yahweh created me at the beginning of his work,

prior to his deeds of long ago.

From antiquity I was established;

from the start,

from before the earth.

I was born *when there were* no deep *oceans*,

when there were no springs abounding with waters.

Before the mountains were settled,

before the hills *were formed* I was born;

when he had not *yet* made the earth and the fields,

or the initial dust of the world;

when he prepared the heavens, I was there;

when he inscribed the horizon above the face of the deep;

when he fixed the clouds above,

when he strengthened the springs of the deep;

when he set for the sea its limit

so the waters would not disobey his command;

when he marked out the foundations of the earth;

then I was beside him growing up,

and I was *his* great delight daily,

playing in his presence at every moment;

playing in the world—his earth,

and full of delight with humankind.

So now, O sons, listen to me;

blessed are those who keep my ways.

Listen to *my* teaching and become wise,

and do not neglect it.

Blessed is the one who listens to me,

keeping watch at my doors day after day,

watching at the entrance to my gates,

because the one who finds me finds life,

and he will obtain favor from Yahweh.

But the one who sins against me is doing violence to his *own* soul;

all those who hate me love death."

Proverbs 8:1–36

Lady Wisdom has built her house;

she has carved out her seven pillars.

She has slaughtered her meat;

she has mixed her wine;

indeed, she has prepared her table.

She has sent out her female servants;

she calls out from the tops of the heights of the town,

"Whoever is naive, let him turn in here."

To the one lacking sense, she says,

"Come! Eat my food,

and drink the wine that I have mixed.

Leave *your* naive ways and live.

And go straight *ahead* on the road of understanding."

The one who rebukes a mocker brings shame upon himself,

and the one who reproves a wicked person *brings*

       injury upon himself.

Do not reprove a mocker or he will hate you;

reprove a wise man and he will love you.

Give *instruction* to a wise person and he will become even wiser;

teach a righteous person and he will increase in learning.

The fear of Yahweh is the starting point of wisdom,

and the knowledge of the Holy One is *the starting point*

      of understanding.

For by me your days will be multiplied,

and years of life will be added to you.

If you are wise, you are wise for your own *benefit*;

and if you mock, you will bear *the consequence* by yourself.

Proverbs 9:1–12

Wisdom is found upon the lips of the discerning,

but a rod *will strike* the back of the one lacking sense.

Proverbs 10:13

Acting indecently is pleasure to a fool,

so also is wisdom for a person with discernment.

Proverbs 10:23

Arrogance comes, then dishonor comes,

but wisdom is with the modest.

Proverbs 11:2

The fruit of a righteous person is a tree of life,

and the wise person takes away souls *from death*.

Proverbs 11:30

The instruction of a wise person is a fountain of life,
that one may turn aside from the snares of death.

Proverbs 13:14

The one who walks with the wise will become wise,
but the one who associates with fools will suffer harm.

Proverbs 13:20

Lady Wisdom builds her house,
but *Lady* Folly tears it down with her hands.

Proverbs 14:1

The wisdom of a prudent person is to understand his road,
but the foolishness of fools is deceit.

Proverbs 14:8

A wise person is cautious and turns away from evil,
but a fool is angry and is overconfident.

Proverbs 14:16

The crown of the wise is *their* wealth,
but the foolishness of fools is *still* foolishness.

Proverbs 14:24

Wisdom rests in the heart of the one who has understanding,
and *even* among fools she makes herself known.

Proverbs 14:33

A wise son makes a father glad,
but a foolish person shows contempt for his mother.

Proverbs 15:20

The fear of Yahweh is what wisdom teaches,
and humility goes before glory.

Proverbs 15:33

How much better to get wisdom than gold!
And to get understanding is to be chosen rather than silver.

Proverbs 16:16

Wisdom is with the one who understands,
but the eyes of a fool are on the ends of the earth.

Proverbs 17:24

The words of a person's mouth *are* deep waters,
a flowing stream, a fountain of wisdom.

Proverbs 18:4

Strength is the splendor of young men,
and gray hair is the majesty of old men.

Proverbs 20:29

Desirable treasure and oil are in the dwelling place of
        the wise person,
but the foolish person consumes it.

Proverbs 21:20

A wise person scales the city of the mighty,
and he brings down the strength of *the city's* confidence.

Proverbs 21:22

Incline your ear and listen to the words of the wise,
and apply your heart to my knowledge,
for it is delightful when you keep them within you,
then they will be established together upon your lips.
So that your trust may be in Yahweh,
I have made *them* known to you today—yes, you.
Have I not written to you 30 sayings
containing counsel and knowledge,

to make known to you true words of faithfulness,
and to return words of faithfulness to those who sent you?

Proverbs 22:17–21

Get truth and do not sell it;
get wisdom and teaching and understanding.
The father of a righteous person will rejoice exceedingly,
and the man who fathers a wise *son* will delight in him;
may your father and your mother be glad,
and may she who gave birth to you rejoice.

Proverbs 23:23–25

By wisdom a house is built,
and by understanding it is established,
and by knowledge *its* rooms are filled
with all precious and pleasant wealth.
A wise man is strong,
and a person with knowledge grows in strength.
For with *wise* guidance you should wage your war,
and with a multitude of advisors there is deliverance.

Proverbs 24:3–6

My son, eat some honey, for it is good,
and honey from the comb is sweet in your mouth;
likewise, know that wisdom is *sweet* to your soul.
If you find it, then there will be a future,
and your hope will not be cut off.

Proverbs 24:13–14

Become wise, my son, and make my heart glad,
so that I may give an answer to the one who reproaches me.

Proverbs 27:11

The person who trusts in his own heart—he is a fool;
but the one who walks in wisdom—he will be delivered.

Proverbs 28:26

A person who loves wisdom makes his father glad,
but the man who gets involved with prostitutes
      destroys his wealth.

Proverbs 29:3

Surely I am more stupid than anyone,
and I do not have the understanding of a man.
And I did not learn wisdom,
nor do I know the knowledge of the Holy One.

Proverbs 30:2–3

She opens her mouth with wisdom,
and instruction about covenant faithfulness is upon her tongue.

Proverbs 31:26

WOMEN/WIVES

Proverbs offers a rich and multifaceted portrayal of women and wives, presenting both warnings and praises that highlight the profound influence a woman can have within a marriage, household, and society. On one hand, Proverbs warns against immoral, seductive women who use flattery and charm to lead others astray. These women are described as dangerous and deceptive, drawing the foolish into regret, ruin, and even death. The path of such a woman is one of secrecy and betrayal, and it leads toward destruction. Only wisdom and moral vigilance can protect a man from being caught by her alluring influence and falling prey to her trap.

In contrast, the virtuous woman is honored as the highest model of strength, dignity, and wisdom. She is the crown of her husband and the foundation of a successful household. Her worth exceeds that of precious gems, and her character is marked by faithfulness, industriousness, kindness, and reverence for God. She manages her home with skill, provides adequately for her family, contributes productively to those around her, honors her husband in the community, and speaks with wisdom and compassion. Her husband and children praise her, and her reputation extends beyond her household to the broader community and all those who know her.

On the other hand, a contentious or quarrelsome wife is like a nagging sore in the household and is compared to an incessant dripping from the ceiling—an unbearable demeanor and temperament to constantly tolerate. Such relationships are marked by tension, frustration, and misery, making even wealth or material comfort in those relationships seem worthless in comparison to the absence of peace. Significantly, the emotional climate of a home, for better or worse, is deeply shaped and affected by the presence and character of the woman within it.

Overall, Proverbs emphasizes that a woman's influence in marriage, family, or society is very powerful. But the influence can be positive or negative—a woman can be either as a source of wisdom, strength, and joy, or as a cause of strife, distress, and problems. The virtuous and excellent woman is one who fears Yahweh, lives with integrity, and enriches the lives of those around her through love, wisdom, and faithfulness.

My son, pay attention to my wisdom;

incline your ear to my discernment,

in order that you keep discretion,

and your lips guard knowledge.

For the lips of the forbidden woman drip honey,

and her mouth is smoother than oil,

but in the end she is bitter as wormwood;

she is sharp as a two-edged sword.

Her feet go down to death;

her steps proceed toward Sheol.

She will not consider the path of life;

her ways are unstable, *yet* she is not aware *of it.*

But now, *my* sons, listen to me,

and do not depart from the words of my mouth.

Keep your road far from her,

and do not go near to the door of her house,

otherwise you might give your honor to others,

and your years to a cruel person;

otherwise strangers might eat their fill from your strength,

and your hard-earned goods *end up* in the house of a foreigner,

and in the end you groan

when your flesh—even your body—are used up.

Then you will say, "O how I have hated discipline,

and my heart has spurned reproof.

I did not listen to the voice of my teachers,

nor did I incline my ear to those instructing me.

I was soon in all sorts of trouble

in the midst of the assembly and congregation."

Drink water from your own cistern,

and fresh water from the midst of your own well.

Should your springs overflow outside,

streams of water in the public plazas?

Let them be for you alone,

and not for strangers with you.

Let your fountain be continually blessed,

and rejoice because of the wife of your youth.

She is a loving doe and a graceful mountain goat;

let her breasts satisfy you at every *opportune* time—

going astray in her love.

So why go astray, my son, with a forbidden woman,

and *why* do you embrace the bosom of a foreign woman?

For a person's ways are before the eyes of Yahweh,

and he weighs all his paths.

The one acting wickedly—his *own* iniquities will capture him, and he will be seized by the cords of his *own* sin.

He will die because of lack of discipline,

and in the abundance of his foolishness he goes astray.

Proverbs 5:1–23

My son, keep your father's commandments,

and do not ignore the instruction of your mother.

Bind them upon your heart always,

tie them around your neck.

As you walk here and there, she will lead you;

when you lie down, she will watch over you,

and *when* you wake up, she will speak with you.

For the commandment is a lamp and the instruction is a light,

and reproofs *that offer* correction are a road *leading to* life,

to keep you from the evil woman,

from the flattering tongue of the foreign woman.

Do not desire her beauty in your heart,

and do not allow her to capture you with her eyes.

For on account of a prostitute *a man is reduced to* a piece of bread,

and an adulteress hunts for a precious life.

Can a man snatch up fire against his chest

and his clothes not be burnt?

Or can a man walk upon hot coals

and his feet not get burned?

So is the one who goes into his neighbor's wife;

all who touch her will not go unpunished.

People do not despise a thief when he steals

to feed himself when he is hungry.

But when he is caught, he will repay seven times;

he will repay with all the wealth of his house.

The man committing adultery with a woman lacks sense;

he who does this is destroying his *own* soul.

He will find affliction and dishonor,

and his disgrace will not be blotted out.

For jealousy enrages a husband,

and he will not spare *him* in the day of *his* vengeance.

He will not be persuaded by any ransom,

nor will he be satisfied when you make many bribes.

Proverbs 6:20–35

My son, keep my words,

and store up my commandments with you.

Keep my commandments and live,

and my instruction as the pupil of your eye.

Bind them upon your fingers;

write them upon the tablet of your heart.

Say to Wisdom, "You are my sister,"

and call understanding, "*my* relative,"

in order to keep you from the forbidden woman,

from the foreign woman *who* flatters with her words.

For at the window of my house,

I looked down through my lattice,

and I saw among the naive,

and I discerned among the youths a young man lacking sense.

He was passing along the street near her corner,

and he was taking steps on the road to her house,

at dusk, in the evening of the day,

in the middle of the night and the *gloomy* darkness,

And look! A woman *comes* to meet him,

dressed as a prostitute and with a cunning heart.

She is boisterous and rebellious;

her feet do not stay in her house.

She is now on the street, now in the public plazas;

she lies in wait at every corner.

So she seizes him and kisses him,

and shamelessly she says to him,

"I *made* peace offerings;

today I fulfilled my vows.

So I came out to meet you,

to diligently seek your face, and I have found you.

I have spread covers on my couch;

embroidered fabrics from Egypt.

I have perfumed my bed

with myrrh, aloes, and cinnamon.

Come, let's drink our fill of lovemaking until the morning;

let's delight ourselves with much love.

For *my* husband is not home;

he has gone on a long journey.

He took a bag of silver in his hand;

he will come home at the full moon."

By her great persuasion she seduces him,

by the seductiveness of her lips she leads him astray.

Suddenly he walks after her,

like an ox goes to the slaughter,

like a stag stepping into a snare,

until an arrow pierces his liver.

He is like a bird rushing into a trap;

and he does not know that it *will cost him* his life.

And now, O sons, listen to me,

and pay attention to the words of my mouth.

Do not allow your heart to turn aside to her ways;
do not wander off onto her paths,
for she has brought down many victims,
and numerous are all her slain.
Her house *has many* paths to Sheol,
descending to the chambers of death.

Proverbs 7:1–27

Like a gold ring in a pig's snout,
so too is a beautiful woman who turns aside from good judgment.

Proverbs 11:22

An excellent wife is the crown of her husband,
but she who acts shamefully is like decay in his bones.

Proverbs 12:4

Lady Wisdom builds her house,
but *Lady* Folly tears it down with her hands.

Proverbs 14:1

He who finds a wife finds a good thing,
and he obtains favor from Yahweh.

Proverbs 18:22

A foolish son *brings* destruction to his father,
and the contentions of a wife are *like* a constant drip.
A house and wealth are the inheritance from fathers,
but an insightful wife is from Yahweh.

Proverbs 19:13–14

It is better to live on the corner of a rooftop
than in a house with a contentious wife.

Proverbs 21:9

It is better to live in a desolate land
than *with* a contentious and angry woman.

Proverbs 21:19

The mouth of the forbidden women is a deep pit;
the person with whom Yahweh is angry will fall in there.

Proverbs 22:14

It is better to sit on the corner of a rooftop
than in a house with a contentious wife.

Proverbs 25:24

A constant dripping on a day of steady rain
and a contentious wife are alike;
whoever can restrain her can *even* restrain the wind,
and can *even* grasp oil in his right hand.

Proverbs 27:15–16

These three things are difficult for me,
and four that I do not understand:
the way of an eagle in the heavens,
the way of a serpent upon a rock,
the way of a ship in the heart of the sea,
and the way of a man with a young woman.
This is the way of the woman who commits adultery:
she eats and wipes her mouth,
and says, "I have not committed *any* wickedness."

Proverbs 30:18–20

An excellent wife, who can find?
For her value is far more than gems.
The heart of her husband trusts in her,
and he will have no lack of gain.

She brings him good and not evil
all the days of her life.
She seeks out wool and linen
and with delight she works with her hands.
She is like the ships of a merchant;
she brings in her food from afar.
She gets up while it is still night,
and provides food for her household
and tasks for her female servants.
She considers a field and purchases it;
from the fruit of her hands she plants a vineyard.
She wraps her waist with strength
and makes her arms strong.
She perceives that her gain is good;
her lamp does not go out during the night.
She stretches out her hand to the distaff,
and her hands grasp the spindle.
She extends her hands to the afflicted,
and stretches out her hands to the needy.
She is not afraid for her household *when* it snows
because her whole household is clothed in scarlet.
She makes coverings for herself,
and her clothing is fine linen and purple.
Her husband is known at the *city* gates,
when he sits with the elders of the land.
She makes and sells linen garments,
and provides belts to the traders.
Strength and majesty are her clothing,
and she laughs at the days to come.
She opens her mouth with wisdom,

and instruction about covenant faithfulness is upon her tongue.

She keeps watch over the activities of her household,

and she does not eat the bread of idleness.

Her children rise up and call her blessed,

and her husband praises her,

"Many daughters have demonstrated themselves to be excellent,

but you have risen up above them all."

Charm is deceptive and beauty is fleeting,

but a woman who fears Yahweh—she will be praised.

Give her the fruit of her hands,

and let her works praise her at the *city* gates.

Proverbs 31:10–31

INDEX

Proverbs 11

Proverbs 12